D0221337

SOCIALISM IN THE CRUCIBLE OF HISTORY

SOCIALISM IN THE CRUCIBLE OF HISTORY

MICHEL BEAUD

TRANSLATED AND WITH AN INTRODUCTION BY
THOMAS DICKMAN

HUMANITIES PRESS
NEW JERSEY

Originally published as *Le socialisme à l'épreuve de l'histoire*
©1982 by Les Editions du Seuil, S.A.

English translation first published 1993 by Humanities Press International, Inc.,
Atlantic Highlands, New Jersey 07716.

This English translation ©1993 by Humanities Press International, Inc.

Library of Congress Cataloging-in-Publication Data
Beaud, Michel.
   [Socialisme à l'épreuve de l'histoire. English]
   Socialism in the crucible of history / Michel Beaud ; translated
and with an introduction by Thomas Dickman.
     p.   cm.
   Translation of: Le socialisme à l'épreuve de l'histoire.
   Includes bibliographical references and index.
   ISBN 0–391–03770–6 (cloth)
   1. Communism—History. 2. Socialism—History. 3. Capitalism—
History. 4. Economic history. 5. Comparative economics.
   I. Title
HX36.B33713 1993
335.43'09—dc20   92–15659
                    CIP

A catalog record is available from the British Library for this book.

Printed in the United States of America

To all those who
have fought and still fight,
have suffered and still suffer,
have been and are now imprisoned,
tortured,
or killed;
to all those who have worked
and still work
for socialism,
bread,
peace,
and freedom.

Believing that one is sincere is not as dangerous as believing that one possesses the truth.

—Igor Stravinsky

CONTENTS

TRANSLATOR'S INTRODUCTION   ix

INTRODUCTION   xiii

CHAPTER 1. THE HOPE FOR ANOTHER SOCIETY / 1
1. Confronting the Wretchedness of the Industrial Revolution   1
2. In the Bright Glare of the French Revolution   4
3. The Power of Utopia   11
   COMMENTS ON CHAPTER 1   17

CHAPTER 2. CLEAR VISIONS OF SOCIALISM / 20
1. The Kaleidoscope of French Socialism   20
2. Marx, or Systematization   29
   COMMENTS ON CHAPTER 2   38

CHAPTER 3. FROM IDEAL TO COMPROMISE / 42
1. Socialism and Unionism   43
2. Immediate Conquests or Revolution   46
3. Internationalism and Patriotism   52
   COMMENTS ON CHAPTER 3   56

CHAPTER 4. THE CHAIN OF EVENTS LEADING TO THE OCTOBER REVOLUTION / 60
1. The Vision of Socialism before 1917   60
2. Within the Movement of the Revolutions of 1917   64
3. In the Name of the Proletariat: The Mechanism of
   Dictatorship   67
4. The Necessity to Produce   71
5. First Warnings, First Critiques   76
   COMMENTS ON CHAPTER 4   81

CHAPTER 5. COMMUNISM AND SOCIALISM / 85
1. The Breakup of the Workers' Movement   86
2. The USSR, "Only Homeland" of the International
   Proletariat   91
3. Workers' Conquests and National Compromises   99
   COMMENTS ON CHAPTER 5   106

CHAPTER 6. INTERPRETATIONS OF THE USSR / 110

1. The Cloak of Official Truth   110
2. Disagreements and Critiques   117
   COMMENTS ON CHAPTER 6   122

CHAPTER 7. A NEW REALITY: STATE COLLECTIVISM / 124

1. A Fundamental Necessity: Accumulate   124
2. A New Dominant Mode of Production   130
3. The Steel Grip of the State   133
4. The Balm of Ideology   137
   COMMENTS ON CHAPTER 7   140

CHAPTER 8. PEOPLES' LIBERATION, SOCIALISM, AND STATE COLLECTIVISM / 142

1. Struggle for Socialism: From One Dependence to Another   143
2. The Chinese Road   149
3. The Flourishing of "Third-World Socialisms"   157
   COMMENTS ON CHAPTER 8   162

CHAPTER 9. THE WINTER OF SOCIALISM / 166

1. In the East, the Great Closing-In   167
2. "Socialist" States against Working Classes   170
3. In the West, the Logic of Compromise   179
   COMMENTS ON CHAPTER 9   188

CHAPTER 10. SOCIALISM AS PROJECT / 191

1. The Hope and the Illusions   191
2. The Gains and the Impasse   195
3. Class Struggles and Compromises   199
4. Directions of Struggle and Guiding Principles   202

CHAPTER 11. BETWEEN THE HAMMER AND THE ANVIL / 209

1. A Clouded Vision   209
2. A Statist System   212
3. New Directions   217

NOTES   225

REFERENCES   233

INDEX   239

TRANSLATOR'S INTRODUCTION

Our memory is both long and short. Long, in the sense that our culture has developed values and beliefs over several thousands of years. Short, in that culture is rarely univocal: competing social interests use events in the recent past in an attempt to invalidate deeply held hopes springing from our longer-term historical experience.

The original edition of *Socialism in the Crucible of History* was published in 1981. The present translation is based on a second French edition, of 1985, and the author's 1989 additions to the final chapter. Despite these updates, voices will predictably rise: "How can a ten-year-old work possibly help us to understand and act in the present turmoil and confusion? Think of all that has happened since 1981 in Poland, Hungary, Germany, the USSR. . . ."

Events in Eastern Europe and the USSR appear to have so overturned the face of contemporary history that we tend to devalue any historical interpretation written before "current" affairs "began." For example, writing in August 1991, the French journalist Jacques Julliard expressed the view that "with a few exceptions all previous works of political economy now appear laughable."

Socialism in the Crucible of History is more a work of history than of political economy, yet the book must be defended against the sort of critique Julliard proposes against "all previous works."

Such a defense may be drawn from persisting cultural memory. Michel Beaud defends the long view of socialism as an extension of several of our culture's most deeply held values: justice, freedom, equality, fraternity. The early chapters of his book develop the view that for the founders of socialism in the late eighteenth and early nineteenth centuries, socialism could be nothing other than a progressive incarnation and realization of these values, variously defined though they were.

In this century the dream of socialism has confronted the reality, in the USSR, of what has been called socialism by both its defenders and attackers. Given this identification of socialism with the USSR, and its never-distant corollary, "socialism equals repression," the dominant view of socialism in this century has greatly differed from the nineteenth-century hope. Such identification is, however, not a given at all, but one axis of socialism's current dilemma.

The other axis is that many of socialism's original values have been achieved within the developed capitalist countries (for example, increased living standards for workers, social security). This achievement has itself occurred not only through workers' struggles but also through the benefits of imperialism and unequal development. The wealth that flowed from periphery to center during the colonial period provided the possessing classes in the developed world with additional financial maneuvering room in their dealings with "their" working classes.

These two sets of circumstances have cut the ground from under a unified socialist politics. The leaders of the USSR continued to describe their country as socialist, even though objectively it was developing along quite different lines. The ruling-class ideology in the developed capitalist world seized upon the immense gap between rhetoric and reality in the USSR and attempted to portray the USSR's specific failure as the necessary failure of any socialist initiative.

Beaud remarks that forecasting the "death of socialism" was for many years the prerogative of the right. By 1981, however, he identified writers on the left, such as Gorz and Touraine, who were thinking of "beyond" socialism and "after" socialism. The strain of defending the values of socialism as well as the excesses of the USSR—this "homeland" of socialism that was to have incarnated these values—became too great to bear. The torturous balancing act, to which the left was resigned from the 1920s through the 1950s, was jettisoned. If *that* was socialism, then we need to seek another goal.

Under the pressure of highly visible political changes in Eastern Europe, this stream of thought has become an apparently irresistible cascade. "Socialism" has been discredited from all sides, and we are left in the 1990s facing a nearly perfect paradox: socialism is proclaimed to have died because it supposedly attacked the very values once considered essentially socialist.

Understanding—not simply explaining away—this paradox is one of the most urgent tasks facing anyone who continues to hope for another society. Beaud attacks this paradox concretely, from three directions.

1. He analyzes the background, reality, and rhetoric of the Russian Revolution.

2. He examines Fordism and the "national compromises" between the capitalist class and the working class that, by 1920, had begun to flourish in the developed capitalist countries. Fordist employment practices paid more than the minimum required for a worker's subsistence,

and, when they were introduced, other employers predicted that they would lead to the downfall of private enterprise; they have instead proven to be one of its most durable guarantees.

3. He considers the internationalization of the class struggle. The burden of absolute misery has shifted, overall, from workers in the developed world to workers in the Third World.

> Thus, the "national compromises" were extended and strengthened from the effort demanded of the producing classes within the nation . . . and from the effort imposed on the producing classes of the dominated countries. . . . Importantly, the compromises placed the trade-union and socialist movements in a fundamentally untenable position regarding the traditional anticapitalist attitude, since maintaining the benefits that had been yielded up to that point depended on the smooth functioning and even the expansion of capitalism.

Workers in the developed world recognize their political stake in the smooth functioning of capitalism on a world scale in order to safeguard their relative position. Of course, the clear counterpoint to the *material* interest of workers in the smooth functioning of capitalism on a world scale is their ideological vulnerability to the ruling-class portrayal of the USSR as the sole definition and limit of socialism.

Trained under the economist François Perroux, Beaud is close to the "world-system" theorists and the paradigm of "center and periphery." His 1987 book, *The Hierarchical National/World System*, works explicitly within a world-system perspective. The defining character of this analytic direction is the thesis that national economic phenomena cannot be reduced to purely national effects, and likewise, that developments on a world level create variable national effects. This may appear straightforward on the face of it, but to integrate different levels into concrete analysis is difficult.

Politically Beaud belongs to a tradition that has remained skeptical of Stalin's claim to have "achieved socialism." At the same time, he is unremittingly critical of imperialism. It is worth noting that this tradition is as old (and older in its attitude) as the Russian Revolution itself, and it includes figures such as Rosa Luxemburg and Karl Korsch. The section of chapter 5 entitled "First Warnings, First Critiques" expresses several of the anarchist and other antiauthoritarian critiques made of the Revolution as early as 1917.

How can this serve as a defense of Beaud, a justification of his book's relevance in the 1990s? Simply this: Beaud carefully constructs a case, beginning with those early critiques, that the USSR developed into "something other" than either capitalism or socialism. He describes the

USSR as "state collectivist," where the state carries the role of the multiplicity of individually competing capitals. This is clearly not an analysis of leaders' subjective intentions but of the working out of revolution in a predominantly peasant, nonindustrialized, and politically absolutist social formation.

If the USSR was not socialist, but was better described as state collectivist, then the changes in the USSR and Eastern Europe must be understood as the disintegration of state collectivism and not of socialism. Yet such an understanding is precisely what is not coming through in most current journalistic accounts. It must be said again: the names we use to describe social reality have been shaped by and in turn shape this reality itself. In class society the ideological use of the present is never innocent. "The whole of history is still action," wrote Merleau-Ponty, "and action is already history." We need to have learned at least this much from Marx: that whatever social transformations are going on, in class society they will be presented according to class interests. Insofar as socialism remains a challenge to capitalism, it is natural that the agonies of state collectivism will be presented as "the death of socialism."

Beaud points out a way beyond our impasse. The description of the USSR as state collectivist is not a verbal dodge. His argument depends on, and contributes to, a tradition that has criticized the Russian Revolution from its earliest days *in the name of socialism*. This is the tradition Beaud recommends we reexamine and deepen, not as "after socialism" but *as* socialism.

Kautsky wrote in 1919 that the task of European socialism was "to assure that the moral catastrophe of a certain method of socialism does not become the catastrophe of socialism in general." If we are now witnessing the shrillest consequences of this all-but-general catastrophe, Beaud offers a realistic understanding of our predicament, surely the necessary first step forward. "The human crisis is always a crisis of understanding," wrote Raymond Williams. "What we genuinely understand, we can do."

A note on the circumstances of this translation: the original French edition was published without page references to keep the book less "academic." Some of these page references have been inserted, but other citations remain less complete. In all cases, however, at least as much information is provided in this edition as is provided in the French edition.

INTRODUCTION

We must reconsider socialism from the ground up.

The word conceals too many realities, leads to too many misunderstandings or ambiguities: Is the USSR socialist? Is China socialist? Is Sweden socialist? In each case convinced supporters can be found who respond affirmatively, while at the same time ardent critics refuse to describe these countries as socialist. Is "planning" socialist while the "market" is antisocialist? Is it as simple as that? Is state intervention socialist, even though the socialist tradition for years and years announced and hoped for the withering away of the state? Is collective appropriation socialist? Even when it allows domination by a privileged class over the producers? These questions must be explored in depth.

The realities are shocking. Oppression, political and police repression, and the gulag have all occurred in the immense country that many called the "homeland of socialism." Total strengthening of the state has taken place where the state was to have declined. Workers rise up, powerful yet vulnerable, against governments that, "in the name of the working class," put them down. War breaks out between two "socialist countries," despite the fact that for generations of socialists capitalism was supposedly the originator of conflict. In the name of socialism the Red Army crushes popular movements, first at Kronstadt and in the Ukraine, more recently in Prague, and even more recently in Afghanistan.

Must one, then, renounce socialism, resign oneself, and repudiate hope? Some overly zealous Stalinists have in fact done just this: upset by the unbearable revelation of what they had for so long agreed to "ignore," they have rejected in a single movement their idol as well as their ideal. And then there are the weather vanes in the world of ideas, some fine and delicate, turning in the slightest breeze, some heavy and grinding, seldom turning but reversing direction completely when they do turn. Here, too, are the pathetic intellectuals who have invented for themselves an ersatz messiah—the proletariat, the USSR, the party, or China—and who one day discover the deception and illusion.

It would be better, as Jean Ferrat advises, to face the errors directly and yet keep the hope:

That socialism was a caricature.
. . . It is another future that we must reinvent,
Without idols or patterns, step by step, humbly,
Without accepted truths or bright tomorrows,
A happiness invented, once and for all.

Without idols or patterns: of course. But we must keep in mind the immense hope that has been—and largely remains—socialism. We must take into account the illusions, due in part to too much generosity, along with the hesitations, the errors, and the disappointments. But we must also consider the achievements and the advances if we are to measure and accept the immense difference between what was attempted and what has been accomplished. Finally, we must analyze the reasons why reality has drifted so far away from the original project if we are to understand the possibilities and the nature of the socialist undertaking in the closing years of this century.

1

THE HOPE FOR ANOTHER SOCIETY

Since the end of the nineteenth century it has been accepted that social-ism is the ideology of the workers' movement. In other words, the working class, exploited in capitalist society, aspires to a socialist soci-ety. How can we question a dogma so universally accepted?

Yet question it we must. A simple glance at the historical record is instructive.

Without going back to Taoism or Plato, without seeking socialist currents in primitive Christianity or Islam, and without lingering on the great "precursors,"[1] one must observe that the principal ideas making up the common ground of socialism were articulated primarily by mem-bers of the middle bourgeoisie, even from déclassé noble families, and from the petty bourgeoisie. And throughout the nineteenth century the main lines of socialist thought were defined by the popular (in the wide sense) strata—craftsmen, shopkeepers, tradesmen—and by the intel-ligentsia, which was often linked to the middle bourgeoisie.

Very early, before the working class could assert itself as such, before the workers' movement could organize itself, the basic elements of socialist thought were formed (though the word *socialist* had not yet been coined): first in England, confronting the ruthless severity of early industrial capitalism, and then in France during the Great Revolution.

1. CONFRONTING THE WRETCHEDNESS OF THE INDUSTRIAL REVOLUTION

The Industrial Revolution had hardly begun, in the last third of the eighteenth century, when attentive minds such as Turgot and François Quesnay in France and Adam Smith in England described the new logic

1

of capitalist accumulation.[2] But at the same time many voices were raised against the new slavery of the mill workers; there arose, opposed to the spectacle of injustice and misery, the intuition and the conviction that another society was possible.

Enclosures drove out landless families and poor country peasants; ever-more-efficient machines put innumerable workers and craftsmen out of work. Uprisings multiplied despite a 1769 law against the destruction of machinery.[3] In 1779 eight to ten thousand enraged workers besieged a spinning mill and destroyed its machines. The textile mill of Robert Peel was also attacked, the machines smashed and thrown into the river. Troops dispersed the rioters; the courts condemned some of them to the gallows. In 1796 the spinning mills of Yorkshire had to be defended by troops, while six years later serious disturbances took place in Wiltshire and Somerset. In 1811 and 1812, when the war and the blockade caused supply difficulties and high prices, the wool shearers in the north of England destroyed machinery, which they accused of lowering wages. At the same time, the Midlands stocking knitters broke up their looms.

In the mills a rigid discipline held sway. Workers accustomed to the flexibility of craft work could not get used to the constraints binding a worker to a single spot day after day. Collective "breaking in" periods were necessary, especially for uprooted country people, women, and children, in order to instill the schedules, discipline, rhythm, and uninterrupted effort required by the mills. The "parish apprentices," poor children given over to the spinning mills, became the earliest victims: they were compelled to work fourteen, sixteen, and sometimes eighteen hours a day, with twenty minutes for a meal and twenty minutes to clean the machine. Exhausted, they suffered hideous accidents, falling into their machines, crushing hands and limbs. They were watched over, whipped, and beaten; some attempted suicide.

Working conditions were extremely unhealthy; the mills were dusty, humid, and smoky, and lacked fresh air. These conditions led to the spread of "mill fever," first observed in the Manchester region in 1784. Mortality from the sickness was high, while those who survived to adulthood remained deeply scarred by rickets, curved spines, mutilations, and premature aging, as well as a lack of culture or education. Workers had few prospects besides unremitting work in a mill. Eden, a disciple of Adam Smith, described them in his book *The State of the Poor* (1797) as proletarians absolutely dependent on the capitalist class: "The man who, in exchange for the real and visible products of the soil, can offer only his labor—an immaterial property—and who can provide for his daily needs only through daily effort, is condemned by nature to be absolutely at the mercy of his employer" (Eden [1797], cited in Mantoux 1959, 440).

Some charitable industrialists, such as David Dale and Robert Owen, attempted to treat the children, and even the adults, whom they employed with humanity. Doctors wrote reports as early as 1784 and 1796 in the hope that laws might establish "reasonable and humane conditions" in the mills. Protests were made by William Godwin in his *Essay on Political Justice and Its Influence on Morality and Happiness* (1793) and in his novel *Caleb William* (1794); by Thomas Spence in his *The True Rights of Man* (1775) and *The Mid-Day Sun of Freedom* (1796); and by Thomas Paine in his *Agrarian Justice* (1796).

Pastor and preacher in a small dissident church, Godwin vigorously denounced injustice and advanced the ideal of equality:

> Equality of conditions, or in other terms, equal access for everyone to the means for self-improvement and joy: this is the law that the voice of justice strictly imposes upon humanity. Any other changes in society are good only if they are aspects of this ideal state and steps on the way toward achieving it. . . . The equality for which we are arguing is an equality that will be realized in a state of great intellectual perfection. So fortunate a revolution may occur only when the public mind has achieved a high degree of enlightenment. And how could men so enlightened not recognize themselves that a life alternating pleasant rest with healthful activity is infinitely superior to a life of abject indolence? Superior, not only in dignity, but in joy. (Godwin [1793], cited in Jaurès 1969, 4:533, 535)

Those who like to attach labels see in Godwin a precursor of communism and anarchism: essentially, with a mixture of idealism and lucidity, he tried to analyze together the twin problems of social justice *and* democracy. Godwin saw the profound link between inequality and oppression, a link that remains today the key problem of socialism.

From this basis grew his mistrust of force as a means, since force attacks individual freedom; from this basis, too, came his theoretical rejection of all government, whether monarchical, aristocratic, or democratic, since Godwin saw all government as an instrument of domination. Similarly, he denounced marriage, not only because it is "a law, and the worst of laws," but also because it is "an affair of property, and the worst of properties."

Even the notion of social contract as the basis of society appeared too oppressive to Godwin. For him, a decision of the

> . . . community is valid only if it is the expression of the general will. All individuals should participate in the decision making. But each individual is bound by the common decision only through his

individual consent. If there is no unanimity, the minority may give in through prudence, wisdom, or in order not to destroy the system of communal decision making. Nonetheless this minority retains the right to pass judgment on the links that connect it to the majority; it is not bound by a contract. Godwin supports the idea that the individual, even at the moment of his submission to the majority, retains a consistent awareness of his right to judge. (Jaurès 1969, 4:515)

Godwin felt that the changes set in motion by machines and engines might one day create more favorable conditions:

At present, in order to cut down a tree, to dig a canal, or to man a ship, the labor of many men is necessary; but will this always be the case? When we think of the complicated machines that human ingenuity has created, of the various sorts of mills, of weaving machines and machines aboard ships, how can we fail to be astonished by the savings in labor these machines produce? Who can say where such progress will end? Today, these inventions alarm the laborers of the community, and though it is true they provoke temporary distress, eventually they will produce enormous benefit to humankind. In a society based on equal work, their usefulness is incontestable.

In the future it is probable that extensive operations may be carried out by a single man, and that a single plough may be adequate for an entire field, accomplishing its work without needing to be watched over. This is what Franklin meant when he said that "one day the mind will be master over matter." The endpoint of the progress that has begun is that eventually manual labor will cease to be necessary. (Godwin [1793], cited in Jaurès 1969, 4:544–45)

2. IN THE BRIGHT GLARE OF THE FRENCH REVOLUTION

In France the Industrial Revolution—the transformation of the entire society by the extension of the capitalist mode of production through mills and, later, factories—had hardly begun. It was within the great upheaval of the French Revolution that the image of another society, beyond the bourgeois society then forming, began to develop.

Jurists, men of letters, scientists, and the sons of the petty and middle bourgeoisie, joined by the younger members of the lower nobility: these were the groups who developed the new ideas of the bourgeois revolution against the old feudal order, against privilege, and against monarchy. They called for equality among the different orders of society and for popular sovereignty. Their slogans were Liberty, Equality, Property!

The voice of the workers was almost inaudible in this tumultuous outpouring:

One is struck, reading the *Notebooks of Grievances* of 1789, to find so few concerned with workers, their needs, or their rights. The main reason for this is, we know, that the workers were not called upon to present their wishes and claims. Some of them participated in the assemblies of the Third Estate in the cities, but their remarks, assuming any were presented to the assembly, were only rarely recorded by the writers, who, in the cities, usually belonged to the cultivated bourgeoisie. (Picard 1910, 95)

A few rare notebooks pose the problems of low wages, lack of work, and competition from machines, inventions termed "harmful in general" that "put many people out of work." "These fine machines enrich a few individuals and ruin an entire country"; they "greatly harm the poor people." These are, perhaps, the comments of craftsmen, of manufacturers in difficulty, or of eminent men listening to the people.

Poor workers and men out of work expressed themselves by demonstrating in the street, as in Lyons, where "thirty thousand emaciated and ashen specters displayed their uselessness and their misery" (Jaurès 1969, 4:169). In Paris, too, the famished common people marched in the streets, calling for bread: "The people must have bread, for where there is no bread, there are no more laws, no more freedom, no more legitimate government" (cited by Bouloiseau 1972, 88). On 4 September 1793 thousands of workers assembled at City Hall; a young typographer, Christophe Tiger, spoke in their name to the governing authorities, at first with deference:

Citizens, the difficulty in finding bread at the bakers is the reason why we have come to interrupt for an instant the important tasks that occupy you. For two months we have suffered in silence, hoping the situation would get better, but instead it gets worse every day. So we have come to ask you to do what public welfare demands: assure that the worker who has worked during the day, and who needs to rest at night, be not obliged to stay up part of the night and lose half of the day looking for bread, and often without finding any.

Tiger's tone then became more vehement:

We are not asking you whether the maximum laws have been carried out, but only that you respond to this question: is there bread, yes or no? (Cited in Jaurès 1969, 4:420–21)

Given the difficulties with supplies, high prices, and low wages, strikes broke out, such as the one in March 1792 by wood cutters and workers responsible for floating logs on the Nièvre and Yonne rivers: the workers dispersed and pursued the armed National Guard, many of whom threw themselves in the river to escape. Later the workers triumphantly paraded the clothes they had taken from the Guard. Other strikes involved workers making weapons in Paris and paper-industry workers in the provinces in the fall of 1793. On 12 December the Committee for Public Safety decreed:

> All alliances or gatherings of workers are prohibited; communications between workers in different shops that are useful or necessary for their work will take place only through an intermediary or with the express permission of the committee on which each workshop depends. . . . Work shall under no pretext be suspended. . . . In no case shall workers gather to voice their complaints; any such gatherings that might form will be dispersed, and their instigators will be arrested and punished according to the law. (Cited in Guérin 1973, 240)

Nonetheless, many strikes occurred in the winter and spring of 1794.

It was in this context that the thought of François l'Ange developed. A silk designer in Lyons, he was condemned to death in 1793, at the age of fifty. He began by asking for the extension of suffrage to everyone: in 1789, in his *Problematic Notions on the General Estates*, he advocated a system of voting by groups of a hundred citizens. In 1790, in the *Complaints and Remonstrances of a Citizen Decreed to Be Passive to Citizens Decreed to Be Active*, he raised this protest:

> Was it not enough to limit the sovereignty of the nation to merely voting for its representatives? Was it necessary beyond this to commit the outrage of excluding us from the primary assemblies on the grounds of our toilsome poverty, from which you draw your wealth? (Cited in Jaurès 1969, 1:486)

He then passionately denounced exploitation, pleading for the rights of workers against the "robbery" committed by what Jaurès calls "idle owners":

> The idlers who call themselves owners can only reap the excess beyond what is necessary for our subsistence. This proves at least our co-ownership. But if we are co-owners and are the sole basis of all income, then the right to cut into our necessities of life and to deprive us of the surplus is the right of a robber. (Ibid.)

In 1792 l'Ange confronted the difficulties of securing provisions with his *Simple and Easy Methods for Assuring the Permanent Abundance of Bread at a Fair Price*; he suggested thirty thousand public granaries, financed by a national subscription. There was to be a granary for every hundred families, stocked at harvest time by the farmers, who, for their part, would be protected against calamity. He described his system minutely and did not hesitate to forecast that if his ideas were adopted the future would be bright:

At that time the land will be well looked after, expenditures for bridges and highways will finally be truly profitable to the nation, all the roads will be beautiful, the rivers and the canals will always be navigable by heavily laden boats, swamps will soon be drained, arid lands will soon be watered, and even the waters of the streams will soon be forced to flow calmly in new pastures: in a word, we will very quickly see France become a terrestrial paradise. (Cited in Droz 1972–78, 1:234)

L'Ange further extended these ideas in his *Remedy for Everything or an Invulnerable Constitution for Public Happiness*. Albert Soboul writes that l'Ange's reforms

were formulated within the general ideological climate of the time. He did not attack property as such, restricting himself to limiting its most flagrant abuses. He affirmed the priority of the right to live, and thus advocated, as did so many others of his time, a whole system of generalized nationalizations for the necessities of life. (Soboul, in Droz 1972–78, 1:257)

What is above all apparent in the writings of l'Ange—and in those of Godwin, too—is their aspiration to social justice and, at the same time, their concern for a real democracy.

The Equals—Babeuf, Sylvain Maréchal, Philippe Buonarotti, and Charles Germain—clearly advanced the claim to equality.

François-Noël Babeuf was born into a poor family in Picardy. As an adult he chose for himself the Roman name Camille and then Gracchus; he named his children Émile, Camille, and Caïus. At times in his life he was destitute, and he felt inequality keenly: in 1779, as an apprentice to a specialist in feudal law (notary/clerk), he was obliged to visit the mansions of the rich wearing torn pants. Later, having become a lands commissioner (1785), he researched the titles of landed nobles and bourgeois and tracked down debtors, as well. Babeuf employed as many as eight or ten assistants and was in daily contact with both great fortunes and extreme misery. He read Rousseau and Morelly and was attracted by Freemasonry, though his request to join in 1787 was opposed by the bourgeois of Roye who controlled the lodge (Dommanget [1922] 1970).

In 1786 he was strongly affected by a leaflet entitled *The Portending Change in the Whole World through Comfort, Good Education, and Prosperity for All Men*, supposedly written by a man named Collignon and printed by Couret de Villeneuve, a member of the Academy of Sciences, Art, and Belles Lettres and a mason in the "perfect union" of Orleans. The following year Babeuf wrote the *Perpetual Cadastre*, which was published in 1789. In it he advocated the creation of a "National Fund for the

Subsistence of the Poor," as well as the division of land, which Babeuf thought should not be inherited but rather should return to the community upon the death of its owner.

In a letter of 1791 to Coupé de l'Oise, who had been recently elected to the legislative Assembly, Babeuf argued forcefully for the agrarian law that "assures the equitable sharing of landed properties." Babeuf maintained that without this law, "freedom, equality, and the rights of man will always remain high-sounding words, but words emptied of meaning." He also knew very well, however, that

> there is hardly anyone who doesn't totally reject the agrarian law; the bias against it is much stronger than the bias for the royalty. Those who have tried to open their mouths on this subject have always been hung. (Babeuf [1791], cited in Bravo 1970, 1:62)

The peasant movement of 1791–92 in Picardy, the suffering of the common people, the radicalization of the Revolution, the meeting with Buonarotti in the Plessis prison, demonstrations by the people for bread: all these led Babeuf to more radical positions. In the *People's Tribune*, which he founded with Buonarotti in the fall of 1794, he wrote:

> Individual property is the main source of all the evils that weigh upon society. . . . Property belongs to usurpers and the laws are made simply by society's strongest members. The sun shines for everyone and the earth belongs to no one. Go then, my friends, and upset, knock down this society that does not suit you. Everywhere, take what pleases you. The surplus belongs by right to him who has nothing. (Babeuf [1794], cited in Leroy 1950, 2:69–70)

Babeuf, who had been upset by the bloody excesses of 14 July 1789, now cried:

> Slaughter without pity the tyrants, the aristocrats, the gilded few. . . . You are the People, the true People, the only People worthy of enjoying the goods of this world. Everything that the People do is legitimate, all that they order is sacred. (Babeuf, cited in Servier 1967, 220)

In 1795 Babeuf, Buonarotti, and their disciples thought of overthrowing the Directory and its regime, which required paying property tax in order to vote. Throughout the Republic, according to the police reports, "hunger and despair have covered with a thick veil the words 'respect for property'" (ibid.). On 30 November 1795 the *People's Tribune* published the "Plebian Manifesto":

> We will prove that the soil belongs to no one, but rather to everyone. We will prove that all ground that an individual takes hold of beyond what is necessary to nourish him is a social theft. . . . The voices of a thousand honorable people will cry: Is it the agrarian law that you

want? No, it is more than that. . . . The only way . . . is to establish common administration, to suppress individual property, to fix each man to the talent or trade that he knows, to oblige him to deposit some of what he produces in the joint warehouse, and to establish a single administration for distribution, an administration for necessary provisions that, keeping account of all individuals and all things, will divide up these goods with the most scrupulous equality. . . . People! Wake up to hope. . . . Rejoice in the vision of a happy future. . . . All suffering is at its maximum; it cannot get worse. Only a total change can redress these wrongs! Let everything be jumbled up then! May all elements be mixed up and smashed together! May everything return into chaos and from chaos may a new and regenerated world emerge! (Babeuf [1795], cited in Droz 1972–78, 1:248–49)

Notices were stuck up on walls during the night. Support and sympathy flourished in the popular strata, even in the army and the police. Songs were written, assuring that the Equals' ideas were widely distributed. They took as their target "the opulent million," and they denounced "the bondage of man to man" and "murderous inequality." They extolled "holy and gentle equality" and repeated forcefully, "The sun shines for everyone."

In the spring of 1796 the Conspiracy of Equals was denounced. Its leaders were arrested and condemned to death. Babeuf and Darthé attempted suicide and were carried, bloody, to the scaffold. Babeuf delivered this final defense to his judges:

Yes, it is one voice that cries out to all: the goal of society is the general happiness. This was the original contract; no more words are needed to express it. The contract is vast, for all institutions should follow, and none should diverge, from this source. (Babeuf, cited in Dommanget [1922] 1970, 348)

In his *Reflections on the French Revolution* (1790), Edmund Burke, a member of the House of Commons and an influential voice in the Whig party, attacked egalitarianism, democracy, and universal suffrage: "It is said that twenty-four million men should prevail over two hundred thousand. Yes, if the Constitution is a matter of arithmetic" (cited in Jaurès 1969, 4:400).

Mackintosh, a doctor who became a lawyer in 1795, replied to Burke in his *Apology for the French Revolution* (1791). Mackintosh saw in the Revolution the promise of a complete political democracy that would concretize universal suffrage through elections. He approved the abolition of privilege and wanted laws to limit inequality, for

even if property is necessary, it is, in its excesses, the greatest sickness of civil society. Wealth grants power, and the accumulation of this power in the hands of a small number of men is a continual source of oppression for the mass of humanity. The power of the rich is further concentrated by their tendency to form alliances, alliances impossible for the poor to create because of their number, geographical dispersion, indigence, and their lack of education. (Mackintosh [1791], cited in Jaurès 1969, 4:410)

An active supporter of American independence and already the author of *Common Sense* (1776), Thomas Paine published *The Rights of Man* in 1791 and his *Agrarian Justice* in 1796. For him monarchy and democracy were irreconcilable: "Monarchy and aristocracy are jokes, and they will be sent to the same grave where all errors are interred: Mr. Burke is dressed in mourning" (Paine, cited in Jaurès 1969, 4:417).

Peace, disarmament, universal suffrage, generalized education about life's hazards: this was Paine's clear program. Paine advocated especially that half the state budget be devoted to a comprehensive insurance that would, through education and assistance to children, through public workshops, and through disability and old age pensions, safeguard workers their entire lives from ignorance, unemployment, and misery. (Jaurès 1969, 4:422, 424)

Throughout Europe people were fascinated and inflamed by the French Revolution.

Johann Fichte—son of a Saxon hosiery dealer, poverty-stricken student who earned a meager living by tutoring, follower of Kant—launched his first political manifesto from "Heliopolis," the "City of the Sun" (Zurich in fact), in the "last year of the old darkness" (1793): *Freedom of Thought Demanded Once Again from the Princes of Europe Who Have Oppressed It until Now*. The same year he published a *Rectification of Public Judgment on the French Revolution*: "The French Revolution appears to me to be important for all of humanity . . . ; [it] is a rich tableau on the theme of the rights of man and human dignity." Yet Fichte did not argue for a violent uprising in Germany:

No, we should first of all acquire an understanding and love of justice, and then diffuse such understanding and love around us, as far as our circle of action extends. It is through an inner effort, a movement from the bottom to the top, that men make themselves worthy of freedom. But liberation itself will come from above. (Cited in Jaurès 1969, 4:245)

In 1795 he published the *Doctrine of Science*:

My system is the first system of freedom. Just as this nation (France) will free humanity from material chains, my system will free it of the essence of oppression, exterior influences, for my system's initial principles treat man as an autonomous being. The doctrine of science was born during the years when political freedom triumphed within the French nation. But the French nation has raised me to an even higher point; it has stimulated in me the strength needed to comprehend French ideas. (Cited in Droz 1972–78, 1:411)

Professor of law at Jena, in 1796 Fichte published the *Foundations of Natural Law*. Accused of atheism, he was forced to seek refuge in Prussia. As a professor in Berlin, in 1800 he published *The Closed Commercial State* and *On the Destination of Man*. Faced with the Napoleonic invasion, he called for a national awakening in his *Discourses to the German Nation*, intended as "lessons on the improvement of education" delivered to the university under the occupation.

In *The Closed Commercial State* Fichte severely criticized liberal capitalism:

> The buyer wishes to wrest from the seller his goods; this is why he calls for free trade, that is to say, the freedom for the seller to over-crowd the markets, to find no outlet for his goods, and thus to sell them necessarily well below their value. This is why he calls for keen competition between manufacturers and merchants, so that they will be forced—due to the difficulties of marketing and maintaining a positive cash balance—to hand over the goods to the buyer at whatever price his generosity might offer to them. If this process takes place, the worker becomes poorer, and working families perish in want and misery, or else emigrate far from an unjust people. . . . In short, an individual is not at all guaranteed stable circumstances through stable employment. Men wish to be free mutually to destroy one another. (Fichte [1800], cited in Denis 1966, 262)

Fichte advocated centralized management of the economy by the state. With society as the owner of mines, the state employs the miners and fixes the number of workers in each branch of industry. The state directs workers to the various productive and administrative tasks; it controls all commercial exchanges and maintains a monopoly on foreign trade. Finally, the state establishes all prices. How can one avoid thinking, reading this, of Campanella's *The City of the Sun* and of the modern statist systems of centralized planning?

3. THE POWER OF UTOPIA

The thought of the great French utopians, Fourier and Saint-Simon, was also formed by the adventure, shock, and trauma of the Revolution.

Born in 1760, raised in aristocratic surroundings in the countryside, Count Claude-Henri de Rouvroy de Saint-Simon was tutored in his youth by d'Alembert. As a member of the French expeditionary corps in

America, he served under the direct orders of George Washington. Yet this man, who openly claimed to be a descendant of Charlemagne, renounced his titles and took the name Claude-Henri Bonhomme. Discovered selling off property belonging to France, Saint-Simon was imprisoned in 1793 and then freed in 1794. In Geneva in 1803 he published his *Letters from an Inhabitant of Geneva to His Contemporaries*. This book described a new society and a new world, governed by a "Council of Newton" composed of "three mathematicians, three physicists, three chemists, three physiologists, three literary men, three painters, and three musicians." This council "will divide humanity into the English, French, German, and Italian divisions; *all men will work*. . . . The Council of Newton will direct the work" (Saint-Simon [1803], cited in Bravo 1970, 1:86, 88).

In his *Parable* (1810), Saint-Simon severely denounced unproductive people who did not work. He speculated that if the important men of the aristocracy, the army, the church, and the government administration, along with the judges and the ten thousand richest property owners, were to disappear, "no political harm to the state would result from this loss of the thirty thousand individuals supposedly most important to the state" (ibid., 92).

On the other hand, if the leading scholars, artists, technicians, bankers, traders, farmers, manufacturers, craftsmen, and essential manufacturing workers—a total of some three thousand persons—were to disappear, then "the nation would become a body without a soul, and would fall immediately into a state of inferiority relative to the nations that are today her rivals. She would remain subordinate to them until she recovered her loss, until she had regrown a head" (ibid., 91).

Saint-Simon concluded that "existing society is in truth a world upside down,

> • since the nation has accepted as its fundamental principle that the poor should be generous to the rich, and that consequently the least well-off should deprive themselves daily of a portion of what is necessary to them in order to increase the luxurious excesses of the biggest property owners;
> • since the most guilty, the generalized thieves, those who put pressure on the citizenry as a whole and who take away three to four hundred million [francs] a year are the ones responsible for punishing small misdemeanors;
> • since ignorance, superstition, laziness, and a taste for expensive pleasures are the privilege of the heads of society, while capable, thrifty, and working people are employed only as subordinates and as instruments;

• since, in a word, in all occupations the incapable men are the ones entrusted to direct the capable. . . ." (Ibid., 94)

In the pamphlet *On the Reorganization of European Society* (1814), Saint-Simon discussed "the necessity and the means for unifying the peoples of Europe into a single political body while keeping for each its national independence." In particular he praised the alliance of France with England. Supported by subscriptions from, among others, the actor François-Joseph Talma, the economist J.-B. Say, and the scholars Delambre, Cuvier, and Berthollet, and by a grant from the banker Jacques Laffitte, he published in 1816 the periodical *Literary and Scientific Industry Linked to Commercial and Manufacturing Industry*, which in 1817 became *Industry: Political, Moral, and Philosophic Discussions*. He then lost his financial support, after which he published *Politics* (twelve issues in 1819), then *The Organizer* (1819–20), *On the Industrial System* (1820–21), and the *Catechism of the Industrialists* (1823–24). Saint-Simon tirelessly emphasized the role of those who create, invent, produce, manufacture, and bring projects to fruition. Thus in *Politics* he opposed the "national and industrial side" to the "antinational side":

The national side is composed
   1. of those who carry out work that is directly useful to society;
   2. of those who direct this work or whose capital is used in industrial projects;
   3. of those who contribute to production through work that is useful to the producers. (Saint-Simon, cited in Alexandrian 1979, 62)

The antinational side is composed
   1. of those who consume but do not produce;
   2. of those whose work is not useful to society and does not help the producers;
   3. of those who profess political ideas whose application harms production and who tend to deprive industrialists of the highest social esteem. (Ibid.)

In society as it is, one must regard "the property owners as the highest class, those who possess an industry[4] as the middle class, and those who have only their arms as the lowest." But Saint-Simon wrote in the *Catechism of the Industrialists*:

what we want, or rather what the progress of civilization demands, is that the industrial class be ahead of all other classes, that all other classes be subordinate to it. For society as a whole is based upon industry. Industry[5] is the only guarantee of society's existence; industry is the only source of all wealth and prosperity. (Ibid., 71)

Saint-Simon concerned himself, too, with workers: in an 1821 pamphlet, *Henri Saint-Simon to the Workers*, he stated: "The principal goal that I set myself in my work is to improve your situation as much as possible." Speaking in the name of the workers, he addressed himself to the leaders:

> You are rich and we are poor; you work with your heads and we work with our arms. There follows from these two basic differences existing between us that we are and should be your subordinates. . . . [But it is up to you] to take the initiative in indicating how our suffering may be ended, suffering that obviously will cease once public affairs are well managed.

Primacy of industry (that is to say, of all creative activities), responsibility for those who have proved their ability (artists, scholars, engineers, dealers, manufacturers, bankers), denunciation of idlers and of those who live off their rents, concern to raise the conditions of the proletarians: one finds all of these in Saint-Simon. Thus, in Saint-Simon one can find roots, not only of socialism, but also of productivism, industrialism, technocracy, and social capitalism.

In later life Saint-Simon wrote *The New Christianity*:

> The primitive goal of the Christian religion was the destruction of slavery. This goal attained, religion must set a new, more advanced goal: to establish a social organization that guarantees uninterrupted work to all proletarians, positive education to all members of society, and enjoyable activities that will develop their intelligence.

After Saint-Simon's death his disciples formed a school, then a church, and finally a sect. Some of them, involved in a cult with Enfantin, waited for the Woman-Messiah; others "went to the people" and labored as workers in order to spread the ideas of Saint-Simon. Some, such as Pierre Leroux, contributed to the development of socialist thought, while yet another group, including the Péreire and the Talabot brothers, became involved—through banking, railroads, and the Suez canal—with the grand projects of nineteenth-century French capitalism.

Charles Fourier, born in 1772, was the son of an important businessman in Besançon, but he had no taste for managing the family business. He made some poor speculative investments during the Revolution, was arrested, and, remaining suspect for a long time afterward, was obliged to work as a traveling salesman and then as a commercial employee in Lyons. As early as 1803 Fourier set himself the task of finishing the work of scholars and scientists:

> The scientists have discovered the laws governing the motion of material objects, which is very fine but does nothing to eradicate

poverty. What was needed was to discover the laws governing social movement. (Fourier, cited in Bravo 1970, 1:100)

In 1808 he published the *Theory of the Four Movements and of the General Destinies: Prospectus and Announcement of the Discovery:*

> I alone will have destroyed twenty centuries of political imbecility and it is to me alone that present and future generations will owe the initiative for their immense happiness. Before me, humanity lost several thousand years in battling foolishly against nature. . . . Possessor of the Destinies, I have shattered the political and moral darkness and, on the ruins of dubious sciences, I raise the theory of universal harmony. (Ibid.)

Following this, he published the *Treatise on Domestic and Agricultural Association* (1822), which was to have been the first of nine volumes in a "Theory of Universal Unity." There then appeared his *New Industrial and Social World* (1829), the denunciations contained in *Traps and Charlatanism in the Two Sects of Saint-Simon and Owen* (1831), and finally *False, Broken-Up, Repugnant, and Deceitful Industry, and the Antidote: Natural, Attractive, Truthful Industry* (1835–36).

Fourier was a visionary, a creator of words and social forms, fascinated by numbers, relationships, equilibrium, and harmony. He wanted to be the Newton of society, of the universe, even of the "polyverse," at the heart of which he saw "our universe" surrounded by an infinite number of others. He generalized the theory of "universal attraction" by advancing the idea of "passionate attraction":

> The passions, like matter and the heavenly bodies, have a double structure, that of social chaos—where our world today is found—and that of social harmony, in which the development of the passions is coordinated with everything else. (Fourier, cited in Alexandrian 1979, 98)

In order to attain "harmony" it is necessary to place men in "passionate gravitation" according to the theorems of "passionate geometry" or, better, the "mechanics of the passions": there are "five sensory passions" (corresponding to the five senses) and "four affective passions" (friendship, ambition, love, and fraternity). Agreement between the different passions is assured by "three little-known and defamed passions": the "cabalist" (the tendency to involve oneself in the affairs of others), the "butterfly" (the tendency toward a frequent change of interest), and the "composite" (the tendency to be interested in several things at once). These three "distributive passions" permit the formation of whole "passionate series" (ibid., 99).

Fourier listed thirty-two possible directions for escaping social chaos, of which six involved "compulsion" and six involved "genius." Among the latter was domestic and agricultural association into a phalanx of 810 or 1,620 "harmonians" living in a phalanstery equipped with all possible comforts. Fourier was not afraid to pass from the most abstract and esoteric vision to the most concrete description. He foresaw the life in a phalanstery:

> Each avenue, each street should lead to some kind of view, either of the countryside, or of a public monument. . . . Every house in the city or central area should have a vacant space—courtyard or garden— equal in surface area to that occupied by the house itself. (Ibid., 114–15)

Taking into account the "butterfly" tendency, he foresaw eight short periods of work per day for each person, all in eight different series, all in eight different possible orders, giving over fifty contrasting occupations during the week.

Thus, all work will become attractive and one

> will see those who are now idle, as well as the smallest householder, afoot by four in the morning, in winter and in summer, devoting themselves arduously to useful work, caring for gardens, farmyards, homes, and mills. At present these mechanics of civil life disgust the entire rich class. (Fourier, cited in Bravo 1970, 1:105)

Through association production would triple. Within the phalanx the "seven industrial functions" would be carried out:

1. domestic work,
2. agricultural work,
3. manufacturing work,
4. commercial work,
5. teaching,
6. study and use of the sciences, and
7. study and use of the fine arts. (Ibid., 1:111)

Besides this, with the partnership system much waste would be avoided:

> Instead of three hundred kitchen fires in three hundred households, there would be only four or five large fires preparing the different sorts of meals suited to the four or five different classes of wealth, for the partnership-state does not at all suppose equality. The present civilized system employs three hundred women working without appreciable mechanical aids. They could be replaced by a dozen experts using such aids in a kitchen designed to prepare meals for eighteen persons (the most suitable number). Such a joining together would leave each person free to go to the variously priced meals available at different tables, without restricting anyone's individual freedom.

The people in this case would spend much less to eat very well than they do today to live wretchedly. Immense quantities of firewood would be saved; this would do more to help restore the forests and vegetation than a hundred unenforceable forest laws.

Household work would be so simplified that seven-eighths of the housewives and domestics would become available and suitable for productive functions.

A communal oven costs much less in masonry and in fuel consumed than a hundred small household ovens, and it would be better managed by two or three experienced bakers than are the hundred ovens by a hundred women who, two times out of three, miss the right temperature for baking bread. (Ibid., 1:109–10, 111)

With this "New World" and its "truthful, attractive, and natural industry distributed in passionate series," the earth would pass through a decisive stage in its history:

On other planets, as on ours, humanity is obliged to spend about a hundred generations in false and divisive processes, comprising four periods: savage, patriarchal, barbarous, and civilized. Humanity languishes there until two conditions are fulfilled:

1. Large-scale industry, high science, and the fine arts are created, these being necessary to the establishment of a partnership system.

2. The partnership process is invented, this new industrial world being opposed to divisiveness. (Ibid., 1:113)

At the beginning of the nineteenth century, with Fourier and Saint-Simon on the one hand, and J.-B. Say and Claude-Frédéric Bastiat on the other, the two powerful utopias that still mark contemporary thought were face to face: the socialist utopia (happiness assured through reason) and the liberal utopia (happiness assured through the market). Both of them may be said to exist within the Newtonian universe of force and equilibrium. For Fourier equilibrium resulted from passionate attraction. In the liberal utopia, harmony resulted from the free play of supply and demand, which in turn assured equilibrium between individual interests.

COMMENTS ON CHAPTER 1

In a third of a century socialism's main ideas appeared and were expressed with both daring and conviction. Fourier, for example, was certain that once his phalanstery was established,

in less than two months the founder will have changed the fate of the entire world. The three societies—civilized, barbarous, and savage—will have been abandoned and the human species will have established the partnership community, which is its destiny. (Fourier, cited in Bravo 1970, 1:117)

The common basis of socialism has been set in place:

• a critique of existing society and its servitudes, injustices, and incoherence;
• the aspiration toward a new, harmonious society, without suffering and without oppression;
• and finally, the will or the desire to assure happiness to the greatest possible number.

But there were already differences springing up. Though all the early "socialists" were unanimous in rejecting social inequality, and though they all aspired to a just society, in general they did not make equality an essential characteristic of the new society. Babeuf and the Conspiracy of Equals did go so far as to question the idea of property itself, but they were an exception. Mackintosh went no further than limiting the unequal distribution of property, and Paine only proposed establishing a system of public assistance to deal with the worst suffering. As for the great French utopians, neither Fourier nor Saint-Simon, who advocated an alliance of workers, scholars, and enterprising men, aimed at equality.

Beyond the question of equality, how was it possible to arrive at a better society, ensuring general happiness? Godwin, Saint-Simon, and Fourier could see very well what mechanical progress, science, and improved technology might make possible. But the Equals, for their part, sought above all for the suppression of the "gilded million." Godwin saw a society where work would no longer be a curse but a joy—the joy of working in a society without injustice and without oppression. Fourier, having discovered the "butterfly passion," counted on a diversity of tasks to make work attractive. Babeuf foresaw public storehouses spread throughout the country, and Fourier conceived of his phalansteries on the scale of small towns. Fichte, however, entrusted the state with the responsibility for organizing production, and Saint-Simon relied on the best scholars, artists, and workers—in a word, on those who produced.

While Paine was committed to the idea of universal suffrage, and though Godwin and l'Ange wanted both social justice *and* democracy— Godwin going so far as to distrust all government, even if it were democratically elected—the problem of democracy was essential neither for the Equals (some of whom recommended abolishing the distinction between those who govern and those who are governed) nor for Saint-Simon or Fourier.

Leadership by the most competent, or effective democracy? Better-distributed property, or communal property? Change as the result of a brutal overturning of the old society, or through its progressive improvement, or through an unfailing adherence to the finally discovered laws of social harmony?

The richness of the socialist movement—in the widest sense—is already present here. And present, too, are many of its areas of contention and division.

2

CLEAR VISIONS OF SOCIALISM

In France many people were fighting for the Republic; in Great Britain capitalist industrialization was wiping out craft work while speeding the development of a working class that sought ways to defend and organize itself. Throughout Europe the affirmation that another society was possible became increasingly explicit, though there were diverse views—systematized by Marx—about what form the new society should take.

1. THE KALEIDOSCOPE OF FRENCH SOCIALISM

What a vast number of struggles were interwoven in nineteenth-century France! In the struggles against the Restoration and the aristocracy's arrogant recapture of the country in 1830, one finds the rising class—the capitalist bourgeoisie—joined together with the middle and petty bourgeoisies, as well as with skilled and unskilled workers from the textile industry.

In the struggles for the Republic, significant fracture lines cut across classes and property-owning strata. Many people were ready to support a constitutional monarchy, while others were definitely in support of a republic; but what kind of republic? A republic of property owners, the eminent, and the talented? No, the Social Republic! Some of the city people supported the central kernel of workers committed to the idea of the Social Republic. But they found themselves too often isolated, as in 1848 when they faced the property owners, who joined together out of common fear of the "sharers." And though the silk workers and other mill workers who demonstrated for work, wages, and bread often found sympathy and support among the common people of the cities, they ran into a hatred sharpened by fear among the rich.

The workers' world at this time of nascent industrial capitalism was weak, diverse, and dispersed. An abundance of socialist ideas proliferated out of this heterogeneous context.

Certainly, there was a common basis in the denunciation of injustice and misery and the unbearable insecurity of life to which so many craftsmen and workers were condemned. This denunciation overflowed socialist circles and could be found, in various forms, among philanthropists, charitable Christians, humanists, and supporters of a republic. Within socialist thought this denunciation increasingly emphasized the gap separating rich from poor, property owners from proletarians.

Thus Enfantin, head of Saint-Simonianism, bitterly described the balance sheet for 1830:

> Who won? It was the poor class, the largest class, the proletarians . . . , in a word, the people . . . [but] the holy revolt that has just taken place does not merit the name of Revolution. Nothing fundamental has been changed in the current social organization: a few names, colors, the national blazon, some titles, a few legislative modifications. . . . Such are the conquests of these days of mourning and glory.

And Charles Béranger, a clock maker, who published his *Petition of a Proletarian to the Chamber of Deputies* at the beginning of 1831, wrote:

> I mean by the people all who work, who have no social existence, all who own nothing—you know what I mean—the proletarians. You have heard talk about them, I'm sure; they have made enough noise in the world for a while, especially on 28 July.

Louis-Auguste Blanqui appeared before the Court of the Seine in January 1832 for a series of articles by the Society of Friends of the People criticizing the government of Louis-Philippe:

> THE PRESIDENT: What is your profession?
> BLANQUI: Proletarian.
> THE PRESIDENT: That is not a profession.
> BLANQUI: What? Not a profession? It is the profession of thirty million Frenchmen who live from their work and who are deprived of political rights.
> THE PRESIDENT: All right then! Clerk, write that the accused is a proletarian.

This notion was widely distributed from then on, as for example in the writings of Victor Considérant, a follower of Fourier and the author of *Social Destiny* (1835–44):

> Society is becoming divided more and more distinctly into two classes:

on the one hand, a small group who possess everything, or nearly everything, in the domain of property, commerce, and industry, and on the other hand a large group who own nothing and who live collectively in absolute dependence on the owners of capital and the instruments of labor. The second group is obliged to hire out, to the feudal lords of modern society, their arms, talents, and strength in return for an uncertain and always decreasing wage.

Lamennais, a priest condemned by the church for his *Words of a Believer* (1834), wrote in *Modern Slavery* (1839):

What is the proletarian today in regard to capitalism? An instrument of labor. Emancipated by present laws, a legally free person, he is not, it is true, salable property that can be bought by his employer. But this freedom is only fictitious. The body is not a slave, but the will is. Should we call it a genuine will that can choose only between an awful, inevitable death and the acceptance of a prescribed law? The chains and the whips of modern slavery are hunger.

And Louis Blanc in *The Organization of Labor* (1839):

Is a poor man a member or an enemy of society? We must respond. All around him he finds the land occupied. . . . What then will this unfortunate man do? He will say to you, "I have arms, intelligence, strength, youth: here, take all of that, and in exchange give me a little bread." This is what the proletarians today are doing and saying. But even here you are able to say to the poor man, "I have no work to give you." What do you want him to do then? You can see very well that he has only two choices: to kill himself or to kill you.

There is another aspect of the "common basis" of socialism:[6] the conviction that another society is possible, the aspiration toward a society ensuring, along with the disappearance of misery and a reduction in inequalities and oppression, dignity for everyone and—dare one write the word?—happiness.

Immediately, however, differences arose about what this new society was to be like, about the priority of various goals, and about means. Socialism at this time presents a fascinating kaleidoscope in which diversity was continually being reborn and cohesion lasted but a moment before bursting apart. One must try to imagine the debates, agreements, confrontations, and compromises; the newspapers and leaflets slipped under doors, the discussions among friends in taverns at night, the gatherings of workers' associations, secret societies, brotherhoods, and mutual-assistance groups. Always, though, there remained the threat of informers and of the police.

Listen once again to the clock maker Charles Béranger in his *Petition* of 1831:

Think of that other proletarian, Christ of Galilee, who preached equality and brotherhood . . . ; he overturned the established order . . . ; he was in a word the greatest agitator ever known. . . . What would become of us, good Lord, if one of these wretches [the proletarians— M. B.] took it into his head to act as did Spartacus or Christ?

In May 1833, when the printers and typographers of Nantes formed a mutual-aid fund, their tone was cordial:

Let it be said to the master printers: we envy neither your fortunes nor your amusements! No, but a wage able to furnish a modest bed, some shelter against the elements, some bread for our old age, and your friendship in exchange for ours. Why shouldn't we gather to speak peaceably of our concerns, of the existence of our families and of our industry?

By the time summer arrived, however, the workers, by ceasing to work, obliged their employers to raise wages and to hire back the printers who had been fired.

In September 1833 Grignon, a tailor and member of the Society for the Rights of Man, spoke to the other tailors:

Until a popular government relieves extreme poverty at the expense of extreme opulence—through a better system of taxation and a sensible organization of work—let us unite to strengthen the bonds of brotherhood, to help the most needy among us, and finally to determine ourselves the maximum duration of work and the minimum value of a day's labor. . . .

Our association must be strong enough and united enough to resist the claims of those who exploit us and to assure for each of us:

1. a wage that allows savings against the slack time and for unexpected expenses;
2. time for the rest necessary for health and learning;
3. relations of independence and equality with our masters.

We must be able to achieve, progressively, a working day no longer than ten hours, and an average wage of five or six francs per day.

Many people will no doubt cry out against our plans; they will find our demands exorbitant.

Grignon then invoked the desperate slogan of the silk workers of Lyons, "Live working or die fighting": "Call to our brothers in the other trades to follow our example, and then the masters will indeed be obliged to accept the law of the worker." The appeals expressed the same year by Jules Leroux to the typographers and by Efrahem, a cobbler, to the workers of all trades advanced similar ideas. The association of the early 1830s was the precursor of the organized workers' movement and of modern trade unionism.

But the association of this time was also the precursor of the cooperative movement. In 1841 Charles Noiret, a worker in Nantes, gave a very
coherent proposal for a cooperative project:

> Since labor is the only source of all production, each person should
> have for himself all the fruits of his labor. . . . Whoever does not work
> should not eat. This is the principle that should serve as a basis for our
> institutions and that will triumph by the organization of work through
> association. . . . This can only occur by our linking together, so that
> we may, ourselves, collect, prepare, and work the raw materials, and
> then deliver them for consumption. In this way, we will be able to
> keep for ourselves all that speculation now takes away from us, and
> we will be rid of those we call our masters.

Noiret saw three levels of cooperation: (1) "partial and special associations" (such as a profession in a single locality); (2) "general associations" (by industries or by locality); (3) the "national association," which
he proposed "dividing up by communes, arrondissements, and depart-
ments" because he feared that without a geographical division of authority "those directing the affair might overstep their bounds."

In 1848 the Society of United Corporations was formed. Article 2 of its
statutes defined its goals:

> *Article 2*: The Society of United Corporations takes as its goal the
> abolition of exploitation of man by man. This will be achieved through
> the immediate association of producers, through the creation of work-
> shops of associated workers. To this end a plan for general association
> will be submitted for consideration to each of the association's sec-
> tions as soon as they are organized.

And in 1849 the association of bronze workers, a trade possessing a
rich and long tradition of struggle, likewise set itself the following goals:

> In ethical order:
> • the emancipation of the workers by suppressing the employers;
> • the uniting of spirit and feelings by substituting emulation for
> hostile or envious competition;
> • a more and more equitable participation by each person in social
> functions and amusements;
> • in a word, the establishment of order in the production by relating
> it to consumption;
> • putting harmony into work, and the Republic into the workshop.
> (Cited by Barbeyer 1980)

Proudhon became the powerful protagonist of this social trend. In
1839, in *The Celebration of Sunday*, he posed the central problem:

> To find a state of social equality that is neither community nor

despotism nor division nor anarchy, but liberty in order and independence in unity. And once this first point is resolved there remains a second one: to outline the best means of transition. This is the whole human problem.

In the *Manual of a Stock Exchange Speculator* (1857) he proposed, in opposition to the existing "industrial feudalism," a plan for an "industrial democracy" in which there would be a "sponsoring of labor by labor, universal reciprocity: an end to the crisis." With his book *On the Federative Principle* (1863), his conception gained strength:

> The federative system is the opposite of the hierarchy, or administrative and governmental centralization. . . . All my economic ideas, elaborated over the last twenty-five years, can be expressed in these three words: industrial, agricultural federation. . . . The workers' association will remain a utopia so long as the government does not understand that public services should be carried out neither by the government nor converted into private and anonymous businesses, but rather bid out and contracted for specified times to companies of jointly liable and responsible workers. No more interference by power in the world of work. . . . In brief, whoever says freedom says federation, or else says nothing; whoever says republic says federation, or else says nothing; whoever says socialism says federation, or once again says nothing. (Proudhon [1863], cited in Gurvitch 1965)

There were others, however, who put their hopes in the state. Louis Blanc, for example, wrote in *The Organization of Labor* (1839):

> There is more: the emancipation of the proletariat is too complicated a matter, is tied to too many reforms, upsets too many customs, conflicts with too many prejudices, and goes counter—not in reality, but in appearance—to too many interests for there not to be folly in believing that this emancipation might be accomplished by a series of partial efforts and isolated endeavors. All the power of the state must be applied here, and even that power is certainly not excessive for such a labor. What the proletarians lack for their emancipation are the instruments of labor: it is up to the government to furnish them. No, without political reform, no social reform is possible; for though the latter is the goal the former is the means. (Blanc [1839], cited in Bravo 1970)

Proudhon reacted against this view, for

> these two propositions—*abolition of the exploitation of man by man and abolition of the government of man by man*—are a single and unique proposition. . . . The time will come when labor will be organized by itself in accordance with its own law; labor will have no more need of legislators or sovereigns: the workshop will make the government disappear.

Proudhon expressed some of the same fears that Charles Noiret, the worker of Nantes, had raised in 1841 when considering the possibility of a "national industrial association":

> In the present state of morals and thinking, where men are used to servitude and domination—a state that may last longer than we suspect—it is to be feared that those directing the affair may overstep their bounds, with the workers not sufficiently resisting such encroachment; little by little those governing the association will substitute themselves for the state and thus become masters of all public resources, disposing of persons and things according to their will. The nation would then become one vast exploitative operation: we would then have a fully developed Egyptian regime in effect, where an entire people work for the individual profit of its governors, receiving for their labor nothing but a little bad food and coarse clothing with which to sustain their venal and debased existence.

Nonetheless, the Republicans were increasingly occupied by the "social question." From the early 1830s men such as Buchez and Pierre Leroux worked to establish the idea that "the true republic is socialism. To want the republic to triumph in France without socialism is absurd." Blanqui, appearing before the Court of the Seine in 1832, asked that

> the thirty-three million French people choose the form of their government, and elect by universal suffrage the representatives who will make the laws. Once this reform is accomplished the taxes that rob the poor to the profit of the rich will be promptly eliminated and replaced by others based upon opposite principles. . . . This, sirs, is what we mean by the republic.

And in 1841 the worker Vabsenter wrote to Flora Tristan:

> We must, with all our strength, call for political reform, or, to express myself more clearly, the universal vote. So long as the poor have no political rights, it will be completely impossible for them to obtain any improvement.

This was realism.

But utopia remained tenacious. In the first volume of *Social Destiny* (1834) the Fourierist Victor Considérant assigned a positive function to utopian thought:

> Just as any judgment always requires a comparison, we are going to briefly sketch an *ideal* society, an order of things in which everything would be for the best, humanely speaking. . . . Let us then construct in thought a society in which the social causes of evil would no longer exist, and in which humanity would employ its energy and force only toward pursuits useful for the happiness of its members. (Considérant [1834], cited in Bravo 1970)

For Considérant the commune was "the cornerstone of the social construction, the basic element in the pattern out of which grow province, nation, and general society." And he saw, for these three levels, separate governments for the first two levels, acting in concert with a unified, overall government that would manage the planet:

> On this world a unified government would be the center for great industrial operations carried out by the nations of different continents; it would be the culminating point in an administrative hierarchy established like a network all around the globe; it would direct the industrial armies whose immense projects would have as their goal the profound modification of the surface of the earth, such as the reforestation of eroded mountain ranges, the agricultural conquest of vast deserts, the establishment of first-class highways, radiating out from the capital of the earth to the continental capitals and linking these latter to each other as well. This central government, through its unified administration, would balance production and consumption of the continents and would supervise commercial exchanges of their foodstuffs and respective products. In a word, it would direct all the general business of the earth, all the operations of the whole; it would be the earth's supreme industrial regulator.

It was also toward utopia that the Republican Étienne Cabet turned. The son of a craftsman, he became a lawyer and involved himself in the struggle for the Republic. He exiled himself to England in 1834, became interested in the ideas of Robert Owen, and wrote a "philosophical novel," *Journey to Icaria*, which was published clandestinely in 1840 and openly in 1842. In 1841 he proclaimed himself a communist:

> Yes, I am a communist! I have never hidden it; I have proclaimed it for a long time and I draw honor and glory from doing so. . . . I am a communist along with Socrates, Plato, and Jesus Christ, . . . with the men who are the light and honor of humanity. (Cited in Alexandrian 1979)

In 1842 the shareholders of his newspaper *Of the People* decided to call themselves "Icarian communists." But this did not prevent Cabet from proposing that

> all the opposition be brought together and centered around Arago, and all the democracy around the opposition; in this way a sort of universal, peaceful, obvious, and legal organization will be created for political and social reforms.

Two years later he launched an appeal in his newspaper to "go to Icaria":

> Since we are persecuted in France, since we are refused all rights, as well as the freedoms of association, assembly, discussion, and

peaceful propaganda, let us seek in Icaria our dignity as men, our rights as citizens, and Freedom with Equality.

The enthusiasm and generosity of the paper's readers supported the project, and on 3 February 1848 sixty-nine communist pioneers embarked for America singing the "Song of the Icarian Departure":

> Soldiers of Brotherhood
> Let us found in Icaria
> The happiness of humanity.

Blanqui, for his part, remained fundamentally convinced that "so far as Freedom is concerned, one must not wait for it, one must take it." And the state was for him decisively important terrain:

> The social state being gangrenous, in order to move on to a healthy state, heroic remedies are needed; for some time the people will need a revolutionary power. The royalty and all the aristocracy must be exterminated, and in their place a republic must be substituted, that is to say, a government of equality. But in order to arrive at this government, a revolutionary power must be used that puts the people in a position to exercise their rights. (Cited in Droz 1972–78)

On 12 May 1839, preparations having been made in greatest secrecy in the Société des Saisons [a secret society—Trans.], three hundred armed men besieged City Hall in Paris. But the Parisians had no advance knowledge of what was taking place and walked calmly by, while Barbès read to a few already-convinced believers the proclamation Blanqui had prepared in their honor:

> People, raise yourselves up, your enemies will disappear like dust before the storm. Strike without pity the vile accomplices of tyranny; take the hand of these soldiers who have emerged from your own womb—they will not turn parricidal weapons against you.

Blanqui was arrested and remained in prison until 1847; though at the people's side in 1848, he was again imprisoned, this time until 1859, and was yet again imprisoned from 1861 to 1870 and from 1871 to 1877. In 1868–69 he finished his *Instructions for a Taking Up of Arms*, which begins as follows:

> This plan is purely military, and does not deal at all with the political and social questions, which are not here at issue: it goes without saying that the revolution should (be made to the profit of labor against the tyranny of capital, and)[7] reform society on a just basis. (Blanqui [1868] 1972)

In 1879—when he was seventy-four, having spent nearly forty years of his life in prison—Blanqui published a newspaper entitled *Neither God nor Master*.

During this period a swarm of diverse views proliferated, inspired by the same ideals of freedom, justice, equality, brotherhood, and happiness. Absolute utopia coexisted with the most immediate claims. And the paths diverged, even among the utopians: were they creating a model for reference or a plan to be put into action right away? Association appeared to many craftsmen and workers as a pathway full of promise, but the question of what sort of association remained: the association of capital and labor, the association of producers excluding the property owners, or the association of workers in order to impose their views on the employers?

Opposed to those who expected nothing from the state were those who saw in the state a powerful tool for change. But was it necessary to conquer the state by force, or to impose the will of the people through universal suffrage? And beyond this question, another: was the state to be conceived as an instrument for reducing the evils of present society, or rather as a sort of lever allowing present society to be overturned so that another society might develop?

Final answers to these questions were not produced during this period. Despite the absence of an organized workers' movement, the energy of popular movements joined together with resolute battles for a democratic republic to create the astonishing richness of thought among French socialists in the second third of the nineteenth century.

2. MARX, OR SYSTEMATIZATION

In England capitalist industrialization was in full swing: in 1815 the cotton-weaving industry utilized 2,500 power looms and 200,000 hand looms; in 1834, 100,000 power looms and 250,000 hand looms; but by 1850, 225,000 power looms and 50,000 hand looms. The number of steam engines grew from 500 in 1780 to 15,000 in 1830 (in France there were 3,000 at this date). The production of coal rose from 10 million tons in 1800 to 16 million tons in 1830 (eight times more than in France or in Germany at the time), 47 million tons in 1850, and 110 million tons in 1870. Pig iron production reached 2 million tons in 1840 (ten times more than in Germany or in the United States at the time) and surpassed 5 million tons in 1860 and 11 million tons in 1880.

The workers' traditions of collective action endured and became richer and more diverse. There were struggles against machines and for a standard wage. Workers' cooperatives grew up, along with helping organizations and provident societies. In 1829 John Doherty founded the General Union of Spinners and Piecers of England, Scotland, and Ireland; the following year he organized a federation open to all existing unions, the National Association for the Protection of Labor, which soon included 150 unions and 80–100,000 members. Thirty thousand copies of his newspaper, *The Voice of the People*, were being printed per issue, though by 1832 the association had fallen apart and disappeared.

In 1831, at the time of the campaign for the Reform Bill, some craftsmen, including William Lowett, a cabinetmaker, formed the National Union of the Working Classes and Others; at the same time the Builders' Union developed, bringing together the different construction trades and representing thirty thousand workers in 1833. The same year the Great Union consolidating different trades was formed; this union joined workers' societies with cooperative associations. Inspired in particular by Owen, it was simultaneously a health insurance institution, a retirement fund, and a means for financing cooperative workshops and strike funds. In the 21 December 1833 issue of its newspaper *The Crisis*, John Fielden, a cotton manufacturer, proposed the idea of a general strike to establish an eight-hour working day. The previous year, William Benbow, one of the moving spirits in the National Union of the Working Classes, had promoted the idea of a "sacred month," a "general strike," a "great national holiday" both to demonstrate—by the absence of production—the absurdity of the idea of overproduction that economists used to explain crises, and to give the producers time to discuss and to come to an agreement about how to establish the reign of equality and happiness.

In 1836 some craftsmen, including Lowett once again, formed the Working Men's Association. The London chapter wrote a "People's Charter" in favor of a true political democracy, including universal suffrage for men (and envisaged for a certain time for women), a secret ballot, the elimination of all poll taxes, the redrawing of electoral boundaries, the establishment of parliamentary compensation (permitting workers to devote themselves to parliamentary affairs once they were elected), and an annual replacement of all members of Parliament. Universal suffrage at this time seemed to be a means for expressing the people's will, and thus for assuring a rapid increase in wages, better housing, and a reduction in the length of the working day.

Carried away by leaders such as the parliamentary radical Feargus O'Connor and the Reverend Mr. Stephens, the impoverished workers of Lancashire and Yorkshire became inflamed. Lowett recommended a peaceful petition. O'Connor advocated the use of force. Reverend Stephens let himself be carried away by his own eloquence:

If those who produce all the wealth do not have the right, in conformity with God's word, to gather for their own use the fruits of the earth which, according to God's word, they have reaped by the sweat of their brow, then let them fight their enemies, who are also God's enemies, by any means necessary. If the knife, the rifle, and the pistol, the sword and the pike are not enough, then may the women take up their scissors, and the children brandish pins or needles. If all else fails, then take burning coals, yes, burning coals [deafening applause], burning coals I say: burn the palaces down! (Cited in Dolléans 1936–56)

Meetings attracted tens of thousands of workers. A first petition was presented in 1839, a second containing more than three million signatures in 1842, and a third with more than six million signatures in 1848. The ruling powers repressed the movement (banishment and prison), threatened it (by sending troops), made concessions (laws enacted governing labor by women and children in the mines and one instituting the ten-hour working day), used force (intervention by troops against outlawed meetings), and benefited finally from divisions within and errors by the workers' leaders: the Chartist movement collapsed, discredited.

In 1842 Friedrich Engels, then twenty-two, went to live in Manchester, where his father owned a textile mill. He met Robert Owen, then seventy-two, who had just published *The Book of the New World*. Engels became involved in the Chartist movement and published articles in the *New Moral World* and in O'Connor's *Northern Star*. He observed and analyzed, and then wrote *The Condition of the Working Class in England*, published in 1845.

In 1844 in Silesia five thousand weavers rose up, destroyed their machines, and burnt the books and titles of property. Karl Marx, in Paris at the time, emphasized the conscious character of this event and saw in it the sign that the German proletariat was to play a leading role in the international workers' movement. The same year Engels sent Marx two articles for the *Franco-German Annals*. Out of Marx's enormous work and his constant exchanges with Engels grew a body of analysis and a worldview that have profoundly affected socialist thought and the socialist movement.

As is true of his analysis of capitalism, the broad directions of Marx's thought about socialism were defined very early. Above all, communism is seen as the negation of capitalism:

Communism is for us not a stable state which is to be established, an *ideal* to which reality will have to adjust itself. We call communism the *real* movement which abolishes the present state of things. The conditions of this movement result from the premises now in existence. (Marx and Engels [1844] 1947, 26)

The actor in this negation is the proletariat:

Where is the positive possibility of German emancipation? Our answer: in the formation of a class with radical chains, a class in civil
society that is not of civil society, an estate that is the dissolution of all
estates, a sphere of society having a universal character because of its
universal suffering and claiming no particular right because no particular wrong but unqualified wrong is perpetrated on it; a sphere that
can claim no traditional title but only a human title; a sphere that does
not stand partially opposed to the consequences but totally opposed
to the premises of the German political system; a sphere, finally, that
cannot emancipate itself without emancipating itself from all the other
spheres of society, thereby emancipating them; a sphere, in short,
that is the complete loss of humanity and that can only redeem itself
through the total redemption of humanity. This dissolution of society
existing as a particular class is the proletariat. (Marx [1844] 1970,
141–42)

This vision is found in many later texts:

The condition for the emancipation of the working class is the abolition of every class, just as the condition for the liberation of the Third
Estate, of the bourgeois order, was the abolition of all estates and all
orders. The working class, in the course of its development, will
substitute for the old civic society an association which will exclude
classes and their antagonism, and there will be no more political
power properly so called, since political power is precisely the official
expression of antagonism in civil society. (Marx [1847] n.d., 146–47)

And again:

The proletariat rallies more and more round revolutionary socialism,
round communism, for which the bourgeoisie has itself invented the
name of Blanqui. This socialism is the declaration of the permanence
of the revolution, the class dictatorship of the proletariat as the necessary transit point to the abolition of class distinctions generally, to the
abolition of all the relations of production on which they rest, the
abolition of all the social relations that correspond to these relations of
production, to the revolutionizing of all the ideas that result from
these social relations. (Marx [1850] n.d., 198)

These two passages clearly show the continuity of thought, but they
also bring to light a problem present in Marx's thought, a problem also
present in both earlier French socialism and in the later development
of socialism: the vision of the emancipation of the proletariat as a
dissolution of "political power properly so called," with the "dictatorship of the proletariat as the necessary transit point" and a provisional reinforcement of political power supposedly opening the way for its
own disappearance.

This is a crucial point. In 1852 Marx took stock of his own efforts:

My own contribution was (1) to show that the existence of classes is merely bound up with certain historical phases in the development of production; (2) that the class struggle necessarily leads to the dictatorship of the proletariat; (3) that this dictatorship itself constitutes no more than a transition to the abolition of all classes and to a classless society. (Marx [1852] 1983, 63–65)

This sequence is, moreover, clearly stated by Marx and Engels in *The Communist Manifesto:*

The distinguishing feature of communism is not the abolition of property generally, but the abolition of bourgeois property. But modern bourgeois private property is the final and most complete expression of the system of producing and appropriating products that is based on class antagonisms, on the exploitation of the many by the few. In this sense, the theory of the communists may be summed up in the single sentence: Abolition of private property. . . . The proletariat will use its political supremacy to wrest, by degrees, all capital from the bourgeoisie, to centralize all instruments of production in the hands of the state, i.e., of the proletariat organized as the ruling class; and to increase the total of productive forces as rapidly as possible. . . . When, in the course of development, class distinctions have disappeared, and all production has been concentrated in the hands of a vast association of the whole nation, the public power will lose its political character. Political power, properly so called, is merely the organized power of one class for oppressing another. If the proletariat during its contest with the bourgeoisie is compelled, by the force of circumstances, to organize itself as a class; if, by means of a revolution, it makes itself the ruling class, and as such sweeps away by force the old conditions of production, then it will, along with these conditions, have swept away the conditions for the existence of class antagonisms, and of classes generally, and will thereby have abolished its own supremacy as a class. In place of the bourgeois society, with its classes and class antagonisms, we shall have an association in which the free development of each is the condition for the free development of all. (Marx and Engels [1848] 1955, 24, 31, 32)

The theoretical coherence of this conception is condensed by Marx in the following passage from *Capital*, vol. 3:

It is always in the immediate relation between the owner, his means of production and the direct producer (a relationship whose various aspects naturally correspond to a definite stage in the development of work procedures, and thus to a certain stage of social productive forces) that one must seek the hidden foundation of the entire social edifice. Consequently, it is this same relationship that underlies the political form of the sovereignty/dependence relationship and, more generally, the basis of the specific form exhibited by the state in a given period.

With the intuition, and then the demonstration, that the logic of capitalist development leads inexorably to the increasing proletarianization of the middle portions of the petty bourgeoisie and at the same time to increasingly severe crises, Marx was able to declare that the economic movement under way ineluctably prepares the establishment of a classless society by strengthening the proletariat.

In 1846 Proudhon, with whom Marx at that time thought of allying himself against Karl Grün, expressed his doubts:

> I profess an economic antidogmatism that is almost absolute. Good God! After having demolished all a priori dogmatisms, let us not in our turn fall into the contradiction of your countryman Martin Luther . . . , let us not ourselves indoctrinate the people. Let us carry on a good and loyal polemic; let us give to the world the example of a learned and far-seeing tolerance; but, since we are at the head of the movement, let us not make ourselves the leaders of a new intolerance. Let us not pose as the apostles of a new religion, even if this be the religion of logic, the religion of reason. Welcome and encourage all allegiances; condemn all exclusions, all mysticisms . . . ; on this condition I will be pleased to associate with you. Otherwise, no! (Proudhon [1846], cited in Dolléans 1936–56)

And Mikhail Bakunin, who, passing through Brussels in 1847, observed the School for German Workers organized by Marx, noted: "Marx is here carrying on the same occupation as before; he corrupts the workers by making dialecticians out of them. It is the same madness for systems and the same unsatisfied conceitedness." Throughout the course of the socialist and workers' movements, differences of ideas and incompatibilities of temperament reinforce each other. At difficult times they produce consuming quarrels, and then, when the social movement is on the upswing, they seem trivial, even though the underlying questions themselves remain decisive.

The revolutionary movement of 1848 pushed back servitude and advanced republican ideals throughout Europe. In France, 1848 resulted in a break between the Republicans and the workers' movement, a break evident in the following exchange between François Arago and some insurgent workers maintaining the barricade in the rue Soufflot:

> ARAGO: Why are you rebelling against the law?
> WORKERS: We have already been promised so much, promises that have been broken so many times that we have no more confidence in words alone.

ARAGO: But why erect barricades? We raised them together in 1832; you no longer remember the Cloister of Saint-Merri?

WORKERS: But, Mr. Arago, why do you reproach us; you have no idea what suffering is, you have never been hungry.

Various forms of repression—isolation, police harassment, arrests, and deportations associated with the 2 December coup d'état—all weakened the French workers' movement. In 1854 Louis Reybaud, a former liberal who helped unify the Order party, wrote: "Socialism is dead; to speak of it is to deliver its funeral oration." But these words forgot the obstinate courage, the daily effort by workers and militants to reform the links between themselves and to reconstitute their organizations. One of these workers, Tolain, a bronze sculptor, wrote in 1863: "The workers claim today, in the name of common law, the freedom to form workers' trade unions in each profession. The workers' trade unions would be, within the economic order, the mother institution for all future progress." Tolain helped to write the manifesto signed by sixty Parisian workers:

> Universal suffrage has brought us to the age of majority politically, but we have yet to emancipate ourselves socially. The freedom that the Third Estate was able to acquire with such strength and perseverance must be extended throughout France, as a democratic country, to all citizens. Equal political rights necessarily imply equal social rights.

In England the organization of the workers' movement made considerable progress. National unions developed (particularly among stone masons, iron workers, steam-engine builders, and mechanics) and began to appoint permanent secretaries and to have sufficient funds available for useful support in case of strikes. They circulated their newspapers and developed information and training networks. In 1860 the Junta, a council of London unions, was formed; in 1868 the first Trade Unions Congress took place, and by 1874 this latter group represented 1,200,000 workers.

The desire to create links between the workers' movements in different countries resulted from diverse traditions and analyses, and led in 1864 to the creation of the International Workingmen's Association (IWA). The composition of the IWA's provisional committee is significant because it united activists from the workers' movement in many different countries; there were twenty-one English representatives, nine French and émigré representatives, ten Germans, six Italians, two Swiss, and two Poles. The provisional statutes affirmed forcefully: "The emancipation of the working class must be the work of the working class itself." Marx wrote the inaugural address, and in it he attempted to find terms that would satisfy both those who gave priority to the internal transformation of society (particularly through cooperation), and those who believed first of all in the conquest of state power:

> Cooperative labor may be fine in principle and practically useful, yet so long as it remains circumscribed within the narrow sector of workers' isolated and dispersed efforts, it will never be able to stop the geometric progression of monopolies, nor free the masses, nor even significantly lighten the burden of misery. . . . In order to free the working masses, the cooperative system must be developed on a national scale, which means that it must have resources on a national scale at its disposal. . . . Given this situation, the primary task of the working class is to conquer political power.

By reaffirming that "the winning of political power becomes the great task of the proletariat," Article 7a of the Statutes of the IWA states explicitly:

> In its struggle against the collective power of the possessing classes, the proletariat can act as a class only by forming itself into a distinct political party, opposed to all the political parties formed by the possessing classes. This development of the proletariat into a political party is indispensable to the triumph of the social revolution and its ultimate goal: the abolition of classes.

At the Lausanne Congress of the IWA in 1867, mutualists opposed collectivists. The motion on the state declared:

> The effort of the nation should be directed toward making the state owner of the means of transport and circulation in order to wipe out the monopoly of the big companies, which, by submitting the working classes to their arbitrary laws, attack the dignity of man as well as individual freedom.

At the congress in Basel in 1869, Bakunin judged the "centralist" camp to be weakened:

> Since 1868, the time when I joined the International, I have led a crusade in Geneva against the very principle of authority, and have argued for the abolition of the state. I have condemned this so-called revolutionary dictatorship that the Jacobins of the International, Marx and his disciples, would have us believe is a provisional measure absolutely necessary to the consolidation and organization of the people's victory. . . . At the congress in Basel we managed a more-or-less complete victory, not only over the doctrinaire and pacifist followers of Proudhon—the individualist, bourgeois socialists of Paris—but also over the authoritarian communists in Marx's school. Because of this, Marx will not pardon us, and this is why, immediately following this congress, Marx and his followers began a war against us aimed at nothing less than our complete destruction.

Once again, personal rivalries embittered the debates and the disagreements. While the First International was splitting apart, the Jurassian Federation stated the underlying problem in these terms:

The question that today divides the International can be summarized in these two terms: federalism or centralism. Two programs for social change are present: one conceives the future society in the form of a centralized popular state [*Volkstaat*] while the other, on the contrary, defines this society as the free federation of free industrial and agricultural associations.

Marx, however, having followed and supported the struggle by the Paris Commune, in his address to the General Council of the IWA on 30 May 1871 stressed the importance of the concrete transformation of the state apparatus that the Commune had carried out:

. . . [T]he working class cannot simply lay hold of the ready-made state machinery, and wield it for its own purposes. . . . The cry of "social republic" with which the Revolution of February was ushered in by the Paris proletariat did but express a vague aspiration after a republic that was not only to supersede the monarchical form of class rule, but class rule itself. The Commune was the positive form of that republic. . . . The first decree of the Commune, therefore, was the suppression of the standing army, and the substitution for it of the armed people. The Commune was formed of the municipal councillors, chosen by universal suffrage in the various wards of the town, responsible and revocable at short terms. The majority of its members were naturally working men, or acknowledged representatives of the working class. The Commune was to be a working, not a parliamentary body, executive and legislative at the same time. Instead of continuing to be the agent of the Central Government, the police was at once stripped of its political attributes, and turned into the responsible and at all times revocable agent of the Commune. So were the officials of all other branches of the administration. From the members of the Commune downwards, the public service had to be done at workmen's wages. . . . The communal *régime* once established in Paris and the secondary centres, the old centralised government would in the provinces, too, have to give way to the self-government of the producers. In a rough sketch of national organisation which the Commune had no time to develop, it states clearly that the Commune was to be the political form of even the smallest country hamlet. . . . The unity of the nation was not to be broken, but, on the contrary, to be organised by the Communal Constitution, and to become a reality by the destruction of the state power which claimed to be the embodiment of that unity independent of, and superior to, the nation itself, from which it was but a parasitic excrescence. . . . The Commune . . . was a thoroughly expansive political form. . . . It was essentially a working-class government, the produce of the struggle of the producing against the appropriating class, the political form at last discovered under which to work out the economical emancipation of labour. (Marx [1871] 1940, 54, 56–58, 60)

This text is important because for Marx and Engels, and then for Marxists in the following decades, the transformation of the state set in motion by the Paris Commune was to become the prime example of the dictatorship of the proletariat. In his letter of 12 April 1871 to Kugelmann, Marx wrote:

. . .[T]he next attempt of the French revolution will be no longer, as before, to transfer the bureaucratic-military machine from one hand to another, but to *smash* it, and this is essential for every real people's revolution on the Continent. (Marx [1871] 1940, 85)

The *Critique of the Gotha Program* reaffirmed the necessity for the dictatorship of the proletariat and, at the same time, the need to transform the state:

Freedom consists in converting the state from an organ controlling society to one completely controlled by it, and thus to-day the forms of the state are freer or less free in measure as they restrict the "freedom of the state." . . . Between capitalist and communist society lies a period of revolutionary transformation from one to the other. There corresponds also to this a political transition period during which the state can be nothing else than the *revolutionary dictatorship of the proletariat*. (Marx [1875] 1933, 43–45)

In 1891, in the introduction that he wrote for the new edition of the Address to the General Council of the International on *The Civil War in France*, celebrating the twentieth anniversary of the Commune, Engels summarized the main points of Marx's 1871 analysis, and he concluded with these words:

The philistine social democrat has lately been seized with wholesome dread when he hears pronounced the words "dictatorship of the proletariat." Do you want to know what this dictatorship resembles? Look at the Paris Commune. That was the dictatorship of the proletariat.

COMMENTS ON CHAPTER 2

This period had a fascinating richness, as well as daring and courage. These visionaries were indeed necessary to socialism: only they were capable of providing a global objective that could both infuse hope and transform various dispersed revolts into a powerful current. Only they could form the conceptual tools that would one day contribute to the toppling of society.

Consequently they were hated, fought against, and condemned. But their ideas—often impoverished by the difficulties of publishing, communicating, and reading—spread within the tumult of popular and workers' movements and there took root, eventually flourishing with a new richness. To abolish the exploitation of man by man: yes, here and now, by creating an association where the producers will be the owners of their instruments of labor and of what they produce. To create a society that establishes human happiness: yes, right now, let us leave to found a community in the New World. To respond, finally, to the immediate desires of the producers, to limit the working day, to raise wages, to protect against life's contingencies: let us obtain universal suffrage in order to impose our solutions on the handful of exploiters.

Everything seems so simple, when one dreams of perfect happiness! Work is no longer a constraining burden. Collective discipline is no longer oppressive.

But as soon as one attempts to express concretely how to advance toward this dream, divergent views come to the surface, revealing different visions of the general future happiness.

The situation of the workers in capitalist industry—at that time in full expansion, particularly in England—was unacceptable to everyone. Their "freedom" was only the absolute necessity to sell themselves to the new masters who employed and exploited them. They endured harsh working conditions, generally degrading living conditions, low wages, and insecurity, and they suffered greatly during times of unemployment. For some, solutions seemed to be within easy reach: coalition against the bosses, association, cooperation, and universal suffrage. These were seen as methods that, in one way or another, would bring a limit to the working day (ten hours here, eight hours there), an increase in wages, and various other protections. For others, *the* solution existed: the overthrow of the old society. Such an overthrow was to be the mission of the proletariat, this new messiah that in freeing itself was going to liberate all the oppressed; that in overthrowing the class that exploited it was going to do away with all class dominations.

In these struggles, and within these perspectives, the socialists in the second third of the nineteenth century came up against the problem of the state. Would winning universal suffrage be enough? A number of leaders of the Chartist movement held that it was, as did Pierre Leroux and Buchez: "Socialism is the republic." Even men as different from each other as Babeuf and Cabet shared this view at certain moments in their struggles. Or would it be necessary to take the state by force, even by conspiracy, as Blanqui was convinced?

And then the next question: should one have confidence, as did Louis Blanc, that this state would reform society? Should one look forward to centralizing in the state's hands the means of production wrested from the bourgeoisie, as Marx and Engels foresaw in *The Communist Manifesto*? Or should one fear, as did Noiret, that the state would impose a new oppression worse than the previous one? What would happen if the state became the owner of all public resources? From this time onward, is it not necessary to consider more closely the concrete realization of what Marx called the disappearance of political power as such? And many socialists in the nineteenth century were in fact trying to do just this: Proudhon, with industrial democracy, universal mutuality, the federation; Considérant, with his three levels of government, from the commune to world government; so many cooperators, with their projects for free associations and for free federations of these associations; Bakunin, with the abolition of state power.

Fundamentally, out of this diversity two lines, two visions become clear. The first is that of seizing central state power and then utilizing this power more or less temporarily: a republican government, a centralized popular state, or a dictatorship of the proletariat. Partisans of this view included Louis Blanc, Blanqui, and Marx, as well as part of the Chartist movement in England and the Republican movement in France. The second vision is that of the dissolution of all political power: using the general strike as the means, shut everything down and create other ways of organizing production, by association and cooperation, as was suggested by Proudhon and Bakunin. Within a single movement both the exploitation of man by man and the government of man by man were to be abolished.

Trying to avoid a serious split at the heart of the workers' movement, Marx attempted the impossible synthesis: if one wants to break the current domination by the bourgeoisie, one must seize the state, though this seizure will be carried out in order to begin a process that will lead to the state's withering away. A dictatorship must be imposed on the former oppressors, though this same regime will be experienced as democracy by most of the people.

To ask this was no doubt to demand the impossible, though at the time it could still appear realistic. Look at the Paris Commune: they in fact took control of the state apparatus *and* began the destruction of this apparatus; the people imposed their will *and* it was democracy. For several decades following the Paris Commune, the "dictatorship of the proletariat" had a concrete reference point.

There remained, however, a silence, something not said—taboo or illusion—about the problem of production in achieved socialism. Of course, there was the formula, "From each according to his abilities, to each according to his needs," but underneath its apparent rationality there reeks a musty Rousseauism: does it not suppose an "innately good" man who, in the new society, would naturally accept hard work if he were capable of it even though, if his needs were small, he would receive very little in return?

Finally, was not Marx—though he contributed greatly to the analysis and denunciation of capitalism by building, in opposition to Fourier's visionary utopia, a powerful and vital rational utopia—the last great utopian?

For with the development of the socialist movement and of trade unionism in the leading capitalist countries, and with the Bolshevik seizure of power in Russia in 1917, socialist ideas and ideals were forced to confront, in these two very different social formations, the inescapable demands of praxis.

3

FROM IDEAL TO COMPROMISE

In the last third of the nineteenth century, capitalist development of industry profoundly transformed many countries, not only Great Britain, which was the workshop and banker to the world despite its diminished supremacy,[8] but also France, Belgium, Germany, and the United States. Along with the increase in production and the increase in the size of the well-to-do classes, the numbers of those without work and those crushed by exploitation also increased. Simultaneously, paternalism, philanthropy, social doctrines, and socialist ideas spread, *and* the workers experienced a long apprenticeship in solidarity, organization, and collective struggle.

In all their various forms, socialist ideas spread and were discussed throughout Europe and North America; they began, at first through the efforts of isolated individuals and small groups of adherents, to penetrate all parts of the world. Intellectuals—often from the middle classes—played a major role in the dissemination of socialist ideas: there were discussion clubs, and groups organized around a single man or around a review. Socialist parties and organizations became more and more involved in political action, particularly in elections and parliamentary activity.

The cooperative, associative, and trade union movements progressed, too, in this period, and though they were more anchored in everyday action and were more concerned with concrete reality than were the intellectuals, they were equally inspired by the grand ideals of socialism.

Thus, in the capitalist countries, the socialist and workers' movements developed, in distinct though related ways, through unions, cooperatives, parties, and discussion groups. And the connections among these

42

powerful forces—especially parties and unions—became decisively important in every capitalist country.

1. SOCIALISM AND UNIONISM

The working classes grew at the pace of capitalist industrialization: in Great Britain there were 5.7 million industrial workers in 1881 and 8.6 million in 1911; during these same years the working class in France grew from 3 to 5 million members, and in Germany, from 5 to nearly 9 million, while in the United States the number of industrial wage earners more than doubled, increasing from 3 to 7 million. The workers' movement organized and strengthened itself, especially in Great Britain (1 million union members in 1874, but 4 million in 1913) and in Germany (300,000 union members in 1890, 2.5 million in 1913), though also in France (750,000 union members in 1905) and in the United States, where, alongside the prudent development of the American Federation of Labor (2 million members in 1912), the advance of unionism was closely tied to strike and wage settlement successes.

The First International having come apart, the socialist movement organized and progressed within the framework of the nation, and here the sort of relations established by the trade union movement became decisively important for the future.

In Great Britain socialist thought and action, though slowed during the period of prosperity from 1850–1875, became vigorous once again during the "great depression" of 1875–1893. This depression particularly affected British capitalism and marked the beginning of Britain's relative decline. The Social Democratic Federation was founded in 1881 by, among others, H. M. Hyndman (who brought a solid family fortune to the organization), Eleanor Marx-Aveling (Marx's daughter), and William Morris, though these latter two broke with the Federation in 1885 to create the Socialist League. During the same period in the 1880s the Fabian Society was also created, by intellectuals such as Sidney and Beatrice Webb and H. G. Wells. It was during this period as well that the first attempts at party organization were made, first by the Scottish Labour party, founded in 1888 by the Scottish miner Keir Hardie, and next by the Independent Labour party, founded in 1893, whose weekly newspaper *The Clarion* was edited by the journalist R. Blatchford.[9] The decisive initiative in these years came from trade union circles, with the decision made at the Trade Unions Congress in Plymouth in 1899 to propose the establishment of a coordinating organization, the Labour Representation Committee, which in 1900 brought together seven trade union representatives, two representatives from the Social Democratic

Federation, two representatives from the Independent Labour party, and one representative from the Fabian Society. Only with great difficulty was this Labour Representation Committee able to get "labor representatives" elected in a two-party system dominated by conservatives and liberals. The labor representatives who were elected in 1906, thanks in part to an alliance with the liberals, then founded the Labour party. The Labour Representation Committee claimed 380,000 members in 1901 and 860,000 in 1903; the Labour party had 1,600,000 members in 1914, of whom 1,570,000 were trade union members. British laborism was, thus, founded very strongly on trade unionism.

In Germany political parties and trade unions developed and organized in parallel with each other. The General Association of German Workers, created in 1863 by Ferdinand Lassalle (from a Breslau manufacturing family), and the Union of German Workers' Associations, formed the same year by Wilhelm Liebknecht (a Hessian intellectual) and August Bebel (a self-taught worker), united in 1875 on the basis of the Gotha Program. Though Social-Democratic parliamentary representation was tolerated, Bismarck and German employers subjected the Social-Democratic movement to systematic repression: residence rights were revoked, obliging many militants to exile themselves, and activists were fired from their jobs, imprisoned, and censured. It was thus on the basis of clandestine organization that German social democracy was able not only to survive but to strengthen itself in the period leading up to 1890, when, following Bismarck's fall, the Exceptional Laws were repealed.

The Social Democratic party, whose votes had declined at the beginning of the period of repression (312,000 votes in 1881 compared to 493,000 in 1877) managed, despite the repression, to expand the number of their sympathizers (763,000 votes in 1887 compared to 1.4 million in 1890). The Erfurt Program, written by Kautsky in 1891, set precise objectives and took up the major themes of Marxist analysis, in particular the ideas about crisis intensification and the dictatorship of the proletariat. With 700,000 members in 1900 and 1.7 million in 1912, and with 3 million votes (81 representatives) in 1903 and 4.2 million votes (110 representatives) in 1912, the Social Democratic party showed itself to be an important political force, and it thus had to face more and more directly the stakes and responsibilities of power, as well as the problem of political alliances.[10] The "equality" accord passed in 1906 between the Social Democratic party and the trade union organizations established a reciprocal obligation to stand together on major policy decisions and to make essential decisions together. Equality and cooperation were, thus, the hallmark of relations between the Social Democratic party and trade union organization in Germany.

At the end of the nineteenth century France was alive with diverse views, debates, invective, accusations, rapprochements, and subsequent breaks in alliances. Following the workers' congress that met from 1876 to 1882, one current of activity led to the formation of the Workers' party of France, which claimed to be Marxist and revolutionary. Jules Guesde (son of a professor and himself a journalist) and Paul Lafargue (Marx's son-in-law) were the leaders of this party. Another current within the workers' movement produced the Federation of Socialist Workers, led by Paul Brousse, a former libertarian who emphasized immediate and "possible" demands, from which came the name "Possibilist." At the end of the 1880s certain activists detached themselves from the Possibilists and formed the Workers' Revolutionary Socialist party, a party strongly influenced by J. Allemane, a typographer and participant in the battles for the Commune. This party put particular emphasis on workers' struggles and economic demands.

The Blanquists regrouped around the Central Revolutionary Committee, founded by Edouard Vaillant, who became the uncontested leader of the group in 1889 after the purge of Boulangist elements. In 1898 this committee became a Socialist Revolutionary party, and in 1902 it merged with the Guesdists into the French Socialist party, which had been formed the previous year by Broussists and Allemanists.

Concurrently, the anarchist tradition remained active, inspired by many local groups and even individuals. The role of many independent socialist personalities should be emphasized here. Their activity often took the form of editing reviews or newspapers; this group included the journalists Jules Vallès (*The People's Cry*) and Lissagaray (*The Battle*); Benoît Malon (a shepherd at age seven and later a dyer), who published *Integral Socialism* and who helped edit the *Socialist Review*; the lawyer Alexandre Millerand (*The Little Republic*); Aristide Briand (*The Lantern*); and the academician Jean Jaurès (*The Toulouse Dispatch*).

Attempts at unification were difficult, delicate, and tense. The establishment of the unified French Socialist party—the French section of the Workers' International—required not only pressure from the Second International but an upswing in workers' struggles and the increasing threat of war. The General Confederation of Workers had been founded in 1895, but its membership did not greatly increase until 1902, when it federated both the job offices and the large national trade federations. A debate opened between the Guesdists, who believed in collaboration between party and trade union, and the partisans of trade union independence. At the Congress of Amiens in October 1906 the latter group prevailed and affirmed the total independence of the trade union movement from employers, the state, and political parties. The preamble to the new statutes was explicit:

1. The Congress affirms the complete freedom of individual trade union members to participate, outside of the union, in whatever form of struggle corresponds to that individual's philosophical or political ideas. The Congress asks reciprocally of the individual only that he not introduce into the union opinions that he professes elsewhere.

2. So far as organizations are concerned, the Congress declares that in order for trade unionism to make the greatest possible impact, economic action should be carried out directly against the employers. The confederated organizations should not, as associations of trade unions, be concerned with political parties and sects that, outside and alongside the confederation, may freely pursue social change. (Cited in Dolléans 1936–56, vol. 2)

France was thus led toward a separation of party and trade union by, on the one hand, the Blanquist and "Gallo-Marxist" currents, and, on the other, by the powerful anarchist-syndicalist tradition.

To summarize, then, in a few words: in Great Britain the Labour party was based on trade unionism; in Germany there was equality and cooperation between party and union; in France a separation heightened by mistrust prevailed between trade unions and political parties. These were the fundamental orientations that characterized the organization of the workers' movement in these three countries for many years.

2. IMMEDIATE CONQUESTS OR REVOLUTION

Whether simplistic or refined, in bare outline or full of detail and qualification, visions of a socialist society continued to develop and to provide hope. John Stuart Mill—too much an economist for the socialists, too much a socialist for the economists—summarized both the ideal and the complexity:

The social problem of the future consists in this: the greatest possible freedom of action for the individual must be made to accord with the universal right of every person to be both owner of the earth's resources and to benefit from labor organization.

Keir Hardie defined socialism with passionate spirit: "Socialism is not a system of political economy. It is life for a starving people." Jaurès joined materialism and idealism, reflection and enthusiasm:

Let us not forget the new and grand character of the socialist revolution, a revolution that will be carried out for everyone. For the first time since the beginning of human history, a tremendous social change will have as its goal not the substitution of one class for another, but instead the destruction of classes, the beginning of human community. What confers nobility upon socialism is that it will not be a minority regime. It then cannot, and should not, be imposed by a minority.

For some, the inevitability of socialism's advent was an absolute certainty, founded on scientific analysis and proof; for others, it was a deeply rooted and unshakable conviction whose sources were more in the realms of belief and faith. For still others, it was a necessary hope, a project that provided strength both for fighting and for putting up with the intolerable. These views, of course, intermingled in countless variations.

As the socialist movement progressed and became more definite, it became necessary to make certain concrete choices, which often meant a split between the ideal and what was immediately possible. Many examples of such choices and situations may be cited: the attempts at agricultural-craft utopias, which degenerated into a predictable outpouring of selfish and personal rivalries; the productive cooperatives by means of which groups of workers attempted to give life to alternative relations of production; the trade union battles, with their martyrs, great victories, and down-to-earth advances, but also their failures; municipal actions to form associations, cultural groups, workers' universities, and organizations for mutual support; and finally, electoral successes and progress in political organization.

At the heart of German social democracy, crucial debates opened up very early, due both to the quality of its supporters' philosophical and theoretical training and to the importance of the immediate stakes in their struggles, stakes that rose along with the number of supporters of social democracy.

In 1895, in his introduction to Marx's *The Class Struggles in France*, Engels described the positive momentum of social democracy in the German elections:

Already, *The Communist Manifesto* had declared the struggle for universal suffrage and democracy to be one of the most important tasks facing the militant proletariat. . . . Universal suffrage allows us to calculate our own as well as our adversaries' strength more exactly, and thus provides us with criteria for action that are far superior to any others. . . . Most importantly, however, it provides us with an unequaled method for gaining contact with the masses where they are still distant from us, and for forcing the other political parties to defend their positions and actions against our attacks. . . . Through this process the bourgeoisie and the government will come to fear the legal action of the workers' party more than the illegal action, electoral success more than victorious revolts. For . . . old-style rebellion, combat at the barricades, which was in all countries the decisive terrain until 1848, has for the most part been surpassed. The time of light-ning-strike revolutions carried out by a small conscious minority of leaders who are then followed by the unconscious masses: this time is over. For the complete transformation of the organization of society to take place, the masses themselves must cooperate. The masses must understand what is at stake, if they are to take part.

The same year in France Jules Guesde proclaimed to the parliamen-tary tribune:

Yes, it is with the political rights of the disinherited, and with the political rights of the proletariat, just as rapidly as the proletariat learns to make use of these rights, that we will penetrate the govern-ment of our decrepit old society and that, soon, in the name of the law, which today you make and which tomorrow we will make, we will transform the regime of anarchy that weighs so heavily upon everyone and will put in its place a regime of comfort and happiness for all. This is our key; we ask for no other.

Engels died in August 1895. In autumn the following year, Eduard Bernstein, still in exile, began to publish a series of articles on problems of socialism, which were published together in 1899 as *Theoretical Social-ism and Practical Social Democracy*. In the preface to the French edition (1899) Bernstein wrote that he wanted to discuss "questions that have become pressing due to the continual growth of the socialist movement in Germany and the political strength the socialist movement has pro-vided to social democracy." Bernstein considered his book to be an "attempt at revision, reconnaissance, and disentanglement." He ques-tioned a number of Marx's analyses and opposed "the spread of the idea that the fall of bourgeois society will soon arrive, and that social democ-racy should base its tactics on this great catastrophe, even subordinating itself to the expectation of such catastrophe" (ibid.).

He declared his political concerns forcefully in the conclusion:

I repeat: the more social democracy decides to present itself as it in fact is, the more it will increase its chances of carrying out political re-forms. . . . Social democracy must have the courage to free itself from the phraseology of the past and to appear as it is in reality: *a party of democratic and social reforms*. (Ibid.)

For Bernstein, "the most exact definition of socialism involves associa-tion. Ultimately socialism is nothing other than the application of de-mocracy to social life as a whole" (ibid.). But

the more the idea of democracy is established and the more it directs general consciousness, the more this idea will signify the highest possible degree of freedom for everyone. . . . Democracy is both a means and an end. It is the means for establishing socialism, as well as the form in which it is realized. . . . Democracy is the condition for socialism; not only a means, but its actual essence. (Ibid.)

This conception, along with his analysis of the development of classes, led Bernstein to question the notion of "the dictatorship of the proletariat." On the one hand, "class dictatorship belongs to an earlier civilization. . . . This is so even before one considers its efficiency or the possibility of putting it into practice" (ibid.). On the other hand, "despite the considerable progress that the working class has made since the time of Marx and Engels, I do not think this class is advanced enough, even today, to take hold of political power" (ibid.).

Karl Kautsky opposed Bernstein's views. In order to defend the Marxist orthodoxy of German social democracy, he used all resources: references to texts by Marx and Engels, lengthy restatements of the theses Bernstein had begun to consider, and biased presentations of Bernstein's positions in order better to repudiate them. And, in truth, Kautsky did not actually respond to the central question of the dictatorship of the proletariat and the indissoluble link between socialism and democracy.

Consider the following evasion: "Bernstein indignantly rejects the idea of the dictatorship of the proletariat. Is it by being full of respect for people such as Prussian Junkers that we will be able to get rid of them?" (Kautsky 1899). And this quibble: "Experience has not yet proved and the forecasts one can make for the future do not lead to the belief that democratic forms make the supremacy of the proletarian class superfluous for this class's emancipation" (ibid.). And this tirade:

> If the great drawbacks to the capitalist mode of production were inherent only at its beginnings and diminished thereafter, if the number of property owners increased, if social inequality steadily decreased, if the proletarians had an increasing possibility of becoming independent or at least of obtaining a satisfactory situation, then what good would socialism serve? If I considered capitalist development in the same way Bernstein thinks of it, then I frankly admit I would consider socialism to be a gross error. If Bernstein could thus convince me of the correctness of his objections to the socialist conception of our mode of production, then I would say: Our place is no longer in the Socialist party but rather in a party that is simply radical, or even, since I would not want to separate myself from my party, I would propose the party adopt a reformist program in place of the revolutionary collectivist program. (Ibid.)

A tradition of dogmatism and intolerance, to which Marx had already contributed, was thus established, strengthened decade by decade with political invective, insult, slander, and exclusion, arriving eventually at the extreme forms of ideological terrorism and political or physical assassination. Socialist thought was in this way tragically boxed in, for how can there be progress toward a free society if the individual cannot freely debate the conditions and directions of this progress?

Once again, Jaurès attempted the impossible synthesis. At a conference organized in February 1900 by the Collectivist Students of Paris, he declared himself to be in agreement "on the whole, with Kautsky," and he recapitulated the main themes of the Marxist analysis of capitalism. Nonetheless, he did not want "to contest the immense service provided to our cause by Bernstein: he has forced us all to reconsider once again our fundamental ideas, or at the very least to make them better accord with reality" (Jaurès 1900). Jaurès manipulated casuistry and dialectic with equal skill: "Bernstein has already greatly affected Kautsky's thinking; there is now in Kautsky a bit of Bernstein, so when I wholeheartedly agree with Kautsky, at the same time I am partially agreeing with Bernstein" (ibid.). Jaurès demonstrated shrewdly that the positions of the two Social Democratic leaders were not as opposed as they claimed them to be. And in a true act of faith, he attempted to reconcile the materialist certitudes of the one with the pragmatic conclusions of the other:

In London a few months ago I heard Liebknecht say: "We have been wrong about only one issue: we underestimated the length of time the capitalist system might last. . . ." Bernstein postpones the transformation of society into the indefinite and shady future; Kautsky declares himself not imprudent in saying that if German social democracy progresses as much in the next thirty years as it has in the previous thirty, then the social revolution has an excellent chance to succeed. But I believe that all calculations so far have been idle and vain, and if we are told today that we are postponing the socialist ideal, that we are making of it a sort of paradise, well then I say that paradise would be very close to the believers if they indeed believed. . . . [Loud approval and applause.] I say that, if they truly believed in it, then paradise would be for them the immediate continuation of their brief existence, or rather that it would be present during their very existence, if they felt that each of their acts, each of their thoughts, each of their words, corresponded to and modified the future events of this paradise. So I ask, then, of socialists, not to specify exactly the date—impossible to determine—when socialism may triumph. I tell them instead to live always in the socialist state of grace. [Loud applause.] We know that the next revolution will be ours, that all our actions head straight toward it, that all our words run toward it like sound waves spreading out on a huge plain without encountering any obstacles. We know that when we walk in the street and we meet our brothers who are suffering or joyous, that when their suffering disappears, it will be because of us! And that when their joy is dignified it will be because of us! (Ibid.)

That same year the French socialist movement was in crisis due to Millerand's entry the previous year into the Waldeck-Rousseau cabinet. The Congress of the Second International took place in Paris and was distinguished by the "Kautsky motion":

> The entry of a Socialist into a bourgeois government does not promise good results to the militant proletariat unless a majority of the Socialist party approves such an act and the Socialist minister remains the representative of his party. In the opposing case, where the minister becomes independent of the Socialist party or represents only one part of it, his participation in a bourgeois ministry threatens to disorganize and confuse the militant proletariat.

Regarding alliances, the motion continued:

> The class struggle prohibits any kind of alliance with any part of the capitalist class, though exceptional circumstances may make occasional coalitions (without, of course, confusing program and tactics) necessary, coalitions that the party should try to keep to a minimum.

This position was reaffirmed four years later at the congress in Amsterdam:

> The congress emphatically rejects revisionist attempts that tend to change our proven and celebrated tactics based on the class struggle, and to replace the forceful seizure of power from the bourgeoisie with a policy of concessions to the established order.

At the heart of the socialist movement, many different debates intermingled and overlapped: the problem of the relation between trade union action, the cooperative movement, and political organization; the alternative between reform and revolution; the implications of socialist electoral successes (budget votes, support for the government, cabinet participation); the question of alliances and the nature of the party (a party of the proletariat or a party of the people). These debates were at heart signs of a growing split between the still dominant view of a global and radical change in society on the one hand, and the increasingly numerous possibilities for change within capitalist society on the other. As the Socialist party, which represented the workers first and foremost, became stronger and able to affect national choices, it could no longer restrict itself to denouncing capitalist exploitation and to extolling the future establishment of a different society. It was incessantly caught up in the logic of the struggle carried out *within* capitalist society regarding issues such as increasing buying power, regulating working conditions, reducing the length of the working day, social security, and education.

Most of those in the Socialist party experienced this situation as a torturous split. Some escaped the split by giving priority to one side of the choice over the other (for some the immediate gains, for others the overthrow of capitalist society). Others managed to get around the split by overlaying their everyday work for immediate gains with revolutionary discourse, or by "staggering" time frames: some social changes today, revolution later on. A few, unfortunately too rare and little noticed amid the general din of certitudes, trials of intentions, and reciprocal condemnations, tried to mesh immediate struggles into possibilities for radical change. Once again, Jaurès found this ground:

> Why is it said that the trade union movement, the cooperative movement, or preparatory reforms hold back the socialist movement? They would hold it back if they were isolated from the central ideas of socialism, but if the trade union, as well as being a union, is also socialist, and considers itself as a means of organization, preparation, and education in order to advance socialism; if the cooperative is socialist, if in the domain of sales and exchange with small stores and shops scattered here and there, the cooperative attempts to become a sort of large popular warehouse; if the reforms we ask for—a limit to the working day, workers' inspection—are understood by the proletariat as new means for increasing its strength on the path toward the definitive society, then in all these cases countless threads connect each of our actions today with the coming revolution.

Here can be seen an essential component of socialist action: the ability to conceive of a global transformation of society as rooted in the struggles of the present moment, and the ability to expand and enlarge the claims and achievements of the present toward the possibility of another society.

3. INTERNATIONALISM AND PATRIOTISM

The approach and the triggering of World War I shifted the terms of the debate and also served as a useful indication of the socialist movement's progress.

Following *The Communist Manifesto* (1848), following the basic texts of the First International in 1864, the principle of internationalism was taken up once again and reaffirmed by the Second International in 1896:

> The congress proclaims the full right to free determination for all nations, and it expresses its sympathy to the workers of all countries currently under the yoke of military, national, or any other absolutism; the congress calls to the workers of all these countries to join the ranks of conscious workers throughout the world, in order to fight

with them in vanquishing international capitalism and in attaining the objectives of international social democracy.

This internationalism could be founded in two ways.

The first was summed up by Marx and Engels in their phrase: "Proletarians have no homeland." Dispossessed of everything, increasingly numerous because of the general spread of proletarianization, and crushed by growing pauperization, the proletarians make up the class that, by freeing itself from domination and exploitation, will free all of the oppressed from all oppressions. From that moment onward, the question of the nation should not slow down the social movement: this is what Marx said in 1869 about Ireland, and this is what Engels said again in 1882 when he discussed friction between French and Germans in Alsace.

The second way to found internationalism is to present it as surpassing patriotism. This was the position of many French socialists, who, though they intended to play a part in the coming socialist revolution, felt themselves to be inheritors of the French Revolution. Thus, the Workers' party in France, led by Jules Guesde, stated in its manifesto of June 1893:

> Internationalism means neither sacrificing nor letting down the homeland. Homelands, at the time they were established, were a first and necessary step toward human unity. . . . One does not stop being a patriot by entering the international path that is now required for a complete flowering of humanity, any more than at the end of the last century one stopped being Provençal, Burgundian, Flemish, or Breton, in becoming French. The internationalists can, on the contrary, call themselves the only patriots, because they are the only ones to understand the expanded conditions that can and should provide for the future and greatness of the homeland, of all homelands, antagonists that have become linked to one another. . . . French socialists are patriots in yet another sense and for other reasons: because France has been in the past and is destined to be in the future one of the most important elements in the social evolution of our species. We wish, then—and are unable not to wish—a France that is great and strong, capable of defending its Republic against allied monarchies and capable, too, of protecting its coming workers' [17]89 against a possible coalition of capitalist Europe.

The following October the Workers' party congress arrived at some very straightforward conclusions:

> No more than workers' solidarity excludes or limits the right and duty of workers to defend themselves against workers who are traitors to their class, international solidarity does not exclude or limit the right

and duty of a nation to defend itself against any government that is a traitor to European peace. If France were attacked, she would have no more passionate defenders than the socialists of the Workers' party who are persuaded of the leading role destined for her in the coming social revolution.

Five years later, in an article in the *Paris Review*, Jaurès further reflected on the relation between patriotism and socialism:

There is no doubt that socialism and the proletariat are held to the French homeland by all their roots. From the time of the bourgeois revolution, the people, though driven into a corner, defended the new France heroically against foreigners; from that time onward the people had a sense of their future inheritance. In addition, national unity is the essential condition for the unity of production and property, which is the very essence of socialism. Finally, all of humanity is not ready for socialist organization, and the nations that have been prepared for the social revolution by the intensity of industrial life and by the development of democracy will accomplish their work without waiting for the burdensome, chaotic mass of humanity. Nations— closed systems, closed whirlwinds among incoherent and diffuse humanity—are thus the necessary condition of socialism. To overthrow nations as such would do away with the sources of distinct points of light, leaving only the unfocused slowness of universal effort; this would suppress all freedom, since humanity would no longer condense its action into autonomous nations and would instead demand unity from a vast Asiatic despotism. A homeland is thus necessary to socialism. Outside it socialism is nothing and can do nothing; even the international movement of the proletariat, which runs the constant danger of losing itself in diffuseness and in the indefinite, needs to find, in the very nations it surpasses, points of contact and support.

Despite this line of thought, the movement of capitalist development itself profoundly transformed the situation. The "great depression" of 1875–1893 and the crises that characterized it were signs both of the rise of new capitalisms (German and North American) confronting older ones (British and French), and of the strengthening of the organized working class, which managed, first in Great Britain but then in other countries as well, to raise real wages and to shorten the working day. The dominant capitalisms escaped from the crisis by developing second-generation industries, by developing new ways to exert pressure on workers, and by a search for foreign markets.[11]

Two different sorts of developments were then related by an underlying connection. On the one hand, the working and living conditions of certain strata or categories of workers became less tenuous and precarious. These workers were able to hope for further improvement, either from an increase in national prosperity or from new national legislation, itself a product of a strengthened national workers' movement. On the other hand, the search for foreign markets brought an increase in international competition (German coal or steel against British coal or steel) as well as a new surge in colonial conquests and national rivalries. In short, with imperialism (and these two developments are not unrelated) some sections of the working class within the dominant capitalisms managed to improve their situation, while at the same time the face-to-face confrontation between national capitalisms—that is, between nations and states—hardened. Given this conjuncture of forces, how could one be sure the working classes would escape a blaze of nationalism if war set Europe on fire?

The leaders of the Second International took up this question, despite their differences in approach and their differing views about the utility of a possible general strike. At the congress in Paris in 1900 they decided "to orchestrate, in all cases of international importance, a uniform and common protest movement including antimilitarist agitation in every country." In 1907 the Stuttgart congress adopted a motion against the war whose final lines were these:

> If a war threatens to break out, it is a duty of the working classes in the countries concerned, it is a duty of their parliamentary representatives, with the help of the international office, through action and coordination, to make all efforts to prevent the war by all means that seem to them appropriate, and which naturally will vary according to the degree of class struggle and the general political situation. In case war breaks out anyway, they have the duty to intervene and end it promptly and to utilize fully the political and economic crisis created by the war to agitate the popular strata at their deepest level and precipitate the fall of capitalist domination.

And in fact, after the incident at Agadir in 1911, socialist meetings were held in Berlin, Paris, and Madrid. Protests against the extension of the war in the Balkans were held simultaneously in Berlin, London, Strasbourg, Milan, and Rome on 17 November 1912.

But in 1914 the constant pressure of events proved too strong and the dike too fragile, with dissension among the German Social Democratic leaders, the assassination of Jaurès, and disagreements about means and methods. The amendment proposed in 1910 by Vaillant and Keir Hardie at Copenhagen called for "a general workers' strike, above all in the industries producing the tools of war (weapons, ammunition, transport) as well as the most active forms of popular agitation and action." But because of basic disagreements and hesitations about the general strike, which many still saw as anarchist inspired, this amendment was sent back for review; it was to have been submitted for a vote at the next congress of the International, in August 1914 in Vienna. As Kautsky remarked cruelly, the International was not made for times of war.

Brutally, the war shifted the debate. Mixed in with the peasants and the middle classes, the working classes of Europe slaughtered each other. The Great War, with its eighteen million deaths, its suffering and its horrors, helped to integrate the working classes into "their" national communities. And while some workers very early on brandished the torch of pacifism and internationalism, this should not hide the fact that the working classes of Europe massively expressed their attachment to "their" homelands.

This theme warranted deeper reflection and analysis: exploitation and class struggle do not prohibit the existence of common interests between the working class and the bourgeoisie of the same country. Thus, when a nation, a national capitalism, is endangered, all classes in the country feel the danger, though each class perceives the threat in its own way.

Beyond the war, once peace returned, the logic of the choice made in the war was to attempt to obtain political rights and social and economic advances insofar as the development of capitalism and the strength of the organized workers' movement allowed such advances. But a new perspective was already opening, since, with the October Revolution, a single country was to become the "homeland of socialism."

COMMENTS ON CHAPTER 3

The vision was uplifting: deprived of everything, radically in bondage, endlessly exploited, the proletariat was invested with the mission of overthrowing capitalism, and, in this same movement, of abolishing class society, class domination, and all other forms of domination and exploitation of man by man.

Who would be capable of describing the immense human richness— the generosity, enthusiasm, courage, labor, great battles, and everyday tasks—dedicated to this fight? Who would be capable of adequately celebrating the heroes and the martyrs of this unending struggle against suffering and oppression, which is at the same time a struggle for justice and the happiness of humanity? And it is not at all a denigration of these men and women if we attempt now to appreciate the role played at the time by illusion and even by error. This is the price we must pay if we wish to conceive, on a new basis, the possibility for the socialist project in our own time.

It was without a doubt an illusion to hope for the overthrow, almost without delay, of the old society, and an equally instantaneous birth of the new. A society is nothing without the men and women who compose it: people rooted in classes, regions, ways of thinking; people possessing areas of knowledge and areas of ignorance, fears and hopes inherited from the past and reproduced through the generations. And though decisive turnings in history may occur in a matter of days, deep social changes take place over generations.

It was an illusion, too, to expect that winning universal suffrage would open a "royal way" permitting rapid adoption of measures sought by the largest class, the class of the oppressed and the exploited. This, however, should not be taken to mean that democracy does not constitute an essential component of any advance toward socialism; it means, rather, that democracy in a diversifying society implies taking into account the plurality of interests of different classes and strata. The ruling class was able very early on to construct alliances that permitted it to maintain power.

There was a final illusion in believing that the expansion and worsening of workers' suffering in the nineteenth century would lead ineluctably to proletarianization and pauperization. In becoming a force, the working class and the workers' movement in general were able to win victories that forced "their" employers to grant important concessions.

Thus the British workers' movement succeeded in extracting major concessions from British capitalism: the Employers and Workmen Act of 1875 replaced the Master and Servant Act of 1867; laws in 1875 and 1876 granted legal status to the trade unions and authorized nonviolent strike picketing. Workers' buying power and living conditions improved; social improvements won locally were eventually generalized by law: workers' retirement and the regulation of home labor (1908), and the institution of unemployment insurance and the expansion of health insurance (1911). In addition the trade unions were a decisive force in the formation and development of the Labour party.

Though individual developments were, of course, specific to each country, the movement as a whole was similar in the other countries where capitalism had first established itself (Holland, Belgium, France) and in the countries where capitalist development occurred later (Germany, the United States). Without anyone at the time being clearly conscious of what was happening, a compromise was being established within the most advanced national capitalisms between the ruling class, the middle classes, and the working class. The working class—by strengthening itself, by organizing itself, and by struggling—managed to reduce the worst aspects of its exploitation and to create living conditions that were more humane and, in certain cases, more pleasant. To what degree were these concessions made "bearable" to the ruling class by the products of activities that this class was developing on a world scale? In other words, to what degree were the national compromises—just beginning to develop in the principal capitalist countries at the end of the nineteenth and the beginning of the twentieth centuries—made possible by imperial domination and the profits accompanying this domination? No one can calculate the answer to this question exactly. No one, however, can deny that the question reveals a fundamental problem.

For once a *national* working class extracts from "its" *national* bourgeoisie certain gains—whether confirmed or not by *national* legislation—how can this working class not be caught up in the logic of the smooth functioning of "its" *national* capitalism? And if this smooth functioning depends on imperial expansion, exploitation, and accumulation on a world scale, then the working class itself will be caught in the following contradiction: the struggle for the reduction of its own exploitation may find a solution very much within the capitalist system, through the development of exploitation on a world scale.

This proletariat, whose emancipation was to assure the emancipation of all the oppressed, may, in the dominant countries, have an indirect interest in "its" capitalism's unfolding itself on a world scale. Is this the case, as Lenin thought, only for a small minority of the working class, which he described as a "workers' aristocracy"? Or is this the case for the working world as a whole, in different forms and with more or less intensity? The debate can be extended endlessly: since, for all its gains, the exploitation of the working class in the dominant countries has not been eliminated, but only reduced; since, for all its advances, this class has not become idle, but has only obtained larger concessions more easily than dividing up national resources alone would have allowed.

Can there not be seen here an objective basis for the involvement of large sections of the working class in the Great War, in support of "their" governments?

Beyond this first question lies another: once the movement of proletarianization and pauperization no longer developed at an absolute rate, once a national working class, through its development and self-organization, was able to win concessions such as better working and living conditions, how was it possible to maintain the idea, the myth, of a radical overturning of society? It was necessary to consider in all its complexity a process that gathered together in a single movement the following elements:

- struggle against the system;
- gains within the system;
- lessening of reasons for fighting the system, and even a growth of reasons for integration into the system.

It was necessary to analyze the conceptual pair "gains/integration," even though the far easier course was to concern oneself with only one of the two faces of this ambiguous movement.

Jaurès attempted to think through the problem's complexities, but in his eyes too many leaders of the socialist movement gave in to facile analyses:

- either by closing themselves into revolutionary intransigence, leading them to scorn advances that were immediately possible;
- or by totally dedicating themselves to struggles on a day-to-day basis, forgetting or setting aside the view of the whole;
- or by attaching revolutionary discourse to reformist practices.

The central problem being thus, in one way or another, avoided, oppositions and confrontations crystallized around biased and simplistic debates. Revolutionaries and reformists confronted one another, the orthodox Marxists clashed with revisionists, believers in class struggle opposed class collaborationists. . . . To all this must be added the extra burden of the "ritual formulae" that little by little grew into the solidified jargon and stock phrases of speeches and congresses, the use in arguments of citations from "the founding fathers," and the games and the tactical stakes that formed the real background of each debate.

The October Revolution, Leninism, and then Stalinism caused yet another shift; not that the former problems had disappeared, but rather that they were reformed in the new confrontation between those who saw in the USSR the homeland of socialism and those who, from many points of view, refused, criticized, and rejected.

For, contrary to the deeper logic of Marxian analysis, it was in Russia that a revolution succeeded, allowing socialists, followers of Marx, to conquer state power. And there, the ordeal of concrete experience was brutal and left no room for verbal dodges or rhetorical cleverness.

4

THE CHAIN OF EVENTS LEADING TO THE OCTOBER REVOLUTION

Jean Jaurès felt it coming. Reflecting on the possibility of advancing toward the "social revolution" "through the means that expanding democracy puts at the disposition of the workers, through the gradual conquest of political power, and through growing political organization," Jaurès had predicted that "the crisis of a great war would completely change this evolution: a war would either submerge socialism and the working class in a bloody torrent of chauvinist passions, or else, through revolution, it would bring to power a daring proletarian minority who would rudely precipitate events." Both sides of his prediction in fact came true.

It was in Russia that a daring minority indeed forced events in a new direction. It is not our concern here to write a history of the entire October Revolution,[12] but instead to try to understand (1) the Bolshevik vision of socialism before October 1917, and (2) how the difficulties and responsibilities of power led them to submit to, to accept, or to decide on the development of a reality very different from their original vision.

1. THE VISION OF SOCIALISM BEFORE 1917

Composed of anarchists, Socialist Revolutionaries (themselves the descendants of a strong populist tradition), and Social Democrats (both Bolsheviks and Mensheviks), the Russian socialist movement at the turn of the century was spurred on principally by certain segments of the intelligentsia. There were many different points of view and endless debates about the agrarian question and the peasantry, about the possibility for socialism in Russia, about minorities and the national question, and about which forms of action were the most useful.

V. I. Lenin (born in 1870) obstinately stressed organization, the party, and the work to be done in educating the working class. He wrote, for example, in 1895:

> In addition to the political explanations of the factory inspectors, we sometimes get still more useful "political explanations" from a Cabinet Minister who reminds the workers about the feelings of "Christian love" which are due the factory owner for the millions he has accumulated from the labour of the workers. Afterwards, to the explanations of the representatives of the state, and to the fact that the workers have learned at first hand on whose side the state is, are added the leaflets, or other forms of information, distributed by the Socialists, so that the workers get a complete political education during the course of such a strike. . . . This, then is assistance the Social-Democratic Party can render to the class struggle of the workers: it must develop the class consciousness of the workers by helping them in the struggle for the satisfaction of their immediate needs. (Lenin [1895] 1943, 1:362–63)

And again, in 1902:

> . . .[T]he organisation of a revolutionary Social-Democratic Party must inevitably *differ* from the organisations of the workers designed for the [economic] struggle. A workers' organisation must in the first place be a trade organisation; secondly, it must be as wide as possible; and thirdly, it must be as public as conditions will allow. . . . On the other hand, the organisations of revolutionaries must consist first and foremost of people whose profession is that of a revolutionary. . . . Such an organisation must of necessity be not too extensive and as secret as possible. (Lenin [1902] 1943, 2:127)

And once again, in 1905:

> The practical question before us now is, first of all, *how* to utilise, to direct, to unite, to organise these new forces; *how* to concentrate Social-Democratic work chiefly on the newer, higher tasks that are presented by the present moment without forgetting for an instant the old, everyday tasks that confront us, and will continue to confront us, so long as the world of capitalist exploitation continues to exist. (Lenin [1905] 1943, 3:432)

In these texts one can sense that Lenin kept in mind the objective of revolution while maintaining his concern with the problem of organization, all the while remaining extremely alert to the conditions of the present moment.

In 1906 a young Bolshevik leader, Joseph Stalin, responding to critics and to objections arising in anarchist circles, published a short work that was both didactic and tainted with a certain dogmatism. This text reveals the predominant vision of socialism then held by the Russian Marxists. After describing and critiquing the capitalist regime, Stalin linked together the following argument:

There can be no doubt that future society will be built on an entirely different basis.

Future society will be socialist society. This means, primarily, that there will be no classes in that society; there will be neither capitalists nor proletarians and, consequently, there will be no exploitation. In that society there will be only workers engaged in collective labour.

Future society will be socialist society. This means also that, with the abolition of exploitation, commodity production and buying and selling will also be abolished, and, therefore, there will be no room for buyers and sellers of labour power, for employers and employed— there will be only free workers.

Future society will be socialist society. This means, lastly, that in that society the abolition of wage labour will be accompanied by the complete abolition of the private ownership of the instruments and means of production; there will be neither poor proletarians nor rich capitalists—there will be only workers who collectively own all the land and minerals, all the forests, all the factories and mills, all the railways, etc.

As you see, the main purpose of production in the future will be to satisfy the needs of society and not to produce goods for sale in order to increase the profits of the capitalists. Here there will be no room for commodity production, struggle for profits, etc.

It is also clear that future production will be socialistically organized, highly developed production, which will take into account the needs of society and will produce as much as society needs. Here there will be no room whether for scattered production, competition, crises, or unemployment.

Where there are no classes, where there are neither rich nor poor, there is no need for a state, there is no need either for political power, which oppresses the poor and protects the rich. Consequently, in socialist society there will be no need for the existence of political power. (Stalin [1906] 1952, 1:335–37)

To support his argument Stalin cited an 1846 text from Marx and an 1884 text from Engels. He then went on to consider the "possible" characteristics of socialism, mentioning the tendency toward the concentration of capital, before stating:

As, however, the private character of appropriation does not correspond to the social character of production, as present-day collective labour must inevitably lead to collective property, it is self-evident that the socialist system will follow capitalism as inevitably as day follows night.

That is how history proves the inevitability of Marx's proletarian socialism. (Stalin [1906] 1952, 1:341)

On this basis Stalin replied to the anarchists:

Thus, from the arguments of the Anarchists it follows that:

1. In the opinion of the Social-Democrats, socialist society is impossible without a government which, in the capacity of principal master, will hire workers and will certainly have "ministers . . . gendarmes and spies."

2. In socialist society, in the opinion of the Social-Democrats, the distinction between "dirty" and "clean" work will be retained, the principle "to each according to his needs" will be rejected, and another principle will prevail, viz., "to each according to his services." (Ibid., 1:359)

Stalin argued by citing Marx and Engels many times (Marx from 1846, Marx and Engels from 1848, and Engels from 1877, 1884, and 1891) and then stated:

. . . [I]n the opinion of the Social-Democrats, socialist society is a society in which there will be no room for the so-called state, political power, with its ministers, governors, gendarmes, police and soldiers. (Ibid., 1:361)

He cited Kropotkin, pardon, "Mister Kropotkin":

We Anarchists have pronounced final sentence upon dictatorship. . . . We know that every dictatorship, no matter how honest its intentions, will lead to the death of the revolution. We know . . . that the idea of dictatorship is nothing more or less than the pernicious product of governmental fetishism which . . . has always striven to perpetuate slavery. (Kropotkin, cited in ibid., 1:366)

Stalin supported his position once again with more quotes (from *The Communist Manifesto* and *The Civil War in France*) and twice cited the closing lines of Engels's introduction to *The Civil War in France*: "Look at the Paris Commune. That was the dictatorship of the proletariat." He concluded:

Clearly, there are two kinds of dictatorship. There is the dictatorship of the minority, the dictatorship of a small group, the dictatorship of the Trepovs and Ignatyevs, which is directed against the people. This kind of dictatorship is usually headed by a camarilla which adopts secret decisions and tightens the noose around the neck of the majority of the people.

Marxists are the enemy of such a dictatorship, and they fight such a dictatorship far more stubbornly and self-sacrificingly than do our noisy Anarchists.

There is another kind of dictatorship, the dictatorship of the proletarian majority, the dictatorship of the masses, which is directed against the bourgeoisie, against the minority. At the head of this dictatorship stand the masses; here there is no room either for a camarilla or for šecret decisions; here everything is done openly, in the streets, at meetings—because it is the dictatorship of the street, of the masses, a dictatorship directed against all oppressors.

Marxists support this kind of dictatorship "with both hands"—and that is because such a dictatorship is the magnificent beginning of the great socialist revolution. (Ibid., 1:371–72)

In this text one can feel not only the strength conferred by the certitudes of dogmatism, but also dogmatism's twin potential for blindness and self-justification.

And as an underlying issue, it is striking to note the break between the frozen and immobile references to what Marx and Engels had been able to write, given the historical movement of their time, and Lenin's vibrant reflections, caught up in action, on the role of the vanguard and the party, on education and the organization of the masses. These two languages could coexist in Bolshevik thought, and even within the thought of Lenin himself. But concrete developments in the Revolution worked to separate the two.

2. WITHIN THE MOVEMENT OF THE REVOLUTIONS OF 1917

The agrarian question, industrialization, and the war deeply affected Russian society. The agrarian question was a fundamental and seemingly permanent fact, with an enormous number of peasants subjected to despotism and feudalism. Capitalist industrialization, which had begun in earnest at the end of the nineteenth century, besides producing a combative working class, also brought a strengthened bourgeoisie who received many of their ideas, including the value of democracy, from the West. And finally, there was the war, with fourteen million people mobilized (of whom nine-tenths were peasants) and two million already dead by the end of 1916. This was the fundamental situation out of which the days of February 1917 grew, leading to the overthrow of the czarist regime, and the formation of a bourgeois government on one hand, and the soviets on the other.

Within this movement several diverging logics are at work. The following three texts from February and March 1917 indicate the various directions of thinking at the time:

The fight continues and should be carried out to its end. The old power should be defeated to give room to a popular government. The salvation of Russia is at stake here. In order to win this combat for democracy, the people should create their own organs of government. (Appeal from the Petrograd Soviet to the people of Russia, 27 February 1917; cited in Ferro 1967–76, 1:119)

The task of the working class and of the revolutionary army is to create a provisional revolutionary government that should put itself at the head of the new regime, the new republican regime that is being born. . . . Throughout Russia, in the cities and the countryside, create the people's revolutionary government. (Bolshevik manifesto, 27 February 1917; cited in Ferro 1967–76, 1:120)

The immediate problem of the Revolution is to liberate itself from all central power, whatever it might be, and to expect complete decentralization, with the flag of social revolution as unifying principle. . . . The hope of the Revolution is found solely in the immediate and public establishment of the Communist regime, and in the reinforcement of direct action. All Russia should form itself into a network of revolutionary and sovereign communes. (Anarchist program, end of March 1917; cited in Ferro 1967–76, 1:126, 128)

Combat for democracy, revolutionary government, direct action . . .

A serious split occurred among the Bolsheviks in April. Some, following Kamenev, thought that the conditions were not yet right for socialism. Believing strongly in democracy, this group thought that the law of the majority should be respected in the soviets. The opposing group, led by Lenin, declared that if the party took power, "no one could force it out": for him, "revolutionary legalism" was not in any case to hinder the party's victory. In the *April Theses*, Lenin rejected the idea of supporting the provisional government and the possibility of a parliamentary republic. He advocated the "republic of the soviets, with delegates who are workers, agricultural wage earners, and peasants, throughout the country, from bottom to top." Among his proposals, the example of the Paris Commune was still very much present:

Elimination of the police, the army, and civil servants (that is: substitution of the armed people for the permanent army). Possible eligibility and recall at any time of all officials; their pay should not be greater than the average wage of a good worker. (Lenin [1917a] n.d., 13–14)

He also proposed "the confiscation of all estates of landed property owners," the "nationalization of all land," the "immediate merger of all the country's banks into a single national bank," and the "control of social production and the dividing-up of production by the soviet of worker-delegates" (ibid.).

The disagreement between the two factions reemerged at the time of the demonstrations in June and July, and again in September during the debate on the insurrection.

Accused of being a German agent, Lenin traveled to Finland, where he wrote *The State and Revolution*. Between the finality of the withering away of the state—to which all followers of Marx must, according to Lenin, remain faithful—and the objective of conquering and controlling state power, which he felt to be within reach, Lenin managed, one might say, to bridge the two extremes: "We do not at all disagree with the Anarchists on the question of the abolition of the state as an *aim*," he wrote (Lenin [1917b] 1932, 21:ii:198). Referring to many texts by Marx and Engels, he emphasized

> Marx's extremely profound remark that the destruction of the military and bureaucratic apparatus of the state is "the precondition of any real *people's* revolution.". . . Thus the Commune would appear to have replaced the shattered state machinery "only" by fuller democracy: abolition of the standing army; all officials to be fully elective and subject to recall. But, as a matter of fact, this "only" signifies a gigantic replacement of one type of institution by others of a fundamentally different order. (Lenin [1917b] 1932, 21:ii:180, 183)

At the same time Lenin took up and developed the idea, supporting his position with many quotations, that "[a] Marxist is one who *extends* the acceptance of class struggle to the acceptance of the *dictatorship of the proletariat*." Thus:

> The transition from capitalism to Communism will certainly bring a great variety and abundance of political forms, but the essence will inevitably be only one: *the dictatorship of the proletariat*.
> . . .[T]he state during this period inevitably must be a state that is democratic *in a new way* (for the proletariat and the poor in general) and dictatorial *in a new way* (against the bourgeoisie). (Ibid., 176, 177)

Though Lenin needed the security of Marx and Engels, he wanted nonetheless to go beyond them. He felt a need to establish coherence between (1) the struggle he was leading for the conquest of the state apparatus; (2) the possibility for the dictatorship of the proletariat; and (3) the finality of the state's disappearance. He did this in a chapter entitled "The Economic Bases of the State's Disappearance." Between capitalism and communism a transition is necessary, and the dictatorship of the proletariat is this transition:

> The dictatorship of the proletariat, the period of transition to

Communism, will, for the first time, produce democracy for the people, for the majority, side by side with the necessary suppression of the minority—the exploiters. (Ibid., 220)

In the initial phase of communist society, commonly called socialism, communal ownership is achieved, and the socialist principles, "Whoever does not work should not eat," and "For equal quantities of work, equal quantities of product" are applied. But "a form of state is still necessary, which, while maintaining public ownership of the means of production, would preserve the equality of labour and equality in the distribution of products" (ibid., 224). Finally, with "the gigantic development of productive forces," the removal "of the antagonism between mental and physical labor," the transformation of "work into the 'first necessity of life,'" and with the realization of the principle, "From each according to his ability; to each according to his needs," when

> [t]he whole of society will have become one office and factory, with equal work and equal pay, . . . [t]he door will then be wide open for the transition from the first phase of Communist society to its higher phase, and along with it to the complete withering away of the state. (Ibid., 225, 230, 231)

On 29 September Lenin published the article "The Crisis Is Ripe." On 7 October he returned secretly to Petrograd; on 10 October he succeeded in persuading the Central Committee of the party, against Kamenev and Zinoviev, to vote for the principle of armed insurrection. The day before, Trotsky, president of the Petrograd soviet, had helped create an autonomous military organization, the Revolutionary Military Committee of Petrograd. The Petrograd garrison supported this Revolutionary Military Committee, and the momentum of events became unstoppable by 22 October. On 24 October the city was in the hands of the insurgents; the workers' and peasants' government elected by the soviets was made up exclusively of Bolsheviks, with Lenin as president.

3. IN THE NAME OF THE PROLETARIAT: THE MECHANISM OF DICTATORSHIP

Fellow workers! Realize that now it is you who direct the state. No one will help you if you do not take all state affairs into your own hands! Your soviets are from now on institutions of state power, provided with full decision-making powers. (Lenin [1917c] n.d., 26:311)

So spoke Lenin in his appeal "To the Population," a few days after the October Revolution.

From October 1917 to November 1918 the Bolsheviks worked to gain control over the soviets. The possibility of forming a joint government with the other socialist forces, reopened under pressure by the pan-Russian railroad workers' union and supported by Kamenev and Zinoviev, was once again ruled out. And though the Bolsheviks had pledged themselves to respect freedom of the press, Lenin had a decree passed that placed all information under Bolshevik control. The elections for the Constitutional Assembly, to which Lenin had been opposed,[13] gave a clear majority to the Socialist Revolutionaries (410 seats) and a definite minority to the Bolsheviks (175 seats). In his "Theses on the Constitutional Assembly" of December 1917, Lenin declared that the needs of the Revolution came before the formal rights of the Assembly; after its first meeting on 5 January 1918, when the Bolsheviks were unable to obtain a majority, the Assembly was prohibited from meeting again.[14] Prepared at the beginning of 1918, the Constitution's Article 9 foresaw a "powerful state" (Desobre 1977, 8): "in order to crush totally the bourgeoisie, to abolish the exploitation of man by man and to establish socialism where there will no longer be either classes or state power" (cited in Desobre 1977, 20); an astonishing shortcut.

At the Seventh Party Congress in March 1918 Bukharin asked that the new party program include a description of "the developed socialist order in which there will be no state." Lenin opposed Bukharin, declaring, "Right now, we are absolutely for the state" (Lenin [1918a] n.d., 27:148). He linked its possible disappearance to

> the realization of the principle "From each according to his abilities, to each according to his needs." But we are still far away from this. . . . We will get there eventually, if we arrive at socialism. . . . We will have time for at least two party congresses before we are able to say: Look how our state is withering away. For the moment it is still too soon. To proclaim in advance the withering away of the state would be to force the historical prospects. (Ibid., 149)

There was of course the war (against Bukharin's opposition, Lenin forced acceptance of the separate peace signed in March 1918); of course there were internal enemies and an onslaught of problems requiring immediate attention. But uppermost in Lenin's mind was the conviction that the Revolution took precedence over everything else: the Bolsheviks, with Lenin as their leader, formed the revolutionary vanguard. Neither previous commitments, principles, adversaries, nor allies should stand in the way of the Revolution he was leading.

The political police, the Cheka, acted against the anarchists in April 1918; repression hit the Socialist Revolutionaries in July, after the Moscow uprising. The fight against the White Terror intensified during the summer; the Red Terror was declared on 3 September and developed throughout the autumn. On the whole, the supremacy of the Bolsheviks over the trade unions as well as the soviets was assured by this time.

There were many who let themselves be convinced by Lenin's arguments, by the references to the English and French revolutions. And there were many who let themselves be carried away by their enthusiasm and faith in the Revolution.

But not all. From her prison cell, Rosa Luxemburg wrote with remarkable lucidity. She criticized the dissolution of the Constitutional Assembly:

> . . .[T]he remedy which Trotsky and Lenin have found, the elimination of democracy as such, is worse than the disease it is supposed to cure; for it stops up the very living source from which alone can come the correction of all the innate shortcomings of social institutions. (Luxemburg [1918] 1961, 62)

For all historical experience demonstrates that

> . . . the living fluid of the popular mood continuously flows around the representative bodies, penetrates them, guides them. . . . And is this ever-living influence of the mood and degree of political ripeness of the masses upon the elected bodies to be renounced in favor of a rigid scheme of party emblems and tickets in the very midst of revolution? Quite the contrary! . . . The basic error of the Lenin-Trotsky theory is that they too, just like Kautsky, oppose dictatorship to democracy. (Ibid., 60, 61, 76)

Luxemburg, in contrast, emphasized the democratic content of the "dictatorship of the proletariat":

> Yes, dictatorship! But this dictatorship consists in the *manner of applying democracy*, not in its *elimination*, in energetic, resolute attacks upon the well-entrenched rights and economic relationships of bourgeois society, without which a socialist transformation cannot be accomplished. But this dictatorship must be the work of the *class* and not of a little leading minority in the name of the class—that is, it must proceed step by step out of the active participation of the masses; it must be under their direct influence, subjected to the control of complete public activity; it must arise out of the growing political training of the mass of the people.
>
> The tacit assumption underlying the Lenin-Trotsky theory of the dictatorship is this: that the socialist transformation is something for which a ready-made formula lies completed in the pocket of the revolutionary party, which needs only to be carried out energetically in practise. This is, unfortunately—or perhaps fortunately—not the case. . . . [W]e know more or less what we must eliminate at the outset in order to free the road for a socialist economy. But when it comes to the nature of the thousand concrete, practical measures,

large and small, necessary to introduce socialist principles into economy, law and all social relationships, there is no key in any socialist party
program or textbook. (Ibid., 77–78, 69, 70)

She made this comment, which sums up at a fundamental level the
essential aspect, too often forgotten, of the struggle carried out in common
by democrats as well as free thinkers, supporters of legitimate government
as well as socialists: "Freedom is always, at the very least, freedom for the
one who thinks differently" (ibid., 69). And she predicted:

. . .[W]ith the repression of political life in the land as a whole, life
in the soviets must also become more and more crippled. Without
general elections, without unrestricted freedom of press and assembly, without a free struggle of opinion, life dies out in every public
institution, becomes a mere semblance of life, in which only the
bureaucracy remains as the active element. Public life gradually falls
asleep, a few dozen party leaders of inexhaustible energy and
boundless experience direct and rule. Among them, in reality only a
dozen outstanding heads do the leading and an elite of the working
class is invited from time to time to meetings where they are to
applaud the speeches of the leaders, and to approve proposed
resolutions unanimously—at bottom, then, a clique affair—a dictatorship, to be sure; not the dictatorship of the proletariat, however,
but only the dictatorship of a handful of politicians, that is, a dictatorship in the bourgeois sense, in the sense of the rule of the
Jacobins. (Ibid., 71–72)

Lenin replied to Kautsky, whose *Dictatorship of the Proletariat* was a
consideration of the problems of the moment, with *The Proletarian Revolution and the Renegade Kautsky* (November 1918). In *The ABC of Communism* Bukharin and Preobrazhensky justified the dictatorship of the
proletariat as well as the forms of power that had been established. Their
key sentence was "*Only* the proletariat struggles for the new world;
everything that gets in the way in this combat is injurious." A terrible
thought indeed, for it invested with unlimited power those, or the one,
who represented or led the struggle of the proletariat.

Then there was the offensive of the White armies; the difficulties of
supplying the cities; the famines in the countryside; a currency-
destroying inflation; the disagreements with and criticism of other
socialist forces; the peasant uprising in the Ukraine; the sailors' uprising
and the Kronstadt Commune.

The anarchist-led peasant movement in the Ukraine was repressed
and put down (November 1920–August 1921); the Kronstadt Commune
was crushed in March 1921. Bolshevik hegemony strengthened compared to all the other parties, which were gradually outlawed. The

antireligious campaigns developed at this time as well. In March 1921, at the Tenth Party Congress, Zinoviev justified matters this way:

> Without the iron dictatorship of the Communist party, soviet power would not have lasted ten years in Russia, nor three years, nor even a few weeks. Every conscious worker should recognize that the dictatorship can be carried out only by the dictatorship of its avant-garde, the Communist party.

And Trotsky, at the same congress:

> The party is obliged to maintain its dictatorship . . . no matter what temporary hesitations may exist even among the working class. . . . The dictatorship is not based at every instant on the formal principle of workers' democracy.

The mechanism of dictatorship was thus engaged. What began as the dictatorship of the proletariat, conceived as an enlarged democracy for the greatest number, had become the dictatorship of the party in the name of the proletariat. And from this time on, the decisive battles were played out within the party itself: the Workers' Opposition found itself isolated, in March 1921, when it defended its positions on the role of the unions and workers in production and on democracy in the party. The group of Forty-Six, which denounced the dictatorial functioning of the party, was condemned in October 1923 at Stalin's urging, and in a few short years Stalin imposed his absolute power over the party and the state. Russia had arrived at Stalinist dictatorship, in the name of the proletariat, in the name of socialism.

4. THE NECESSITY TO PRODUCE

Socialist thinking had hardly tackled the question of production and incitement—much less compulsion—to work. Either man, supposed to be good, was to work of his own accord once capitalism was overthrown, or work was to become attractive, or the wealth taken away from the privileged classes was to suffice, or, finally, the development of productive forces was to provide what was needed.

The capitalist employers, on the other hand, were increasingly concerned at the end of the nineteenth and the beginning of the twentieth centuries by the problem of production. Their situation was marked by the rise of the workers' movement and by increasingly stiff competition between capitalists. They resorted to systems of bonuses and fines, various methods of remuneration, and rational and scientific organization of work (for example, those of Fayol and Taylor). When a meeting on Taylorism was held at an Institute of Engineers in Petrograd, Lenin denounced it in a 1913 article in *Pravda* as "a scientific system for pressuring workers" that exhausted the workers and increased unemployment (Lenin [1913] n.d., 18:618). He returned again to Taylorism in a 1914 article in which he expressed once more his earlier critique and contrasted this "rational and reasoned distribution of work within the factory" to "the state of chaos into which capitalist production as a whole finds itself plunged" (Lenin [1914] n.d., 20:157). In his view, by its own rationality, "Taylor's system is preparing the time when the proletariat will take control of all social production and will designate its own commissions, workers' commissions, charged with dividing up and judiciously regulating social labor as a whole" (ibid., 158).[15]

Soon after the October Revolution, the decree on land ownership was made, peasant debts were annulled, and workers' control over businesses was established. In December the monopoly over foreign trade was decided along with nationalization of the banks. But scarcities and supply difficulties soon revealed a disastrous economic situation. Lenin, in his *Immediate Tasks of Soviet Power*, published at the end of 1918, declared himself convinced that soviet organization, "by passing from the purely formal democracy of the bourgeois republic to the *effective participation of the working masses in the duties of management*, confers on competition for the first time its fullest possible scope." However, he regretted, "it is much easier to do this in the domain of politics than in the economic domain. Yet the success of socialism depends more on the second of these" (Lenin [1918b] n.d., 27:269). There remained discipline:

. . . all large-scale mechanical industry, which in fact forms the source and material base for socialist production, requires a rigorous and absolute unity of will, regulating the combined work of hundreds, of thousands, and of tens of thousands of men. On a technical, economic, and historical level this necessity is evident, and all those who have thought about socialism have always acknowledged this necessity as one of the conditions for socialism. Yet how can such a strict and harsh unity of will be assured? By the submission of the will of thousands of people to the will of a single person. . . . The Revolution has just broken the oldest, heaviest, and most solid chains imposed upon the masses by the regime of brute force. That was yesterday. But today the same Revolution requires . . . precisely in the interests of socialism, that the masses obey without reserve the single will of the labor leaders. It is obvious that such a transition will not take place in an instant. (Ibid., 278–79)

Given this perspective, recourse to Taylorism finds its place:

The task lying before the Soviet Socialist Republic may be briefly summed up as this: we must introduce Taylorism, along with the scientific increase—in American fashion—of labor productivity, into all of Russia. But this must be accompanied by a shortening of the working day, by the utilization of new procedures for production and for labor organization, all without causing the slightest damage to the labor power of the working population. (Lenin [1918c] n.d., 42:64–65)

The expropriation of heavy industry was decided on in June 1918. During the summer, forced deliveries of agricultural products were organized. The length of the working day for industrial workers was increased from ten to eleven hours. In January 1919, workers, mobilized on the spot, were prohibited from leaving their jobs. At the Ninth Party Congress (1920), Trotsky succeeded in getting the congress to vote to allow single individuals to manage business enterprises, but he ran into opposition from workers and unions when he advocated the militarization of work. Fines were assessed against workers found guilty of absenteeism. The first government established in the name of the working class found itself in a situation where the entire population, and first of all the workers, suffered from scarcity, hunger, and cold; it had no other recourse than to urge, and if necessary, force, the workers to produce. In addition, the new workers arriving from the countryside were put to work, a situation itself involving force. A terrible contradiction can be seen here. In February 1921, during a meeting held at a large metals factory in Petrograd, the workers demanded an increase in food rations and an immediate distribution of shoes and winter clothes. The president of the trade union council of the city—a Bolshevik—who had come to persuade them to go back to work, was forcibly attacked. The movement spread to other factories in the city.

Following this the sailors of Kronstadt took up the call. They drew up a relatively moderate program, which demanded the dissolution of the soviets; new elections by secret ballot; freedom of the press and of assembly for the Socialist parties, the anarchists, and the trade unions; and the end of requisitions and searches in the countryside. During the Kronstadt Commune, fourteen issues of *Izvestia* were published by the provisional revolutionary committee. In the 7 March issue one can read the following:

> In making the October Revolution the working class had hoped to gain its freedom. But out of this Revolution will come an even greater slavery of human individuality. . . . The Communists . . . rather than bequeathing freedom have instead given the people fear of the Cheka's prisons. . . . They have put their hand as well on the thinking and the ethical life of the workers, forcing everyone to think according to their phrases and expressions alone. With the help of the nationalized unions, they have fixed the workers to the machine and have transformed work into a new kind of slavery, rather than making it

agreeable. To the protests of the peasants (which have gone so far as spontaneous revolts), and to the demands of the workers (forced to strike because of their living conditions), the Communists have responded with mass shootings and with a ferocity that the czarist generals would have envied. . . . It has by now become evident that the Communist party is not, as it pretended to be, the champion of the workers. The interests of the working class are foreign to it. Once having obtained power, it has only one concern: not to lose power. For this task it considers all means to be fair: slander, deceit, violence, assassination, and vengeance against the families of rebels. (Cited in Voline [1947] 1972, 2:238–39)

It took the Red Army ten days, from 8 to 18 March, to crush the Kronstadt Commune.

The announcement on 15 March of the New Economic Program (NEP) was also required in order to win over to the regime soldiers who were ready to give out. Among other things, the NEP provided for a limitation and regulation of goods demanded from the peasants, a liberalization of exchange (a new currency was created the following October), and the acceptance of private capital in commerce and small businesses. The NEP was fundamentally a tactical reversal designed to restore the necessary bases for production on the basis of an alliance between the working class and the peasantry (an alliance that itself concealed an "armistice" between the Bolshevik power and the peasants). Lenin wrote in May 1921:

As soon as we have definitively repelled the foreign enemy, another task rises up before us: the task of building an *economic* alliance between the working class and the peasantry. . . . Either the peasantry cooperates with us, in which case we will grant it economic concessions, or else we will be fighting the peasantry.

The NEP was also, for Lenin, a turning back toward capitalism, for

[t]he sole and real basis for developing capitalist society can only be heavy industry. Without large capitalist factories, without highly organized heavy industry, one cannot speak of socialism in general; this is even more so regarding an agricultural country.[16]

Lenin analyzed the measures that had been taken as a retreat, a detour through state capitalism:

The entire theoretical and practical question is to find the right methods to orient, in the direction of state capitalism, the inevitable (to a certain degree and for a certain length of time) development of capitalism. Thereafter in the near future we must establish the necessary conditions for, and then assure, the transformation of state capitalism into socialism. (Lenin [1921a] n.d., 32:367)

He came back to the question in October: "We realized clearly in the spring of 1921 that it was necessary to abandon building socialism immediately, that it was necessary in many economic spheres to turn back toward state capitalism" (Lenin [1921b] n.d., 33:89). Within Lenin's logic this choice was perfectly in keeping with his vision of a monopoly capitalism preparing the way for socialism, of a capitalist concentration or centralization establishing the condition and bases for socialism.

Though for Lenin the NEP was a momentary and tactical retreat, it was for Bukharin the beginning of a necessarily very long detour. He wrote in 1925:

> We must advance slowly, very, very slowly, dragging behind us our heavy peasant cart.
> To the peasants, to all the peasants, we should say: enrich yourselves, develop your farms, do not think that compulsion will fall upon you! (Bukharin, cited in Carrère d'Encausse [1972] 1979, 194)[17]

On the basis of this peasant enrichment, Bukharin saw the possibility of extracting a surplus allowing industrialization. The whole process implies continuing and enlarging the NEP for some time. Preobrazhensky opposed this position: "The idea that a socialist economy can develop by itself without tapping the resources of the petty-bourgeoisie and the peasantry is a reactionary idea, a petty-bourgeois utopia" (Preobrazhensky [1926] 1966, 114, 134). He was convinced that a period of "primitive socialist accumulation," requiring coercion of the peasantry and restriction of consumption, was needed first, in order to give priority to heavy industry (ibid., 180).

In 1928, in the face of the food crisis, new coercive measures were taken against the peasants. The First Five-Year Plan began; the order for collectivization was given. Bukharin, who, in his "Notes of an Economist" had favorably judged the NEP in *Pravda*, was excluded from the political committee. The fight against the peasants intensified during the winter. From this moment on, it was within a framework of collectivization and planning giving priority to industrialization that the means for inciting or forcing the producers to produce more and more—including a surplus—were sought and became intensified and systematized.

There were some who saw in this a brutal return to capitalism; others who saw in it the admirable and necessary effort of building socialism. The facts themselves were undeniable: in the name of socialism, the leaders of the Communist party imposed, not only on the peasantry but on the working class as well, an inflexible discipline, which extended in some cases to pitiless oppression.

Up to this time, the transformation of small independent producers into industrial workers, the compulsion to surplus labor permitting the extraction of a surplus—necessary to accumulation in industry—had been carried out in England, Europe, and the United States within the framework of commodity societies utilizing two sorts of pressure:

1. pressure of the "free market," the labor market, the market of commodities, which condemned the unemployed proletarian to misery, without any one person appearing responsible;
2. pressure from "discipline" in the mill and then in the factory, itself legitimized by the law of competition and thus of the market.

These pressures created misery and intolerable suffering; they also produced, in reaction, the development of the workers' movement and of socialism.

And now the inheritors of a revolution made in the name of socialism found themselves at the head of a state hated by the bourgeoisies of the entire world. These leaders were forced to engage in a process of industrialization, using state-imposed force as the means for compelling the productive classes to produce more and more in order to extract the necessary surplus. Many remained convinced that they were in the process of building socialism; groping, they invented and put into place the elements of a new mode of production: state collectivism.

5. FIRST WARNINGS, FIRST CRITIQUES

Cries of alarm were raised and disagreements were expressed while the Revolution was taking place: for example, Rosa Luxemburg's 1918 text written from prison. Other critiques were published as well, in particular by anarchists, Mensheviks, and German and Austrian Social Democrats.

These texts, however, were burdened with a terrible handicap: to criticize a revolutionary movement at the very moment this movement is the object of hatred and attack by ruling classes and other reactionary forces—is this not, objectively, to play into the hands of the forces of reaction? Wouldn't it be wiser to put off certain debates, certain critiques, until a later time, and to devote oneself entirely to the fight against the main adversary?

So many half-truths were passed, so many voices kept silent or were actively stifled under the cover of this argument! And though obviously the silenced voices themselves have left no record besides certain distorted interpretations written after the fact, some of the voices that were raised are well worth noting.

Consider first Voline, writing in 1917 in the anarchist journal *Golos Truda*:

Once their power is consolidated and legalized, the Bolsheviks . . .
will begin to organize the life of the country and the people using
governmental and dictatorial methods. . . . Your soviets will become
little by little nothing more than executive organs for carrying out the
will of the central government. We will witness the establishment of
an authoritarian political and statist apparatus, which will act from
above and which will begin to crush everything with its iron fist. . . .
Woe to anyone who disagrees with the central power! (Voline, cited in
Guérin 1970, 3:134)

In 1919, in a letter written to Georges Brandès, Kropotkin wrote:

Concerning our present economic and political situation, the Russian
Revolution, as the continuation of the two great revolutions of England and France, tries to progress where France stopped, at the point
of establishing equality-in-fact, that is to say, economic equality. Unfortunately this attempt has been carried out in Russia under the
extremely centralized dictatorship of a single party, the maximalist
Social Democrats. The experience has been carried out in the same
way as the Conspiracy of Babeuf: extremely centralized and Jacobin-
ist. I must tell you frankly that in my opinion this attempt to build a
communist republic on the basis of a strongly centralized state communism, and under the iron law of a party dictatorship, is ending in a
fiasco. We are learning in Russia how communism should not be
introduced, even for a population weary of the old regime and opposing no active resistance to the initiatives of the new leaders. (Kropotkin, cited in Guérin 1970, 2:163)

And in 1920 a meeting of the Ukranian anarchists of the Nabat Federation reaffirmed their position:

Anarchy is irreconcilable with any kind of dictatorship, even the
dictatorship by class-conscious workers over other workers and even
if the goal of this dictatorship is the advancement of workers' interests. (Cited in Guérin 1970, 3:155)

They evaluated their active participation in the Soviet Revolution:

In their constant struggle against all forms of the state, the anarchists
of the Nabat Federation accept no compromises and no concessions.
For a while we behaved differently toward the "Soviet power." The
vigorous spirit of the October Revolution, the anarchist phraseology
of the Bolshevik "leaders," and the urgency of the struggle against
world imperialism, closing in with an iron circle upon the Revolution
that had been born in turmoil: all these factors reduced our opposition
to the Soviet power. We asked peasants and workers to consolidate
the Revolution, we gave our advice to the new dominators, and
submitted critiques made by the comrades to them. But when the

Soviet power, born out of the Revolution, becomes in three years a powerful machine of domination, the Revolution has been strangled. The "dictatorship of the proletariat" (without the bourgeoisie) has substituted in place of the bourgeoisie the dictatorship of a party and a tiny fraction of the proletariat over all the working people. This dictatorship has stifled the will of large masses of workers. Because of this the creative force that alone could have resolved the various problems of the Revolution has been smashed. (Cited in Guérin 1970, 3:155–56)

The criticism is harsh. Yet the reaffirmation of belief in "the creative force that alone" could resolve the different problems of the Revolution, the "will of large masses": do these not constitute two more of those facile expressions to which socialist and revolutionary thinking regularly sacrifice themselves? Faced with problems piling up on one another, it is always easy and tempting to trot out a "sacred expression," a sacrosanct phrase guaranteed to win approval of some sort, from strong and vigorous applause to ambiguous silence. For whoever might begin to question the sacred phrase will be already suspect and, given the difficulty and depth of the questions raised, it will be easy to isolate and condemn the doubter as a traitor, or at the very least as a suspicious character guilty of doubting what everyone else believes, or pretends or declares to believe.

The refusal of sacrosanctity, the right to criticize freely and to criticize even at difficult moments: these should be the golden rules of all those who wish to change society for the better.

At the same time that the anarchists were raising their voices, the Russian Mensheviks (such as Plekhanov, Liber, Maslov, and Dallin) and the German and Austrian Social Democrats were criticizing and denouncing the unfolding events in Russia. Their critique was often made in the name of Marx, and their arguments were often supported by references to Marx's writings.

Plekhanov, writing in 1917, did not believe a socialist revolution to be possible in Russia, for the development of capitalism was as yet insufficient:

Marx says clearly that a determinate mode of production can in no way be superseded in a given country so long as this mode of production stimulates rather than hinders the productive forces of the country. One may then ask oneself whether such is the case for capitalism in Russia. Are we indeed able to say that capitalism has fully inhabited Russian society, that it has attained the point where, unable to further activate the productive forces, it has instead become an obstacle to these forces? Russia suffers not only from the existence of capitalism, but also from the fact that the capitalist mode of production is in

Russia insufficiently developed. And this undeniable truth has not yet been contested by any of those who in Russia call themselves Marxists. (Plekhanov, cited in Bukharin [1925–27] 1974, 249)

Dallin, and Maslov as well, believed that "the revolution that Russia has been undergoing for five years now was from the start and will remain to the end a bourgeois revolution" (Dallin, 1922, cited in Bukharin [1925–27] 1974, 251). And it was in Germany, in England, and in America that Liber saw propitious terrain for socialist advances:

For those socialists who have not been "reeducated," there is no question that socialism can be first implemented only in the countries that have reached the highest degree of economic development. (Liber, 1919, cited in Bukharin [1925–27] 1974, 251)

The weight and force of the dogmatic attitude, propped up where necessary by reference to the master, lead in any case to an already established conviction.

This approach can be found among the German Social Democrats, for example in Parvus: "For the establishment of socialism, the development of industry and the maturity of the working class must have attained a certain degree" (Parvus, 1919, cited in Bukharin [1925–27] 1974, 15).

Heinrich Ströbel insisted upon the influence of the Russian peasantry:

The peasants . . . represent at least seven-eighths of the Soviet Russian population. The weight of their number and of their economic importance will definitively decide the fate of the Revolution! After admitting this, how much fantasy and blind faith in miracles must one have to consider the Russian Revolution as a *Communist* revolution by its internal *character* and its final result! (Ströbel, 1921, cited in Bukharin [1925–27] 1974, 247–48)

Otto Bauer drew from this observation the conviction that the domination of the proletariat in Russia could only be temporary:

The temporary domination of industrial socialism in peasant Russia is only a flame inviting the proletariat of the industrial West to struggle on. Only the conquest of political power by this proletariat can assure the lasting domination of socialism. (Bauer, 1921, cited in Bukharin [1925–27] 1974, 246)

Considering the progress of the Bolshevik Revolution, Bernstein made every effort to remain moderate:

Bolshevism may be defined as an attempt to speed up social evolution, during a certain period, by authoritarian measures. In the case of Russia, a predominantly agricultural country where the proletariat is only a slight minority, it was a case of imposing socialist rule by means of a dictatorship that was designated, using Marx's term, the "dictatorship of the proletariat." In fact it was only the dictatorship of a party supported by certain categories of the working class. This party violently took hold of the state apparatus and put the other parties, whether socialist or not, under its domination. (Bernstein [1920] 1974, 244)

Kautsky was more brutal:

The Bolsheviks have arrived at the point of living off of their domination and exploitation of the proletariat. But they have no wish to cede this position to the capitalist class. That is why they are now above the proletariat and above capital as well, and seek to turn each of these groups into their tools. (Kautsky, 1925, cited in Bukharin [1925–27] 1974, 327)

Kautsky then made the following comparison, which was particularly galling to the Bolsheviks:

Of course, Bolshevik despotism differs from the despotism we have known up to now in that the new despots were formerly our comrades. . . . Still, in America there are many millionaires who were extremely poor proletarians in their youth. Their proletarian origins have not in the least prevented them from becoming in later life the most cynical and pitiless exploiters of the proletariat. It is the same for the Bolsheviks. The fact that they have raised themselves from the lowest level of the proletariat up to unlimited power does not at all guarantee that they respect or think in the same way as the proletariat: they are distinguished from other ruling classes only by a particular cruelty and brazenness. (Kautsky, 1925, cited in Bukharin [1925–27] 1974, 321)

The elimination of all democratic life from Soviet Russia was particularly shocking to the Austrian and German Social Democrats. Otto Bauer attempted to make sense of the situation while still maintaining his hope:

It is in the vital interest of the Russian proletariat and the international proletariat that the inevitable elimination of the dictatorship be accomplished peaceably, and not through a violent overthrow of the Soviet regime. This is why we should above all support the Soviet Republic against every counterrevolutionary threat. . . . But our solidarity with the great Russian Revolution imposes upon us another duty: the duty to support, within the Revolution itself, with all the intellectual weaponry we possess, the forces pushing the government of the Soviets toward a timely and voluntary elimination of the dictatorship, which alone can prevent its violent overthrow. (Bauer [1921] 1968, 83)

Kautsky, on the other hand, thought the die was cast and there was nothing left to save:

> No world revolution, no foreign aid, would be able to prevent the economic collapse of the Bolshevik economic method. The task of European socialism in regards to "Communism" is quite different: it is to assure that the moral catastrophe of a certain method of socialism does not become the catastrophe of *socialism in general*, and that a clear distinction be made between this method and the method of Marxism, and further that this distinction be clearly presented to the consciousness of the masses. (Kautsky 1919, 218)

Bukharin, while still a member of the ruling Bolshevik group, distilled the analyses that social democracy had made of the Soviet Revolution into this phrase: "The Russian Bolsheviks are not building socialism but are rather preparing the ground for the birth of a new capitalist regime" (Bukharin [1925–27] 1974, 248).

A caricature that was intended to be caustic toward the social democratic positions, this short formula is interesting, at least, because it indicates the limits, within Marxist thought at the time, constraining the statement of the problem. Socialism or capitalism? Such was the alternative.

COMMENTS ON CHAPTER 4

Our purpose is not to award certificates of socialism; it is to sort out, with as much clarity as possible, the tangled mass of "official truths" and criticisms of these "truths," of imagined projects and concrete accomplishments, of established facts and interpretations of these facts. In other words, our objective is to understand the gap between the fine simplicity of socialist hopes in the nineteenth century and the complexity of situations and problems confronting socialists in the late twentieth century.

A close examination of the October Revolution appears to us to be extremely useful for this task because of the light the Revolution casts on two fundamentally important questions: first, that of power and the state, and second, that of production and labor.

By the beginning of the nineteenth century, socialist thinking was split over the question of political power. Though Godwin and l'Ange paid as much attention to democracy as to social justice, the Equals placed absolute priority on the objective of equality, and Saint-Simon willingly entrusted the task of governing to those most competent. There were also many who saw the state as the instrument of social change. Some, such as Blanqui, thought it necessary to seize state power; others sought control of the state through democratic means, which in principle would follow from universal suffrage, since the oppressed and disinherited were the majority of the population. But others, such as Bakunin and Proudhon, were suspicious of the state; they felt that the abolition of exploitation of man by man was inseparable from the abolition of government of man by man. In addition, vast numbers of shopkeepers, craftsmen, and workmen put their hopes in free association and in a social structure rebuilt, not from the top down, but from the bottom up, through the free federation of these free associations.

Marx analyzed the relations between classes; he believed that capitalism could not be overthrown without a clash between proletariat and bourgeoisie. Victorious, the proletariat was to impose its will as a dictatorship over the handful of previous rulers. But at the same time Marx saw the proletariat, this oppressed and absolutely exploited class, as the force that in liberating itself would liberate all the oppressed and all the exploited: a historical savior whose uprising would open the way toward a society without classes. This is what allowed him to think of the advance toward socialism as a movement leading to the withering away of the state.

Thus, a dictatorship of the proletariat—temporary, and democratic for the majority—was to lead to the disappearance of the state. Hadn't the Paris Commune concretized the beginning?

Until 1917 the Russian Social Democrats remained faithful to this vision. Stalin basically pursued such an argument in his discussion with the anarchists in 1906, and Lenin followed this path as well, though he emphasized the essential necessity of revolutionary organization.

But then implacable reality scattered illusions like dust in the wind. Once state power was won, this power had to be organized; there were struggles to be taken up immediately, decisions to be made without delay, and compulsions to be imposed. All this needed an iron will. The withering away of the state? That was put off until later, while at the moment the state was required "absolutely."

And once having successfully carried out the proletarian Revolution, assailed by reactionary forces, facing the war and provisioning problems, counterrevolution, and popular discontent; having been right so many times against all odds and while still maintaining control of this state: how could decisions be left to float according to the preferences of one group or another? How could the uncertain game of democracy be trusted? How could even the idea be maintained of a "dictatorship of the proletariat, which would be democratic for the majority"? To be responsible for a revolutionary state, for the state of the working class, to act in the name of the Revolution and the working class: this meant the elimination of other political parties and forces, and then the elimination of opposition or competition within the party itself. It meant, finally, dictatorship in the name of the proletariat, dictatorship over even the working class.

Seventy years later, the state is omnipresent, oppressive, and repressive. A state oligarchy continues to rule in the name of the working class. Beyond the issue of conditions in Russia and in the USSR themselves, the whole question remains: does not the call for a society without classes, without political power, derive from a utopian vision? And further, from a utopia that can turn itself absolutely upside down, since it allows a tiny handful—the problem of political power supposedly being no longer an issue—to seize power and to exercise it limitlessly, in the name of the Revolution, the working class, or the people? In the world as it is, a revolution led by a vanguard, by an organized minority, can only get rid of the former oppressors—which can by itself be a positive accomplishment—but such a revolution can in no case abolish the necessity of power.

And if we try to conceive the withering away of political power—the progressive disappearance of government of man by man occurring under favorable social conditions—then we see hardly any path possible other than patiently infusing democracy into all aspects of social life. For any of this to be thinkable, the contradictions of society would have to be overcome to a sufficient degree, which would imply adequate production, relative equality, the acceptance of diversity, and multiple networks of solidarity. Within such a framework, the citizens could contribute to the withering away of political power by actively investing themselves in the different loci of power within political life, as well as within production and social life as a whole. This could not be done without pluralism, decentralization, and federalism—themselves dependent on the creation and patient learning, through generations of time, of new values and new principles of social life.

The second question posed by the October Revolution is that of production. The socialists of the nineteenth century could dream: Godwin thought each person would work joyfully, and Fourier believed that a diversity of tasks would make all work attractive. The Bolshevik leaders had not the leisure to indulge in this kind of thinking.

By 1917 Lenin had relegated to a second phase of Communist society the time when, work having become for each person a "vital need," the principle "From each according to his abilities, to each according to his needs" could be applied. The compulsions of the reality he faced were impossible to resist and the principles that had to be followed were severe: "Whoever does not work should not eat," and "For an equal quantity of labor, an equal quantity of products."

Very quickly, it was necessary to produce; supply the cities; equip the transports, the army, the factories; make the peasants work and prevent them from keeping for themselves all that they produced. It was necessary to make workers work who were fatigued, disappointed, badly fed, and subjected to difficult working conditions. They had to produce and then produce still more. It was necessary to transform into workers people who had never done industrial work before; they had to be trained and "broken in"—just what nineteenth-century English capitalism had so cruelly and so pitilessly accomplished . . . and precisely what so many socialists had risen up against.

In all countries where the leaders have come to power in the name of socialism, these leaders have found themselves, and find themselves still, confronting this same problem. Until labor becomes a joy, one of the very first vital needs, and so long as it is still, for many people, tiring, numbing, unpleasant, and unattractive, is it possible to speak of a "socialist" mode of production? Can one speak of "socialist" means of compelling labor, or of "socialist" forms of extracting a surplus? The question is important, central in our eyes, and we will return to it.

5

COMMUNISM AND SOCIALISM

In 1915, in the middle of the war, Lenin raised the cry against reformism:

The revolutionary situation is an accomplished fact in most of the advanced countries and great powers of Europe. . . . The duty of socialists is then to use the crisis in order to precipitate the fall of capitalism. . . . The failure to carry out this duty reveals the betrayal of the currently existing political parties, their political death, the abdication of their role, their passage to the side of the bourgeoisie. . . .

The failure of the Second International, which indicates the total victory of opportunism, the transformation of Social Democratic parties into national-liberal workers' parties, is simply the culmination of the entire period covered by the Second International. . . . The crisis created by the Great War has torn the veil, swept away the conventions, popped the already ripe abcess. It has exposed opportunism in its true role as the ally of the bourgeoisie. The opportunism of the Second International must now be completely separated and detached, on the level of organization, from the workers' parties. (Lenin 1915)

In 1919, when, in the eyes of many, the Soviet Revolution represented a major step forward in humanity's progress toward socialism, Karl Kautsky expressed his disagreements and concerns about the Bolsheviks' approach and method. He wrote that, admittedly, "democracy itself does not exclude coercion, but the only kind of coercion it allows is that imposed by a majority upon a minority" (Kautsky 1919). Kautsky judged that Bolshevism would stay in power only by giving up its revolutionary objectives and by receiving support from the army and the new strata of bureaucrats. Kautsky believed that the task of European socialism henceforth was, as we saw peviously, "to assure that the moral catastrophe of a certain method of socialism does not become the catastrophe of socialism in general" (Kautsky 1919).

The essential terms of the debate were thus expressed.

That which, a few decades earlier, had remained a disagreement among theoreticians, between schools of thought, or even between rival organizations, became the center of an ideological and political war that affected all of Europe and that soon extended to all five continents.

1. THE BREAKUP OF THE WORKERS' MOVEMENT

Within the various workers' and socialist movements at the end of the nineteenth and the beginning of the twentieth centuries, there existed many different conceptions, tendencies, nuances, and sensibilities. The war brought further division, bitterness, and opposition between national movements. When war was declared, and even more strongly after 1917, a split developed between patriotic and pacifist positions. The Russian Revolution—"a vehement proclamation of gigantic expectations" (Brice Parrain)—inspired a strong wave of hope: "The Russian Revolution has reawakend hope in me," proclaimed Victor Serge. But at the same time the Revolution elicited hesitations and reserve, particularly on the part of those suspicious of this "Blanqui-ism served with tartar sauce."

"Long live the world socialist revolution!" cried Lenin to the Petrograd soviet the night of 6–7 November 1917. Later on he expanded: "The complete victory of the socialist revolution is unimaginable in a single country; such a victory requires the most active collaboration of at least a few advanced countries, among which we cannot count Russia."

By 1918 Communist parties had been created in other countries: Finland and Latvia (August); Holland, Hungary, and Austria (November); and Poland and Germany (December). The pressures toward revolution in Austria, Germany, and Hungary appeared to be answering Bolshevik hopes.

But at the same time signs of the coming split began to appear.

In January 1919, at a meeting in Italy, Filippo Turati emphasized the necessity to prepare people's minds and consciousness for the coming of socialist society and to carry out a gradual transformation of society. A voice interrupted him: "It takes too long!" Turati: "If you know a shorter path, tell me . . ." Other voices: "Russia! Russia! Long live Lenin!"

In France, while preparing for May Day 1919, the leadership of the General Confederation of Workers (CGT) proposed as an objective the concrete establishment of the eight-hour day. The minority, however, wanted to discuss revolution, which would be "possible, soon to arrive, inevitable, irresistible."

At the Congress of the CGT in September, the motion proposed by the confederated committee, and approved by a large majority, pointed out that syndicalism was a revolutionary force, and then continued on:

> The Congress of Lyon cannot let it be thought that trade union action finds its correct and appropriate expression in acts of violence and surprise. Nor can one consider trade unionism as a weapon open to use by outside groups. The trade union movement affirms the necessity for the working class to take up its responsibilities in managing society.

Léon Jouhaux remarked: "Revolution is not only the catastrophic act, it is also the long preparation, the long penetration, the long undermining of bourgeois society." Nonetheless the minority resolution declared:

> It is in the flowering of the Russian Revolution, in its extension to all countries, that the hopes of all the martyred proletariat, exhausted by five years of unprecedented, exterminating warfare, lie. . . . All the revolutionary energies that the proletariat possesses should be transformed into acts.

Two views, two attitudes . . .

In January 1919, in a "Manifesto to the Workingmen of the Universe," thirty-nine parties, factions, and groups taking their stand from the "point of view of the dictatorship of the proletariat in the form of the power of the soviets" were invited to an "International Communist Conference." By the time the conference met in March, the Spartacist movement in Germany had been crushed, Karl Liebknecht and Rosa Luxemburg had been assassinated, and the two Soviet republics in Bavaria and Hungary were defeated. The Communist International, the Third International which Lenin had wished for since 1914, gave itself at this time the task of

> generalizing the revolutionary experience of the working class, of ridding the movement of impure mixtures of opportunism and of social patriotism, of uniting the strengths of all the truly revolutionary parties of the world proletariat, and by these means facilitating and speeding the victory of the Communist Revolution throughout the world.

Militants proclaimed their concurrence and enthusiasm. Clara Zetkin was among them: "The old International has died in shame; it cannot be brought back to life. . . . I will not spend the last years of my life there where death is, but where the forces of the future lie."

At the International's second congress, in 1920, the direction and the choices became more definite:

> The Communist International has taken up the cause of Soviet Russia. The international proletariat will not return its sword into the scabbard until Soviet Russia has become one of the links in a federation of Soviet Republics spanning the world. . . .
> The Communist International concentrates the will of the worldwide revolutionary proletariat. Its task is to organize the working class of the entire world in order to overthrow the capitalist order and establish communism. . . . The world political situation today is such that the time has come for the dictatorship of the proletariat.

The Communist party was defined here as the "conscious interpreter of the proletariat in its struggle against the yoke of the bourgeoisie"; its central goal was "the fight against bourgeois democracy, whose hypocrisy must be uncovered." Twenty-one conditions for membership in the International were stated. They had to do with the formation of Communist parties that were to be solidly organized and directed, acting as a single body in the principal areas of struggle:

> The parties belonging to the Communist International should be organized on the basis of democratic centralism. In the current period of acute civil war, the Communist party will not be able to fulfill its duty unless it is organized in the most centralized manner possible, with an iron, even military, discipline holding sway. The inner circle of the party . . . must be granted the widest possible authority and powers. (Condition 12)

They had to call themselves "Communist parties" (Condition 17), purge reformist elements from posts of responsibility (Condition 2), and elect a new central committee with at least two-thirds of its members endorsed by the Third International (Condition 20). Excluded from the party were those who rejected the conditions of membership in the Communist International (Condition 21); this was not only a question of breaking with "blatant reformists" but also of assuring the periodic purge of petty-bourgeois elements (Condition 13).

These parties were to combat both the bourgeoisie *and* reformism at the same time and were to demonstrate the necessity of the dictatorship of the proletariat; propaganda and agitation were to possess a "truly Communist character" (Condition 1); legal action was to be combined with illegal action (Condition 3) and was to be carried out within the army (Condition 4), the countryside (Condition 5), and the trade unions (Condition 9), which meant combating the "yellow" trade union International, called the Amsterdam International (Condition 10). The action of the parliamentary group was to be strictly controlled (Condition 11).

Communist parties were to denounce social patriotism and social pacifism (Condition 6) and were to support emancipation movements in the colonies (Condition 8).

Finally, these parties were to submit to the authority of the International: "All decisions of the Communist International, including the decisions of its executive committee, are binding" (Condition 16). Important documents of the International were to be published by the Communist party of each country (Condition 18). Each party was to meet within four months to decide on membership in the Communist International (Condition 19). In addition, the programs—developed in accordance with conditions in each country—that individual parties planned to adopt were to be ratified by the International (Condition 15). Each party was expected to give unreserved support to the Soviet Republics in their struggles against the counterrevolution (Condition 14).

Léon Blum analyzed this program with lucidity:

> You have before you a doctrinal whole. . . . This is a new socialism in all essential points: organizational conception, conception of the relation between political organization and economic organization, conception of revolution, conception of the dictatorship of the proletariat. . . . In my opinion it is based on ideas that are false in themselves, and that are contrary to the essential and unvarying principles of Marxist socialism. Besides this, the program is based on the vast factual error that consists in generalizing from a certain number of notions drawn out of a single and localized experience, the Russian Revolution, to international socialism as a whole.

Though for some there could be no question of not remaining faithful to the ethics and traditions of democratic socialism, for others there could be no question of not being in the camp of the Revolution.

At the congress in Tours, 25 December 1920, under the banner "Proletarians of all countries, Unite!" the socialist delegates clashed with one another.

Rappoport expressed the dominant feeling when he declared: "Bolshevik Russia has become the engine and the soul of all revolution; toward it turn all nations in which revolutionary ferment is ready to break out."

Clara Zetkin was present as well, having come out of hiding: "In Russia, faith in world revolution has become a religion. By all means, legal or illegal, you should help this revolution."

She tried to shake up those who hesitated because of the possibility of a split: "Unite with the reformists, with the centrists, with the social patriots? Impossible. Your unity is a house in ruins, a prison in which the right keeps the left chained up."

A telegram signed by Zinoviev, Lenin, Trotsky, Bukharin, and Rosmer denounced those who advocated membership in the International "with reservations": "They have been and remain the determined agents of bourgeois influence over the proletariat." But what led a majority of delegates to support membership in the Third International was a deep sense of solidarity and belonging, something Frossard well understood:

> The Russian Revolution exercises over the working class, whether you wish it to or not, such prestige and influence that you will not be able to prevent workers' organizations from seeing membership in the International as one of the ways to affirm, against bourgeois governments, solidarity with this very Revolution.

Against these voices the analyses of Léon Blum were barely heard. Blum recalled the traditions of freedom in the Socialist party, the tradition of autonomy between trade unionism and the party, the constant effort to unite reform and revolution into a single movement. He rejected the

> tactic of inorganic masses following the Communist vanguard. . . . It is dangerous because any move toward taking power depending on the sheeplike violence of inorganic masses is based on a very fragile foundation and could easily backfire. . . . You will not make the Revolution with these herds that run after all the horses. You will make it with millions of organized workers who know what they are after and what methods they will use to get to the goal, and who are ready to accept the necessary suffering and sacrifices.

Blum saw two approaches opposing one other: "One sees the transformation as the goal with the winning of public power as a means, and the other sees the winning of power as the goal."

Henceforward, said Blum, the dictatorship of the proletariat, acceptable if it is the dictatorship of a class, organized on a temporary basis "by a party such as ours," is unacceptable if it becomes a long-lasting system of government, the dictatorship of a committee, to which the Bolshevik conception of a party leads.

> In the party that they want to make for us, the central power will ultimately belong to a secret committee appointed . . . under the control of the executive committee of the International itself. Who will make decisions about the most important issues in the life of the party?—Men whom you will not know.

The vote on membership in the International precipitated the rupture: on one side the majority of the congress established itself as a Communist party, the French section of the Communist International. On the other side the minority re-formed the Socialist party, the French section of the Workers' International. The two tendencies were implacably bound together by the rivalries, fights, and hatred of those who, with differing conceptions and methods, led a struggle for similar objectives on shared terrain.

In Germany a Communist party was created in December 1918 from the remains of the Spartacist movement. Weakened by the assassinations of its leaders Rosa Luxemburg and Karl Liebknecht and then by internal dissension, the party merged with the majority of the Independent Social Democratic party (USPD), which declared itself, in December 1920 at the Halle Congress, in favor of joining the Communist International. The German Social Democratic party, called upon to assume governing responsibilities, had then to reckon with a strong Communist party.

In Switzerland, after deciding to join the Communist International in August 1919, the Socialist party went back on its decision in December 1920, with the refusal to join confirmed by referendum in January 1921. In Italy the Socialist party had similarly voted to join the International in April 1919, but after the twenty-one conditions were made public, an unscheduled congress was convened in January 1921: the party broke into three groups, with a strong minority creating the Italian Communist party. In Spain the Socialist Youth separated from the Socialist party in 1920 in order to found the Spanish Communist party; they were joined by a minority of the Socialist party after this party rejected membership in the International in 1921. In Belgium, too, the Communist party was created out of a minority group within the Socialist party.

In Great Britain, confronted by the Labour party, the Communist party was able to play only a limited role. Similar situations existed in Holland, Denmark, and Sweden, where the Social Democratic parties took much of the ground away from the Communist party.

From then on, in Europe and throughout the world, two conceptions of socialism clashed with each other; two forms of political organization; two families of trade union organizations.

2. THE USSR, "ONLY HOMELAND" OF THE INTERNATIONAL PROLETARIAT

Paradoxically, after the end of 1921, once the break had occurred and the Communist parties were formed, one of the first directives of the Communist International aimed at a rapprochement with those for whom, yesterday, no words had been harsh enough. No doubt this was due in part to the failure of revolutionary movements in Germany and in Hungary, and of strikes in Italy, France, and Czechoslovakia. But it also involved accompanying the NEP, which had begun in the USSR, with the formation of a "united proletarian front" organized around the theme: "More bread and peace." This first turnaround was not accepted without dissension and disputes.

In 1924 Stalin made the phrase "socialism in a single country" respectable. Allied at the time with Zinoviev and Kamenev against Trotsky, he strengthened his hold over the leadership of the Communist party of the USSR. Factions were prohibited and a campaign of "verification and purging" was launched. The Fifth Congress of the Communist International decided on the Bolshevization of the Communist parties:

> The essential objective of this period of the Communist International is the Bolshevization of its sections. . . . Bolshevization of the parties signifies the transfer into the sections of everything within Bolshevism that has been, and is still, of international significance. (Resolution of the Fifth Congress [1924], cited in Lazitch 1956)

> Purges struck in Germany, Poland, France, Italy, China . . .

At this same congress, social democracy was sorely accused:

> Between the political heads of the bourgeoisie and those of revolutionary social democracy, there is only a division of labor: the former create the appearance of being democratic-pacifist, while the latter work to develop democratic-pacifist illusions within the working class. (Resolution of the Fifth Congress [1924])

And again:

> It is historically false to speak of the victory of fascism over social democracy. Fascism and social democracy (insofar as one considers its leaders) are the right and left hands of contemporary capitalism, unsettled by World War I and the first worker uprisings. (Resolution of the Fifth Congress [1924])

From this viewpoint,

> the tactic of a united front is simply a means for mobilizing and agitating the masses for a certain period. To try to interpret this tactic as a political coalition with social democracy is opportunism refused by the Communist International. (Resolution of the Fifth Congress [1924])

This was the period when the Communist party of the USSR carried out a new wave of repression against the Mensheviks and the Socialist Revolutionaries. The SFIO (French Section of the Workers' International) during its Twenty-First Congress in February 1924, adopted this motion:

> The Congress of the Socialist party (SFIO) renews its protests against the imprisonment and persecution of Russian Social Democrats and

Socialist Revolutionaries who are fighting the Bolshevik regime. The congress expresses its sympathy to all those who are victims of a dictatorship violating the best traditions of socialism. (*Reports of the Twenty-First Congress of the Socialist Party* 1924)

The previous month, at its Third Congress, the French Communist party (SFIC) appealed to the workers:

The decline of Western imperialism stands in striking contrast to the uninterrupted expansion of the great Union of Soviet Republics. This Russian Revolution—put down, shamed, ridiculed, calumnified, and so weighed down with domestic and foreign enemies—is still standing, stronger than ever after six years of struggle, unbeaten, invincible. Only the Soviet Republic, dedicated to peaceful and constructive work, gives to the world the example of prosperity, creation, and true greatness. . . . Communists around the world are proud of their Russian brothers and hope only to equal them. (*Addresses and Resolutions of the Third Congress of the French Communist Party* 1924)

In 1928 a new step was taken. Stalin had the Communist party in hand by this time; with collectivization in the countryside, the First Five-Year Plan, and priority given to heavy industry, a new stage began in the construction of socialism in the USSR. The Communist party asserted itself as the leading party of the world Communist movement. At the Communist party's Sixth Congress, which met from 17 July to 1 September in Moscow, the program of the Communist International was adopted:

The duty of the international proletariat, of which the USSR is the *only homeland*, the bastion of its conquests, the essential factor in its international emancipation, is to contribute to the success of building socialism in the USSR and to defend the USSR by all means against attacks by capitalist powers. (*Program of the Communist International* 1928)

This congress also approved the *Theses on the Struggle against the Imperialist War and the Tasks of Communists*, in which the world was seen as divided into two camps,

on one side the entire capitalist world, on the other the USSR, around which gather the international proletariat and the oppressed peoples of the colonies. (*Theses on the Struggle against the Imperialist War and the Tasks of Communists 1928*)

In case of an imperialist war against the USSR,

the proletariat of the imperialist countries should not only fight for the defeat of their governments in this war; the proletariat should actively seek the victory of the Soviet power. . . . The Red Army is not an "enemy" army; it is the army of the international proletariat. The proletariat of the capitalist countries, during a period of war against the USSR, will not let itself be intimidated by the bourgeoisie—which will accuse it of high treason—and it will not, under the threat of war, renounce the USSR. (Ibid.)

Within this perspective, the attacks against social democracy became harsher:

The essential role of social democracy is now to undermine indispensable unity in the struggle of the proletariat against imperialism. By splitting and dividing the united red front of the proletarian fight against capital, social democracy is imperialism's main point of support within the working class. International social democracy of all kinds—the Second International and its trade union subsidiary, the Trade Union Federation of Amsterdam—have thus become the reserves of bourgeois society, its most dependable safeguard. (*Program of the Communist International* 1928)

Henceforth,

the tactic of the united front, the most efficient method of struggle against capital, for mobilizing the masses in class action and for unmasking and isolating reformist leaders, is one basic tactic of Communist parties throughout the revolutionary period. (Ibid.)

The dominant line of thinking during this period was in fact summed up by the phrase "class against class." Because social democracy was seen as a defense and point of support for the bourgeoisie, social democracy had to be combated, and the alliance it proposed with the liberal parts of the bourgeoisie was to be rejected. The tactic of the united front, calling on proletarians in all countries to support the construction of socialism in the USSR, supposedly would cut off the Social Democratic leaders from their own workers.

In Germany this line of thinking was applied all the more strictly as the Communists won more votes: 3.3 million votes in 1928, 4.6 million in 1930, nearly 5 million in March 1932. Although the rate of increase in votes for the Nazis was even steeper (800,000 in 1928, 6.4 million in 1930, 11.3 million in March 1932), the proletarian revolution appeared to be within sight, and success seemed only a matter of preventing social democracy from once again rescuing the bourgeoisie. Hitler's taking power, the establishment of a National-Socialist state, and the systematic repression against leaders and militants of the workers' movement opened, in fact, a very different historical path.

In France the phrase "class against class" was applied to the elections of 1928 (the Communist party gained votes but lost seats) and to the

1932 elections (the party lost both votes and seats). It was affirmed in a tone that testifies to the harshness of the battle:

> Social democracy was, after the war, the shield of the bourgeoisie. It disoriented the revolutionary movement of the masses who were leaving the trenches, still worn out from handling guns and grenades. It broke the great strikes of 1920. . . . After the Moroccan war the role of the Socialist party changed and became more clear. *While before it had been an instrument of defense of the bourgeoisie, it then became the instrument of* CAPITALIST ATTACK AGAINST THE WORKING CLASS. . . . DEFEND YOURSELVES AGAINST THE SOCIALIST PARTY, AGAINST SOCIALISM WHICH PREPARES FOR WAR, AGAINST SOCIALISM THE STRIKE-BREAKER, AGAINST REACTIONARY AND POLICING SOCIALISM. (*Manifesto, Theses, and Resolutions of the Sixth Congress of the French Communist Party [SFIC] 1929*; typography as in original.)

And again in 1932:

> The congress confirms the tactic "class against class," which has been verified by all elections since 1928. The relentless and systematic combat against social democracy will not be fulfilled unless the party as a whole turns definitely toward the socialist workers and the masses influenced by social democracy, convincing each socialist worker through constant practice of the single front at ground level. (*Theses and Resolutions of the Seventh Congress of the French Communist Party [SFIC] 1932*)

Of course, there were disagreements, militants who were uneasy, discontented; there were departures from the party as well as exclusions. Membership in the Communist party fell from 110,000 in 1921 to 52,000 in 1927–28, and then to 30,000 in 1931. But the party apparatus, in France and elsewhere, held together.

The Communist parties applied the successive positions adopted by the Communist International: the struggle against fascism and the creation of popular fronts; then, after the signing of the German-Soviet nonagression pact, action against the imperialist war; and then combat once again against Nazi Germany once hostilities began between Germany and the USSR.

Our concern is not to follow the establishment of these successive positions any more than it has been to recount the history of the Communist International or the Communist parties. Our intention is rather to show how, after 1919, a portion of the workers' movements throughout the world, though especially in Europe, committed itself to unconditional support of the USSR. This was a crucial phenomenon in this period, a fundamental phenomenon that we must consider further.

For throughout this period, hundreds of thousands of militants in the world were the active partisans of the USSR and saw the construction of socialism in the USSR as the keystone of their own fight for socialism.[18] Taking into account those lost through purges, departures, and abandonments, millions of men and women consecrated a part of their lives to the cause of the USSR, in the certainty that they were working for socialism. And tens of thousands of workers, wage earners or otherwise, along with young people and intellectuals, have been inspired— for a few years or for their whole lives—by this hope.

And there were many who devoted themselves to this cause with an undivided generosity of spirit: work, discipline, risks—in some cases prison or death, and in many cases the anguish of accepting or putting up with the intolerable because the movement demanded it. Militants attacking—sometimes with iron bars—their socialist comrades/adversaries, or becoming reconciled later with those whom they had earlier attacked—all this on command. Intellectuals keeping quiet, hiding the truth, clouding the truth, forbidding certain questions, refusing to look at reality, such as the trials or the camps. Leaders held in the grasp of the apparatus, with the constant threat of being broken or excluded if they disapproved or rebelled.

The process required, throughout the workers' movement, that faith, hope, and reason—forces able to bring about individual commitment— be united with the rigor of state organization and power.

Faith and hope: understood in their widest sense these are the profound impulses that move every socialist to believe in the possibility of a just society—or at least a society less unequal; a fraternal society—or at least a society less cruel, from which exploitation will be abolished in the long term and limited in the short term. After 1917 this faith took the form, at least for one segment of the men and women believing in socialism, of faith in the USSR: not only was socialism possible in general, but it was being achieved at the moment, where the proletarian revolution had been carried out, in the USSR.

Listen to the report of a worker just returned from a journey organized by the Association of Friends of the Soviet Union, a worker still feeling the emotional effects of the May Day parade:

> They were coming from all directions, singing, greeting us and taking our hands. Ah, my friends, when you think that you have to come back to this dirty, stupid capitalist country after that! I would have stayed ten years there. Forever! (Cited in Kupferman 1979)

This flame was, of course, maintained by the Communist party:

> The Seventh Congress of the French Communist party . . . enthusiastically salutes the heroic effort of the proletariat of the USSR,

shock brigade of the world revolution, which is preparing, through the realization of the Second Five-Year Plan, to carry out the historic task of abolishing classes and founding a classless society. (*Theses and Resolutions of the Seventh Congress of the French Communist Party [SFIC]* 1932)

In a similar vein, Maurice Thorez reflected in 1937 on his earlier trips to the USSR:

I admired [in 1925] this universe under construction, these cities rising up out of the ground, these factories working to increase productivity. "We have done all this without bosses," proclaimed the proud faces of workers, both men and women. . . . Everywhere [in 1927] the image of true democracy offered itself to my eyes. (Thorez 1937)

And Henri Barbusse, a member of the Communist party since 1923, accorded the remarkable privilege of being received by Stalin, recalled Stalin's "frank cordiality," his "goodness" and "tact." Stalin appeared to him a "clear and shining man" whose "gaiety" caused him to "laugh like a child." This author, who had denounced the horrors of the Great War with such force, stated:

The Russian people are the first people who know themselves to be occupied with saving people everywhere; the USSR, the only socialist experiment, is giving a real proof, a constructed proof: socialism is feasible, here on this earth. (Barbusse 1936)

Though this flame was maintained by the party, by its leaders and intellectuals, the flame itself was born in the denial of capitalist society, of injustice, of crises and unemployment.

Proceeding from the analyses of Marx and Lenin, the Communist movement rationally explained the defects and problems of capitalism and went on to predict, no less rationally, revolution and the establishment of socialism:

Imperialism is rotting and dying capitalism and is in general the last stage of capitalist evolution, the prelude to world socialist revolution. The international proletarian revolution thus follows from the conditions of the development of capitalism in general, and from its imperialist phase in particular. The capitalist system leads as a whole to a definitive collapse. The dictatorship of finance capital perishes, making room for the dictatorship of the proletariat. (*Program of the Communist International* 1928)

But the proletarian revolution and the dictatorship of the proletariat open the way toward socialist society. And there, rational deduction rejoined the faith and hope that had nourished the socialist movement for more than a century:

The abolition of classes and private property abolishes the exploitation of man by man. Labor ceases to be accomplished for the profit of the class enemy and as nothing but a means for existing: it is transformed into a vital and primordial need. Poverty, economic inequality, the suffering of the dominated classes, the miserable level of material life in general: these all disappear. The hierarchy of men in the division of labor and the contradiction between intellectual labor and manual labor disappear, along with any traces of social inequality between the sexes. Organs of class domination—state power first among them— disappear at the same time! The incarnation of class domination, the state dies as classes and all forms of compulsion disappear. (Ibid.)

For some, there was more hope and enthusiasm; for others, more analysis and reasoning. In any case, a coherent ideological whole was in place and available, from which an individual could find reasons and motives for commitment. Following this, the logic of faith, of bonds formed, and in some cases of gain and ambition, did the rest within the immense machine of the organization.

For by themselves ideology and belief hardly lead beyond the sect. But in this case they were joined by the science of organization, of organization disciplined with a strictness and coherence inspired by wartime armies: the proletariat, was it not at war with the bourgeoisie? And this organization itself was linked to a state apparatus, continually strengthened and controlled by Stalin's steel hand: a state apparatus with its methods, police, agents, and resources.

Thus, an exceptionally powerful movement developed on a world scale, a movement rooted in the revolt against capitalist society. It was nourished by socialist ideas and ideals, and it was inspired by deep commitment and hope. But the ideals and hopes were channeled, organized, guided, and mobilized by the Communist parties under the direction of the Communist International and Stalin.

There was the daily struggle and the hope for a better tomorrow; the camaraderie and the warmth that come from working with fellow believers; for the intellectuals, there was the feeling of being at the service of the people, of the poor, and of finding one's salvation by accepting the discipline of the "party of the working class"; there were the campaigns, the critiques, the purges, the exclusions, the liquidations (political or physical), the trials, the camps.

Some activists accepted everything, in the name of the struggle for socialism; others had doubts and asked themselves serious questions. Others became torn between belief and doubt, and would carry this open wound with them their entire lives. For still others, the tension became unbearable: they killed themselves.

In the name of socialism, what generosity of spirit and what human richness! But what a tragic waste as well!

3. WORKERS' CONQUESTS AND NATIONAL COMPROMISES

Confronted by the disaster of the war that they were unable to prevent, despite so many repeated pledges to the contrary; facing the flag of socialism so hurriedly raised in Russia, which filled so many young people, intellectuals, and workers with passion, and to which so many militants and responsible figures devoted themselves enthusiastically; in the uncertainty of postwar crises and turnarounds, European socialists hung on to their past, obstinately repeating the phrases hallowed by decades of debates, motions, and congresses. There were, for example, the French socialists who stayed—or came back to—the "old house," or the German Social Democrats who, at Heidelberg in 1924, adopted a program largely inspired by the Erfurt Program of 1891. In addition, having assumed parliamentary and sometimes governmental responsibilities, European socialists, in varying national contexts, also had to take up and deal with the contradictions and limits of the present.

In Great Britain, the dominant capitalist power until the end of the nineteenth century, the workers' movement—mainly the trade unions, which had provided the major impetus toward creating the Labour party—had won substantial concessions from the employers and the ruling class before World War I. Weakened by the war, for the most part surpassed by North American capitalism, which was at the time in full expansion, and in competition with new and rising capitalisms, British capitalism was determined to regain the leading position it had occupied in the international monetary and financial system. The return to pre-1914 parity for gold convertibility of the pound was the symbolic objective, while an increase in competitiveness—through greater productivity, pressure on buying power, restructuring, and if necessary, unemployment—was the principal method. In other words, the very existence of the social compromise that had begun at the end of the nineteenth and during the first years of the twentieth centuries in Great Britain was directly challenged in the 1920s: would the compromise be greatly cut back to a few trivial concessions, as a large fraction of the employers wished, or would it be expanded and increased, as the labor leaders hoped?

In fact, directly after the war, these leaders adopted an explicitly socialist program. What came to be known as "The House of Tomorrow" was supported by "four pillars":

1. a "national minimum" (full employment, minimum wage, forty-eight-hour workweek);

2. "democratic control of industry," in particular, mines, railroads, ports, electricity;

3. fiscal reform, including taxes on large incomes and on capital;

4. appropriation of part of the national surplus by the community to be used for the "common good," especially education and culture.

It was thus a question, not of changing society, but of obtaining transformations within present society advantageous to the working world and to the popular classes; transformations to be obtained within the framework of the "national compromise."

On the other hand, for the British employers the objective was not only to concede as little as possible, but to go back on earlier concessions. For example, in 1920 the railroad workers, through striking, had obtained a forty-eight-hour workweek and an increase in wages, though they did not manage to obtain nationalization of the railroads. But the following year the mine owners tried to reduce wages by as much as a third, and resorted to lockouts; confronted by strikes, the government called out the armed forces. In 1925 the mine owners wanted to reduce wages once again and to lengthen the working day from seven to eight hours: the 1926 general strike in support of the miners was broken when the government skillfully manipulated public opinion and, in addition, met strikers and their supporters with military force. In 1927 a law was passed limiting trade union rights (especially for civil servants) and the right to strike and prohibiting solidarity strikes and strikes aimed at putting pressure on the government. In addition, the general strike was declared illegal.

Throughout this period unemployment was high: there were more than a million unemployed during the 1920s (12 percent of the active population) and three million at the beginning of the 1930s. Unemployment compensation was increased several times (in 1920, 1922, and 1930). Under the unyielding pressures of the employers, nominal wages fell from 1920 to 1922 and stagnated from 1920 to 1929, though productivity steadily increased. However, due to decreases in prices, especially for food products, wage earners who did have jobs were able to maintain and even increase their buying power, especially between 1924 and 1939.

That Labour managed to achieve governmental responsibilities in 1924 and 1929 was due to the support of the Liberal party, but as a minority party they were unable to enact their full program of social reforms. They were, however, able to develop and put into operation a welfare-housing construction program and a reduction in the miners' working day from eight to seven-and-a-half hours. The health insurance program was strengthened in 1921, protection of widows and orphans was improved in 1925, and universal suffrage was extended to women in 1928.

Though the "social compromise" was damaged by the employers' offensive and the resolve of the conservative governments, the essential substance of the compromise was not itself destroyed. The central measures were preserved, in a period when British capitalism was subjected to strong foreign competition and a vigorous economic program designed to restore the pound. Preservation of the compromise may be ascribed to the power of the trade union movement and to advances by the Labour party.[19] To what degree was this preservation of the "national compromise" in Great Britain made possible by the profits resulting from domination on a world scale?[20] No one can say exactly, but similarly no one can deny that these profits facilitated the maintenance of the national compromise.

If this compromise is situated in the perspective of a socialist project, it is a project clearly different and distinct from what was developing at the same time in the USSR. A text published by Clement Attlee in 1937 gives a clear view of this difference:

> The goal of socialism is to give greater freedom to the individual. British socialists have never raised the state up as their idol, nor have they ever asked that individuals be sacrificed; they have never taken the beehive or the anthill as their ideal. . . . On the contrary, they believe that the value of a society, far from being found in uniformity, is due rather to its diversity. The herd travels in the direction opposite to that of progress. . . . Socialists advocate state intervention not as a goal in itself, but because such intervention is necessary in order to prevent the oppression of certain individuals by other individuals, to assure that the freedom of some people does not hinder the freedom of others nor conflict with the common good of society as a whole. (Attlee 1937)

In the Scandinavian countries as a whole, a similar sort of compromise was set into place. For example, in Sweden, with the support of the liberals who defended the positions of the advanced wing of the bourgeoisie, universal suffrage for men was adopted in 1909 for elections to the lower chamber, and in 1919 universal suffrage for men and women for elections to both chambers was adopted. The socialist-led minority government was unable in 1920 to institute profound reforms, though after 1932 the government that was founded on an alliance between socialists and peasants began a policy of increased buying power and major public-works projects, with deficit financing and credit development, which simultaneously facilitated the movement of agricultural products and allowed for an improvement in living conditions, a resurgence in economic activity, and a reduction in unemployment.

Some measures were carried out by changes in the laws: for example, those having to do with work-related accidents (1916), work-related illnesses (1929), collective bargaining (1929), and unemployment insurance (1934). But the bulk of the important issues were negotiated between the workers' union and the employers' union and were adopted using collective bargaining. The subsidiary collective agreements, signed by the labor federations, had to do with wages, hiring and firing policies, the length of the working day, overtime hours, annual holidays, and various sorts of aid. In addition, agreements were signed by the labor confederations on procedures for arbitrating social conflicts (1938), firing and dismissal conditions (1938), and work safety and health (1942).

Here again, on the basis of balancing forces, within the framework of capitalist society, a "social compromise" was set into place that assured the working world a certain number of gains.[21] Workers' struggles were symbolized by the Adalen strike of 1931, when troops fired at the strikers. In addition, the workers made a successful alliance with the peasants. Economists such as Gunnar Myrdal hoped "without doctrine that blinds us, but also without false prejudices, to do all that one can reasonably do to make the economy more stable" (cited in Tingsten 1973). Per Albin Hansson, leader of the party, declared in 1932: "I do not believe that between social democratic politics and bourgeois politics there is a gulf that would force our paths to separate." And in 1936 he stated:

> I believe that we will more easily attain our goal of a society without classes if we utilize all possibilities for negotiation and cooperation to solve conflicts. So far as I am concerned, a policy trying to achieve a socialist order can only be a policy of consensus. (Cited in Buci-Glucksmann and Therborn 1981)

Again:

> Social democratic politics may very easily be politics that attempt to let us benefit from the immense strengths present in private enterprise, while being at the same time a politics relying on state and social action. (Cited in Tingsten 1973)

Thus, in the name of socialism and within the perspective of an advance toward a classless society, there developed in Sweden an acceptance of capitalism, though it was a capitalism modified by state action, negotiation, and cooperation.

In Germany, directly after World War I, the Social Democrats held a similar attitude: to consolidate, strengthen, and widen, upon the basis of a solidly established democracy, the compromise whose elements had been set in place before the war. But . . .

But . . . democracy and the Republic had been founded in a climate of defeat and humiliation, and in many people's eyes democracy retained the mark of humiliation. But . . . the revolutionary movements ran the risk of clouding the possibilities, barely opening at the time, for a Social Democratic democracy, and it was within social democracy that the German revolutionaries found their Versailles. But . . . the defeat, the conditions of the peace, and the reparations weighed heavily upon the early years of the Weimar Republic . . .

At the congress of Görlitz, in 1921, the Social Democratic party abandoned the essentials of Marxist doctrine and proclaimed itself the "party of the whole people." But four years later, at Heidelberg, the party adopted a program inspired for the most part by the Erfurt Program of 1891.

The Social Democratic party contributed to the establishment of the most democratic democracy in the world, with universal suffrage for men and women at the age of twenty, proportional voting for the Reichstag, the right to popular initiatives, and the possibility of making final decisions by referendum. Schooling was compulsory and free, and an extensive social security system, to be managed democratically, had been announced. On the one hand, free enterprise was recognized and rights to property and inheritance were guaranteed, while on the other hand, labor power, including the right to organize, was protected. In addition, the possibility existed of collectivizing certain businesses, and a system of comanagement had begun (see Rovan 1978).

But there was insufficient national commitment to this democracy, and in addition, significant sectors among the employers and the army rejected the democracy. Thus, Fritz Thyssen in 1924 said, "Democracy, for us, means nothing." One might say it was a democracy without democrats.

The Social Democratic leaders did indeed seek compromise. They sought it with the army, which they avoided purging and to which they left the business of maintaining or reestablishing order. But the leaders of the military maintained intact their arrogance and their spitefulness, not to speak of their hatred and their taste for authority, hierarchy, and power.

The Social Democratic leaders would have welcomed compromise with the employers. However, except for the middle-level employers, German employers as a whole were hostile to compromise, as this declaration by Hugo Stinnes in 1919 shows: "The great industrialists, and all the leaders of economic life, will one day recover their influence and their power. They will be called back by the sobered-up people, half-dead from hunger, who will need bread and not words."

In 1923 there were still more than one-and-a-half million unemployed; there were two-and-a-half million in 1929 and six million in 1932. The Communist party used all possible means in their opposition to social democracy. And the National-Socialist movement, at least in its early years, took over certain themes and symbols from the socialists.

The economic, social, and political situation made impossible in Germany a "social compromise" such as had been established in Great Britain or in Sweden, and this was the fundamental cause, when the great crisis developed, of Hitler's rise and the expansion of National Socialism, though Hitler was supported additionally by a segment of large capital. Thus a consensus was established on a quite different basis between the major employers, entrepreneurs as a whole, large fractions of the middle and small bureoisie,[22] and the working class. The consensus was founded on nationalism and xenophobia; on feelings of superiority, anti-Semitism, and expansionism; on a taste for order, the army, and the greatness of Germany; and, as well, on a resurgence of business activity and a return to full employment through major strategic public-works projects, rearming and then over-arming, militarization, and the march toward war: a consensus that, through violence, propaganda, coercion, and state repression, was transformed into totalitarianism.

It was a consensus that opened and unchained logics of hatred, madness, and domination, which eventually became uncontrollable and led to the horror.

In France, capitalism in the 1920s underwent significant growth, with a 5.8 percent annual growth rate between 1922 and 1929. Productivity increased steeply, and thus so did the intensity of labor for industrial workers. But the working class, who supported the burden of these additional profits, managed to benefit from some of them as well; first of all by the reduction of the working day (with the establishment of the eight-hour day in 1919, the slowdown in economic activity after 1919, and finally with the establishment of the forty-hour week and paid holidays in 1936), and then by the increase in buying power, which averaged 2.2 percent per year from 1920 to 1930 and 1.5 percent per year from 1930 to 1937.

These concessions were obtained on the basis of a balance of forces clearly more favorable in 1936 than in 1919.[23] They were concessions obtained, year after year, by action within businesses, and, despite the break between the CGT and CGTU in 1921, through the development and strengthening of trade union action.[24]

The electoral victory of the Popular Front in 1936 and the accompanying strikes permitted these concessions to be suddenly extended. Léon Blum recounted:

M. Lambert-Ribot, who had been my comrade for many years in the State Council . . . contacted me through mutual friends . . . so that I might, as quickly as possible and without wasting a second, work to establish contact between the highest employers' organizations . . . and the CGT. Without a doubt, I would have attempted myself what has come to be known as the Matignon accord, but the truth is that the first initiative came from the large employers. (Cited in Ligou 1962)

The elections took place in April; the strike movement broke out on 26 May and quickly spread: there were 500,000 workers on strike on 5 June; the Blum government was installed on 6 June.

The Matignon accord between the General Confederation of French Production and the CGT was signed in the night of 6–7 June. It provided for wage increases between 7 and 15 percent, free exercise of trade union rights, rights of workshop representatives, free discussion of collective contracts, and negotiations that would continue while workers, in the meantime, went back to work.

In ten weeks, several important laws were passed: on retirement for former combatants, paid holidays, collective bargaining, a forty-hour workweek, the dissolution of leagues, new status for the Bank of France, an extension of the age for school studies, nationalization of war-related industries, social insurance, retirement for miners, the organization of state markets, and the Grain Office. At the end of 1936 two more laws were also passed, having to do with conciliation, arbitration, and the possibility of extending collective agreements.

Finally, negotiations took place within each business or industry: more than a thousand collective agreements were signed in 1936 and more than three thousand in 1937, in contrast to the early 1930s when only a few dozen collective agreements were signed each year.[25] These negotiations allowed workers to widen and strengthen the gains they had made in many areas.

Thus, throughout the 1920s and again in 1936, the workers' movement in France forced some important concessions to be made. But no workers' organization situated itself, doctrinally, within the perspective of a "national compromise"—neither the Communist party, whose strategy went along with the schema laid down by the Communist International, nor the Socialist party, which remained, doctrinally, anticapitalist and revolutionary.

Thus, in the speech outlining his program, Léon Blum denounced capitalism:

The cause of our common suffering lies in a bad social system. . . . [Capitalism] is incapable of getting agreement between, and consequently of fulfilling, the natural functions of all human societies: allocating and distributing. Out of human progress, which should be a cause of well-being and joy, it creates a cause of injustice and suffering. In its hands, science, the honor of our race, gives rise only to waste, degradation, destruction, and misery.

Against this bad society Blum opposed good society:

Socialism, for its part, refuses to mutilate the gifts of nature and the contributions of intelligence. . . . Its motto is "to open up to all of humanity the collective benefits of nature and of progress." This is the highest and most noble work that men can propose to each other. (Cited in Ligou 1962)

A mind as fine as Blum's must, at some level, have seen the limits of this dichotomy. Was such a simplistic and overdrawn contrast felt to be necessary for electoral success? Or was this the ritual repetition of an anthem inherited from the past, repeated more out of tradition than from a clear analysis of present realities?

In any case, in France as well, the "national compromise" took form under the banner of doctrinal anticapitalism.

COMMENTS ON CHAPTER 5

A new split developed among those who hoped to change the world.

There were those who saw the USSR as the homeland of socialism and its rulers as the leaders of the international Communist movement. The October Revolution, the organization and the leading role of the Communist party, Marxism-Leninism, collectivization of the means of production, centralized planning—these were all seen as patterns to be adopted, as far as possible. Similarly, it was right to defend the USSR, forward bastion in the combat for socialism throughout the world.

And yet, in the space of a few decades, what a swing in thought! The proletariat was supposed to have no homeland; now it had one: the USSR. The movement toward socialism was supposed to have a chance to succeed only through revolutions carried out in several developed countries; now socialism was being constructed in a single country, and this despite its low level of development. The dictatorship of the proletariat was supposed to be democratic for the greatest number; now a few men—one man—ruled in the name of the proletariat.

Faith and hope, reason and ideology, the feeling of devoting oneself to a grand cause: these had helped fuel the socialist movement in the nineteenth century. Now these same deep human impulses served as the basis for the commitment of hundreds of thousands of militants to a "socialism" incarnated by the USSR.

There were also those who, whatever their sympathy or their judgment of what was being built in Russia, saw the Revolution there as an experiment profoundly marked by conditions peculiar to Russia itself. They remained the adherents of an approach, within the leading capitalist countries of Europe, that combined a widening of the gains won by workers and the popular strata along with a strengthening of democracy.

The gap was huge between the hope—which some people nourish still—for a change in society, for a classless society without injustice or oppression, and the struggle carried out *within* capitalist society to make this society less cruel, less unjust, less oppressive. This was a struggle that, insofar as it succeeded, weakened the reasons for overthrowing capitalism.

Here, several points need to be emphasized. First, the "compromise," which was a product of this struggle within capitalist society, did not flow intrinsically from social democracy. Throughout the nineteenth century and into the early twentieth century, a policy of high wages had appeared to employers to be contrary to their own interests; nonetheless such a policy became the key element of a plan guaranteeing capitalism favorable conditions for functioning and reproduction.

For example, in the United States, Henry Ford, confronted by absenteeism, personnel instability, and poor production quality, granted a high wage (the Five-Dollar Day) to assembly-line workers. Certainly this involved in part the creation of lasting ties with good, selected workers, but it was also a matter of creating new conditions for the reproduction of the working class itself:

> By underpaying the men, we will produce a generation of both physically and morally underfed and underdeveloped children; we will be left with a generation of physically and morally feeble workers who, for this very reason, will prove ineffective once they enter industry. In the end, it will be industry that pays the price. (Ford, cited in Coriat 1978, 101)

In addition, the Five-Dollar Day improved the functioning of the capitalist economy, because once the Five-Dollar Day became generalized, consumers' demands increased:

> I believe in the first place that, all other considerations aside, our own sales depend in a measure upon the wages we pay. If we can distribute high wages, then that money is going to be spent and it will serve to make storekeepers and distributors and manufacturers and

workers in other lines more prosperous, and their prosperity will be reflected in our sales. (Ford 1922, 124)

Henry Ford thus put into place one of the essential elements in the modern version of the "national compromise." Franklin D. Roosevelt, trying to find ways to deal with the major crisis of the 1930s, moved in the same direction: he went further by establishing a minimum wage, prohibiting child labor, limiting the working day, and strengthening the rights of unions. These were all measures against which large sections of American employers protested, yet they contributed, as Roosevelt remarked during the 1936 presidential campaign, to "saving the system of private profit and free enterprise."

John Maynard Keynes can be viewed within this same perspective. As an escape from the crisis of the 1930s he proposed getting economic activity moving again through supplementary injections to buying power. This formed the theoretical justification for the policies of building and investing in great public-works projects and the welfare state.

We see, then, that the compromise between classes, within the framework of the developed capitalisms, was not an "invention" of the social democracies. This compromise is found, in different forms, even in countries where social democracy did not become a strong force (the United States, but also, in another way, France). Thus, the "social democratic compromise" has been only one particular form of the "national compromise" carried out in all the leading capitalist countries. The specificity of the social democratic compromise is that the representative organizations of the working class, and more generally of the working world, (1) have renounced the idea of overthrowing capitalism and aim instead, by transforming capitalism, at obtaining substantial benefits for the working world and the popular strata; and (2) have renounced the idea of a revolutionary seizure of power and have committed themselves to strengthening and expanding democratic life, with all that this implies, including pluralism and succession of power.

The whole process has been very much a compromise between major social forces: between classes. In the interwar period the compromise was maintained in Great Britain, despite the difficulties encountered by British capitalism. The compromise became established as well in the Scandinavian countries, particularly Sweden, but was defeated in Germany's Weimar Republic.

These "national compromises" allowed for the satisfaction—more or less—of the immediate claims and deeper hopes of the working world and the working class.

But can they still be considered, as Hansson thought, within the perspective of an advance toward socialism, toward a society without classes? Quite the reverse: who does not see that even if they improve capitalist society—because they improve it—these compromises strengthen and solidify capitalism? And can one extol socialism at the same time one compromises with capitalism?

This is hardly possible, unless one abandons a Manichean vision in which capitalism is evil and socialism good, the passage from one to the other taking place through an absolute break; unless one thinks that, through transformation after transformation, reform after reform, conquest after conquest, not only may the damages inflicted by capitalism be limited, but also a progressive process leading toward the socialist ideal may be successfully carried out.

Between the two wars there were in fact many socialists who thought as did Henri de Man: "To put an end to capitalism, it is less important to be able to defeat capitalism than to replace it" (de Man [1926] 1929). One finds here the problems of production, of labor, of incitement and compulsion to labor. And everything takes place as though, not knowing how to "replace" capitalist methods in this domain, the socialists of the developed countries left it to the employers to be the ones to experiment, to hire, to direct production, and to compel workers to produce ever more, while they, the socialists, tried only to limit the excesses, and obtain some reciprocal agreements, assurances, and benefits. Social democracy (in the countries where it has become a strong force), the left in France, and the trade union movement: all of them—even when they have assumed governmental responsibilities—have behaved as a kind of "opposition to His Majesty Capital."

Finally, the question remains open of how much the "social compromise" was made possible by the profits that the developed capitalisms were able to extract from their domination on a world scale, from colonial exploitation and unequal exchange. For it was precisely in the two major countries defeated in 1918, weakened and deprived of their colonies, that the "social compromise" fell apart (Italy and Germany). And it was in the dominant capitalisms—Great Britain from the end of the nineteenth century, the United States from the time between the two wars, France, and Sweden—that these compromises, in one way or another, became established.

While in the USSR the Bolshevik leaders reinvented or took up capitalist methods for compelling labor, in the leading capitalist countries the socialists sought only the attenuation of these methods, accompanied by a more equitable division of wealth. For socialists who agree to examine the situation head-on, the abyss is immense between the ideal and what has in fact been accomplished. Past the nice ideas, the good intentions, and the fine sentiment, the ordeal of reality has been pitiless.

6

INTERPRETATIONS OF THE USSR

Is it possible, today, to speak calmly about the USSR? Is it possible to be heard and to debate without raising passions, without spilling over into polemic? Our own efforts are placed within the field of understanding, of concrete analysis of a historical reality. Yet an element of this reality has been an immense, prodigious hope. What meaning can there be to the phrase "the reason for hope"?

We must accept a certain amount of mystery, a certain amount of incomprehensibility. For there is an area of spiritual generosity, of enthusiasm, and of believing in a better world that makes it possible for those on the bottom of society to bear their suffering, and that gives to many sensitive men and women of the middle class a consciousness of the injustice and advantages from which they benefit.

So it is not a question here of judging those who have persisted—and sometimes still persist—in seeing the USSR as the "homeland of socialism," as "realized socialism," or recently, with greater modesty, as "actually existing socialism." It is rather a question of seeing how contradictory views have considered the reality of the USSR, and especially how an official truth has been hammered out, a sacred myth that has weighed down socialist and workers' movements throughout the world for many years. Along with this first movement, there has been a second: the critiques of the USSR, denunciations made in the name of socialism but which were often pushed too far by bitterness, deception, or hatred.

1. THE CLOAK OF OFFICIAL TRUTH

As we have seen, Lenin interpreted the NEP as a detour through state capitalism. This was a coherent vision with a conception of a necessary

110

succession of modes of production in which the development of capitalism inexorably prepares the establishment of communism. Bukharin and Preobrazhensky summarized the process with pedagogic clarity:

> Capitalism . . . digs its own grave. For it creates its own grave-diggers, the proletarians. The more it develops, the more does it multiply those who are its mortal enemies, and the more does it unite them against itself. But it does not merely breed its enemies. It likewise prepares the ground for a new organization of social production, for a new economic order that will be comradely and communistic. How does it do this? . . . [Through] a centralization and concentration of production, [which] actually paves the way for cooperative production after the proletarian revolution. . . . The further capitalism has developed and the more highly centralized production has become, the easier will it be for the proletariat to manage production after the victory.
>
> Thus, *capitalism does not merely create its own enemies and does not only lead to the communist revolution, but it brings into being the economic basis for the realization of the communist social order.* (Bukharin and Preobrazhensky [1919] 1968, 66, 68)

In trying to conceive of the historic movement in which his own action was inscribed, Lenin occasionally went even further:

> Socialism is nothing other than state capitalist monopoly employed in the interest of the entire people, and ceasing to this extent only to be a capitalist monopoly. . . . Capitalism has created a system that is tightly connected to the banks and the industrial trade-unions—coal, metals, sugar, etc.—a system that carries out a great labor of registering and inventorying, if one may so express it. This system cannot and must not be broken up. Without the large banks socialism would be unrealizable. The large banks constitute the state mechanism, which we need in order to establish socialism, and which we take over from capitalism ready-made. The capitalism of state monopolies is the most complete *material* preparation for socialism; it is the *ante-chamber* of socialism. (Lenin, cited in Dolléans 1936–56, 2:254)

But by 1920, drawing conclusions from the failure of the Hungarian Revolution and analyzing the difficulties and errors with remarkable lucidity, Eugene Varga emphasized that "the passage from capitalism to socialism is carried out through difficult struggles and privations of all sorts" (Varga [1920] 1922, 196). Further on we find this analysis:

> The evolutionist interpretation of Marxist doctrine leads to the persistence of a passive and fatalist mentality among the proletarian masses. The Marxist doctrine of the fatal fall of the capitalist mode of production, its economic proof of the coming of socialism: these have been poorly understood when one attributes to them the idea that the fall of

capitalism could happen automatically, without an active revolutionary struggle on the part of the proletariat. This is a fatal error. (Varga [1920] 1922, 197)

Throughout the 1920s, within the movement itself of building socialist society, the debate and the questioning continued.

In the name of socialism, Trotsky in 1920 praised forced labor:

It is said that forced labor is not productive. If that is true, then all of the economy is condemned, for no other pathways lead to socialism besides the forced dividing-up, by an economic center, of all the labor force of the country, in conformity with the needs of the economic plan of the state as a whole. . . . If this labor power, organized and directed by force, is not productive, then you can erect a cross over socialism. (Trotsky, cited in Heller 1974)

In the name of socialism, Trotsky in 1923 spoke in favor of a statist economy:

By statist economy we naturally mean—besides industry—transport, statist foreign trade, domestic trade, and finance. The whole complex—as a whole and in parts—is adapted to the peasant market and to the isolated peasant as a taxpayer. But this adaptation has as its fundamental object the strengthening and developing of *statist industry, the cornerstone of the dictatorship of the proletariat and the basis of socialism.* (Trotsky [1923a] 1972, 138)

In the name of socialism, the Workers' Opposition was by 1921 demanding a greater role for the trade unions. Shlyapnikov said:

The basis for the disagreement resides in the path by which our party, at the present moment of transition, puts into practice its political economy: either the mass of workers organized into unions, or else, coming down from above, the bureaucratic path relying on civil servants who have been directly invested with power. (Cited in Kollontaï [1921] 1974, 64–65)

And Alexandra Kollontaï insisted:

When the comrades think about it, is it possible to achieve and build communist economy and production using the hands and spirits of individuals belonging to an outside class who are shot through and through with the traditions of the past? (Kollontaï [1921] 1974, 65)

In the name of socialism, Bukharin in 1925 advocated the maintenance of the worker-peasant alliance, though "there is a direct opposition between the interests of the working class and the interests of the peasants," especially concerning the establishment of agricultural and industrial prices (Bukharin [1925–27] 1974, 131). At the same time, however, the fundamental interest of these two classes is in the establishment of socialism. . . . Accumulation in our industry goes along with accumulation in the peasant economy. . . . The development of industry is a function of the development of agriculture and vice versa. [Thus], mutual assistance between industry and agriculture constitutes the primordial condition for the worker-peasant alliance, without which it is impossible to progress toward socialism. (Bukharin [1925–27] 1974, 132, 133, 135)

In the name of socialism, Preobrazhensky developed the theory of primitive socialist accumulation that required severe contributions from the peasants. For

the more a given country, going toward a socialist organization of production, is economically backward, petty-bourgeois, and agricultural, the less the proletariat of the country at the moment of the social revolution will inherit into its fund for socialist accumulation—and the more, relatively, the socialist accumulation will be obliged to depend on the extraction of surplus from pre-socialist forms of economy. In the same way the part of accumulation specifically coming from its own base of production will be reduced; that is to say accumulation will be based less on the surplus of workers in socialist industry. (Preobrazhensky [1926] 1966, 180)

In the name of socialism, so many differing views . . .

Stubbornly tightening the screws, Stalin put an end to this cacophony. Priority to industrialization, the collectivization of agriculture, the fight against the kulaks, and more generally, the test of strength against the peasantry, centralized and authoritarian planning, the elimination of opposition, even of those who could be suspected of joining the opposition, police terror, deportation, gulags: the more social reality diverged from the ideal put forth in earlier times, the more Stalin broadcast the official truth that this was socialism being built. He wrote in 1933:

The basis of our regime is social property, in the same way that the basis of capitalism is private property. The capitalists have proclaimed private property sacred and inviolable, and have managed at present to consolidate the capitalist regime; we Communists should proclaim all the more that social property is sacred and inviolable, so as to stabilize the socialist forms in the economy in all branches of production and commerce. (Stalin [1933] 1977, 637)

Stalin, 1936: The "socialist ownership" of the instruments and means of production "is from now on the unshakeable foundation of socialist society" (Stalin [1936] 1977, 812).

And the Soviet Constitution of 1936 confirmed this official truth:

The Union of Soviet Socialist Republics is a socialist state of the workers and peasants. . . . The economic basis of the USSR is constituted by the socialist economic system and by socialist ownership of the instruments and means of production. . . . In the USSR the principle of socialism, "From each according to his abilities, to each according to his needs," is being realized. (Cited by Desobre 1977, 51, 53)

Stalin knew that following such a declaration, it was enough to keep pushing in the same direction. This he did stubbornly, and he made sure that the ideologists, especially the economists, applied themselves to the task.

Stalin, 1938: "Under the socialist regime, which for the moment has been put into practice only in the USSR, it is social ownership of the means of production that forms the basis of the relations of production" (Stalin [1938] 1968, 57).

The authors of the collectively written article in 1943 on teaching about the economy echoed Stalin's views:

In conformity with the Constitution of the USSR, the economic base of the USSR is the socialist economic system, and socialist ownership of the instruments and means of production, established by the liquidation of the capitalist economic system, the abolition of the exploitation of man by man. (Cited in Chavance 1980, 506)[26]

In 1952 Stalin wrote as though reciting a catechism:

Is there a basic economic law of capitalism? Yes, there is. What is this law, and what are its characteristic features? . . . Most appropriate to the concept of a basic economic law of capitalism is the law of surplus value, the law of the origin and growth of capitalist profit . . . : the securing of the maximum capitalist profit through the exploitation, ruin, and impoverishment of the majority of the population of the given country; through the enslavement and systematic robbery of the peoples of other countries, especially backward countries; and lastly, through wars and militarization of the national economy, which are utilized for the obtaining of the highest profits. . . .

Is there a basic economic law of socialism? Yes, there is. What are the essential features and requirements of this law? . . . [T]he securing of the maximum satisfaction of the constantly rising material and cultural requirements of the whole of society through the continuous expansion and perfection of socialist production on the basis of higher techniques. (Stalin 1952, 42, 43, 45)

This was also the time of certitudes:

. . .[W]ith the abolition of capitalism and the exploiting system, the antagonism of interests between physical and mental labor was also bound to disappear. And it really has disappeared in our present socialist system. Today, the physical workers and the managerial personnel are not enemies, but comrades and friends, members of a single collective body of producers who are vitally interested in the progress and improvement of production. Not a trace remains of the former enmity between them. (Stalin 1952, 31)

As for the workers and the peasants, they of course

do represent two classes differing from one another in status. But this difference does not weaken their friendship in any way. On the contrary, their interests lie along one common line, that of strengthening the socialist system and attaining the victory of communism. It is not surprising, therefore, that not a trace remains of the former distrust, not to speak of the former hatred, of the country for the town. (Stalin 1952, 30)

Following Stalin's death, Stalinist truths saturated treatises and handbooks for many years. First came the *Handbook of Political Economy*, the first edition of which was published in 1954. After considering precapitalist and capitalist modes of production, the third part took up the "socialist mode of production," and here the cloak of "official truth" thickened:

Socialism is a regime founded on social ownership of the means of production.

In becoming social property, the means of production ceased functioning as capital. The exploitation of man by man was abolished.

To the social character of production there corresponds, in a socialist regime, collective and socialist ownership of the means of production.

As for the state,

the character of the socialist state is determined by the economic base of socialism. The socialist system of economy, the social ownership by working people over the means of production, have as corollaries the political power of the workers led by the working class. (*Handbook of Political Economy* [1954] 1956, 347, 447)

These "Stalinist truths" persisted well after de-Stalinization. For example, in the *Political Economy of Socialism*:

Socialist relations of production as a whole form the economic base of socialist society. Under socialism, these relations are based upon social ownership of the means of production. . . . Socialist property is property of the collectivity. It belongs to the whole society, and consequently expresses an equal relation by all members of the society toward the means of production. (*Political Economy of Socialism* 1967, 39, 40)

As for the state, under socialism its economic role expands greatly, which "follows from the nature of the socialist regime itself":

> In contrast to all previous states, the socialist state is the owner of the principal means of production, which radically changes the character of this state. To the political functions of the state the socialist socialization of the means of production adds the duty of managing the national economy. The primary function of the socialist state, of the workers, is to organize social production, to direct the economy and cultural life, to exercise, in the interest of the workers, control over the extent of labor and consumption, to assure the well-being of the population, to educate the workers in the spirit of a new discipline of work, a communist attitude toward work. (*Political Economy of Socialism* 1967, 58–59)

To which was added the fact that the socialist state is "the instrument that creates socialist and communist relations of production" (*Political Economy of Socialism* 1967, 59–60).[27]

In the *Political Economy of Communism* one finds:

> With the establishment of the political domination of the working class, power is transferred to the popular masses for whom the abolition of the capitalist order is a vital interest. From a tool that subordinates and subjugates society, state power becomes a living force of society. The political domination of the working class creates the political form which is that of the social emancipation of all the people. . . . In none of its historic phases does the socialist state place itself above the people. The members of socialist society legitimately declare: "The state is us." (Roumiantsev 1969, 535, 538)

The dogma is there: socialism has been realized in the USSR. What difference does it make that the state has strengthened itself when it was supposed to begin to wither away: one calls the state socialist while observing how it is strengthened. What difference does it make that classes maintain their existence when differences between them were supposed to be reduced in the socialist period: one declares that in socialist society classes are no longer antagonistic. Commodities? Socialist! The law of value? Not inherent to capitalism. Nationalizations? Careful here, there is a subtle point: nationalizations are capitalist in capitalist society, but socialist in socialist societies. Accumulation? Socialist! Surplus labor? Socialist! And quite naturally, one ends up talking about socialist enterprise and, finally, about socialist capital. When the official truth becomes this heavy, no room is left for analysis or discussion. One agrees or one rejects. Sometimes what occurs is an about-face brought to fruition by the very excesses of official truth: yes, indeed, this is socialism! "Socialism = totalitarianism," "socialism is the gulag."

2. DISAGREEMENTS AND CRITIQUES

During the 1930s, confronted by the reality of the USSR, it was hardly possible to "keep one's reason": the pressure—affective, ideological, political—was such that a reasoned debate could not be conducted.

On one side there were the unconditional supporters of the USSR: essentially the members of the Communist parties and their "fellow travelers." Socialism was being built in the USSR; the USSR was the homeland of workers; Stalin was the "father" of people throughout the world.

On the other side there was the revenge-seeking and hate-filled right, the right that took fright when the workers became angry or made demands, and which approved heartily when the forces of order crushed and repressed workers' movements. This was the right that denounced the Soviet hell, "the man with the knife between his teeth," the bloodthirsty oppression.

Between the two, within the workers' movement and more generally within the democratic and "progressive" movement, no space remained. Anyone who attempted to see clearly was immediately accused of providing comfort to the "class enemy." André Gide tried nonetheless:

> Good and bad alike are to be found there; I should say rather: the best and the worst. The best was often achieved only by an immense effort. . . . Sometimes the worst accompanies and shadows the best; it almost seems as if it were a consequence of the best. And one passes from the brightest light to the darkest shade with a disconcerting abruptness. . . . I do not hide from myself the apparent advantage that hostile parties . . . will try to derive from my book. . . . Falsehood, even that which consists in silence, may appear opportune, as may perseverance in falsehood, but it leaves far too dangerous weapons in the hands of the enemy, and truth, however painful, only wounds in order to cure. (Gide [1936] 1937, xiii–xvi)

Because he did not give unconditional approval, Gide became the target of the supporters of the USSR. Georges Friedmann, for example, published an open letter to Gide: "You have not brought back 'the truth' from the USSR. The truth requires more patience and self-effacement. Some of us think your short book has only 'wounded' without being capable of 'healing'" (Friedmann [1937], cited in Kupferman 1979, 118). Fernand Grenier, leader of the group Friends of the Soviet Union, became indignant:

> If Gide does not understand certain aspects of the Soviet problem, I think he would have found better explanations through talking with a metal-worker in the outskirts of town than with the Trotskyist

gentlemen who too often get in the way of those who, without pretension, try to do something as well as they can. (Grenier [1936], cited in Kupferman 1979, 119)

This was a forbidden debate, an impossible debate, between those who believed in the USSR and those who were skeptical, between those who agreed and those who still searched and doubted. For there was the strength of conviction and support; above all there was the split in the workers' movement, and the unending attacks, the hatreds rekindled. What dialogue, in these conditions, was possible?

Thanks to the will to speak despite everything, and, at the deepest level, the passion for truth—the "truth about socialism" that has inspired so many lives and given strength to support so many sacrifices— there remain however some isolated reflections, reflections that have been distorted, whether one likes it or not, by the force of the reigning prohibitions.

For example, Emile Vandervelde, toward the end of a life committed to the socialist movement in Belgium, tried to take stock of the situation of socialism throughout the world. He summarized his conclusions about the USSR in these words:

It is possible to have differing opinions about the present and the future of the Russian Revolution. However, even if one agrees that what is being built in the USSR is socialism (a matter, after all, of definition), it is impossible to deny that this dictatorial, bureaucratic, hyper-statist socialism established in a country where capitalism existed only in embryonic form, has nothing in common with democratic socialism as Marx and Engels had always conceived it. (Vandervelde 1933, 206)

Trotsky, from exile, tried to localize the point of contradiction:

The means of production belong to the state. The state "belongs" in some degree to the bureaucracy. . . . [But this bureaucracy] is obliged to defend state ownership, which is the source of its power and its income. Through this aspect of its activity, the bureaucracy remains the instrument of the dictatorship of the proletariat. Because [this] state that has taken up the task of the socialist transformation of society is obliged to defend inequality—that is to say, the privileges of the minority—with force, [it] remains to a certain degree a "bourgeois" state, though without bourgeoisie. . . . The bourgeois norms of distribution, by speeding up the growth of material power, should serve socialist ends, though the state immediately acquires a two-sided character: socialist insofar as it defends collective ownership of the means of production; bourgeois insofar as the distribution of goods takes place according to capitalist standards of value, with all the consequences that flow from this fact. Such a contradictory definition will perhaps dismay dogmatists and scholastics; to them we can only express our regrets. (Trotsky [1936] 1963, 478–79)

Against the cloak of official truth, against dogmatism, a small group of intellectuals worked to keep Marxist thought alive. They published their thoughts in 1934 under the title *Theses on Bolshevism*. On the basis of a class analysis of the Russian Revolution and of Soviet social reality, they arrived at conclusions that the workers' movement, as a whole, was not ready to hear: "Bolshevism shows all the characteristics of a bourgeois revolution, but intensified by a thorough understanding, drawn from Marxism, of class struggle. . . . The Bolshevik economy is statist production employing capitalist methods" (Korsch, Mattick, and Pannekoek [1934] 1973, 31, 49). They pushed their analysis further:

The state becomes a huge trust, which, because of its hyperorganization, pushes aside the obstacles opposing an expansion of production. . . . But the Russian example proves not only that official socialism is in reality just state capitalism. . . . It has also revealed the formation of a new ruling element, which does as it likes with statist property and so manages to occupy a privileged position. The interests of this element lie in seeing state power increase, since it is precisely state power that assures this element its privileged social position. (Korsch, Mattick, and Pannekoek [1935] 1973, 61, 62)

This group then proclaimed the necessary development of "class struggle between workers and state bureaucracy" (Korsch, Mattick, and Pannekoek [1935] 1973, 63).

Some of Trotsky's followers produced analyses tending in the same direction. For example, Bruno Rizzi, in *The Bureaucratization of the World*, described the USSR as a

bureaucratic collectivism, a new type of society, ruled by a new class. . . . Property, collectivized, belongs in fact to this class which has established a new—and better—system of production. Exploitation passes from the realm of the individual to that of the class. . . . The Soviet state, instead of becoming socialized, has become bureaucratic; instead of disappearing gradually into a classless society, it has swelled immeasurably. Fifteen million individuals are already glued to the trunk of the state, whose sap they suck. The proletarian class is exploited, as a whole, in conformity with the transformation of ownership. The bureaucratic class exploits the proletarian class and fixes the standard to which the proletarian class must adapt its way of living, through wages and the selling price of commodities in the state stores. The new dominating class has bought the entire proletariat. Nothing is left to the workers, not even the freedom to offer their "labor power" to various entrepreneurs: it is an extremely monopolizing bureaucracy; it is the bureaucracy which has perfected the system of exploitation. The Russian proletarians have fallen from the frying pan into the fire. (Rizzi 1939, 26)

This system, whose arrival was explained by "the political immaturity of the proletariat," was seen by Rizzi as taking place within a more general, worldwide movement of bureaucratization.

Max Shachtman, in *The Bureaucratic Revolution*, also described the Soviet regime as a bureaucratic collectivism, leading to an enslavement of society to which the concentration camps, under Stalin, bore witness.

Continuing his denunciation of Bolshevik tyranny, Voline, too, came to use the expression "state capitalism":

The state provides this citizen with work and appoints him to a job; the state feeds him and pays him; the state watches over him; the state uses and molds him as it wishes; the state educates and trains him; the state judges him; the state rewards or punishes him; employer, nourisher, protector, guardian, educator, instructor, judge, jailer, executioner—everything, absolutely everything, in the same person: that of a state that, with the help of its civil servants, wants to be omnipresent, omniscient, omnipotent. God help anyone who tries to escape it! We emphasize that the Bolshevik state (the government) has taken hold not only of all existing material and spiritual goods, but what is perhaps more serious, it has made itself the perpetual holder of truth, in all domains: historical, economic, political, social, scientific, philosophical, and all others. . . . The Bolshevik party tries to construct socialism by means of a centralized and authoritarian state, government, and political action. It is arriving only at a monstrous, murderous state capitalism based on the hateful exploitation of "mechanized," blinded, unconscious masses. (Voline [1947] 1972, 147, 149)

Leading figure of *Socialism or Barbarism*, Castoriadis carried out an analysis of the Soviet social formation and class relations. Relying on the authority of Engels and Lenin, he stressed that

Until 1930, no one in the Marxist movement had ever considered that state ownership formed, in itself, a basis for socialist relations of production, or even that state ownership tended to become such. No one had ever thought the "nationalization" of the means of production was equivalent to the abolition of exploitation. (Castoriadis [1949] 1973, 1:221)[28]

He then examined

the fundamental relation of production in the Russian economy. This relation presents itself, from a legal and formal point of view, as a relation between the worker and the "state." But the legal state is an abstraction for sociology. In its social reality, the state is first of all the group of persons who form the statist apparatus, in all its political, administrative, military, technical, and economic ramifications. The "state" is above all a bureaucracy, and the relations between the worker and the "state" are in reality relations with this bureaucracy. (Castoriadis [1949] 1973, 1:250–51)

He drew these conclusions: "Two social categories thus confront one another: the proletariat and the bureaucracy. . . . There is, then, a class relation in production, and exploitation, an exploitation that knows no objective limits" (Castoriadis [1949] 1973, 1:251, 254).

In the course of a discussion about the above text Castoriadis expanded:

The Russian bureaucracy "plans" the economy by orienting it toward the satisfaction of its own needs, by providing it with its own class content. The goal of Russian planning, as avowed by even the most open apologists of the bureaucracy such as Bettelheim, is the realization of the maximum military potential and the satisfaction of the bureaucracy's consumption needs. This orientation is found concretely in the Russian plans, in which the development of heavy industry has priority and luxury industries (or industries considered as such in Russia) are secondary, while production of major consumer goods remains practically static. Stalinist planning carries to the highest degree of perfection the capitalist ideal: the workers work a maximum for minimum pay. (Castoriadis [1949] 1973, 2:15)

Castoriadis interpreted the Soviet regime as the "last stage of capitalist production":

One could then define it as the regime of bureaucratic capitalism, if one emphasized that once arrived at this stage, capitalism appears completely different from traditional capitalism and in several characteristics appears as its complete opposite. (Castoriadis [1949] 1973, 2:16)

The interpretation of Soviet reality as state capitalism is the most useful interpretative scheme for anyone wishing to remain within the framework established by Marx and Lenin. Bettelheim systematizes this view on the basis of a rigorous reexamination of legal relations (state ownership) and relations of production (economic).

To attempt to go beyond these limits, it is necessary to widen, in at least one respect, the interpretative frameworks that have heretofore existed: we must admit the hypothesis that capitalism is not the last class society in the history of humanity and that another mode of production—in some ways similar to capitalism and in others ways distinct—has arisen within the stirrings of contemporary history.

COMMENTS ON CHAPTER 6

Seen from the nineteenth century, opposed to the awful reality of capitalist industrialization, the socialism to follow was splendid: the abolition of the exploitation of man by man, the abolition of alienated labor, of suffering, of inequality; an end to the domination of man over man; the withering away of the state and of political power; a classless society; liberation; the establishment of a fraternal society. Many roads toward this future were foreseen: an uprising by the people, action by a determined vanguard, cooperation, association, federation, democratic dictatorship of the proletariat over the handful of former oppressors. . . . But, beyond this diversity, there existed a shared project.

This project was the overthrow, the destruction, of capitalism, and through such a movement the destruction of all class societies, all oppressive and exploitative societies. This was to lead to a new era. Humanity would at last emerge from darkness; the sun would at last shine upon the wretched of the earth.

But now, who would deny the evidence? The socialism just described exists nowhere today. Is one permitted to say this calmly, without aggressiveness, and with no other heartbreak beyond that of being obliged to make such a statement? Is it possible for one to say this without being immediately accused of being anti-Soviet, anticommunist, or more generally, hostile to this or that country, this or that regime calling itself socialist?

Nonetheless, one only has to open one's eyes. Classes are everywhere: the working class, the peasantry, the organizing and ruling techno-bureoisie.[29] The state apparatus, omnipresent, often excessive, invading, oppressive, repressive, sometimes totalitarian, is everywhere. Everywhere the workers are driven: by crude methods or refined methods borrowed from capitalism; by old methods inherited from former societies, as well as by ideological-political incentives and pressures. A minority dominates the "masses," the working class that is supposedly *the* ruling class; everywhere inequalities are maintained or renewed: chains. And everywhere, forever reborn, the hope for liberation, social justice, equality, a different, other, society . . .

As signs of this hope, some curious expressions have arisen, such as "socialism with a human face," "democratic socialism," "socialism in freedom." Curious, for what socialist in the nineteenth century could have conceived of or accepted the idea of an inhuman, oppressive, tyrannical socialism? And by what reversals of thought is it possible to arrive in our time at such aberrant conceptions? Was not socialism to be—and should it not always be—a decisive advance for humanity?

Was it not a synonym for liberation, the fulfillment of a new society of free men; should it not remain so?[30]

What then can be said of these societies that, from decade to decade, represent a growing segment of the earth's inhabitants? Some thinkers, in order to indicate their conviction—and sometimes their disappointment—that these societies are not socialist, describe them instead as capitalist: bureaucratic capitalist or state capitalist. Others, by contrast, describe these societies, despite everything, as socialist: "actually existing socialism"; countries that, from the point of view of socialism, represent an "overall positive balance-sheet"; and all the "socialisms" enclosed within quotation marks. Still others have limited themselves to cautious circumlocutions: countries with planned economies, the Eastern bloc, countries calling themselves socialist.

We propose to explore here another hypothesis, that these countries have developed on the basis of a new mode of production, state collectivism, which is *similar* to capitalism in that it, too, is organized around the accumulation of dead labor in industrial equipment, technology, and weaponry. Thus, it is a class society involving domination and compulsion to surplus labor. But it is *different* from capitalism in that accumulation is organized by the state apparatus within a framework characterized by the statist and collective appropriation of the means of production, and by the ideological structuring of reality around the theme of "socialism being constructed," or "socialism that has been achieved but is still to be improved" or "to be defended."

7

A NEW REALITY:
STATE COLLECTIVISM

With the 1917 Revolution the czarist regime and Russian capitalism were swept away.

In order to govern, men can be changed. In order to produce, the peasantry and the working class have always been called upon: lacking a socialist mode of production, either the earlier methods were reverted to—and this was the NEP—or else a new mode of production and accumulation was invented—and this was state collectivism.

1. A FUNDAMENTAL NECESSITY: ACCUMULATE

Most of the nineteenth-century socialist authors considered the problem of production within socialism very little, if at all. Either liberated work would become so productive that abundance would blossom; or, with inequality and luxury abolished, the needs of all the people would be easily satisfied; or, capitalism having carried productive forces to an extremely high level, the historical conditions for a close-knit and liberated society would be fulfilled. Yet it was in agricultural and backward Russia that a revolution broke out, allowing a Marxist vanguard to seize state power.

Once rival forces were eliminated or neutralized, once the struggles against foreign and domestic enemies were over, the Bolshevik power confronted the immensity of the task to be accomplished: with more than twelve million dead, a hostile or disheartened peasantry, a working class whose numbers fell from three million in 1916 to one million in 1921, despite hunger, cold, and epidemics, production had to be started up again and industry and transport systems had to be reconstructed. The intention, the objective, the project, was socialism. Immediate ne-

124

cessity required production, and the extraction from this production of enough to equip, construct, and modernize, so that it would be possible to produce even more: to produce and to accumulate in order to produce still more.

From this time on, by improvising and through an incredible process of social experimentation, the Bolsheviks tried to reconcile intention with necessity. Lucid in the face of every situation, Lenin remained, as we have seen, faithful to the Marxian conception that capitalism would develop productive forces to a stage sufficient to make it possible to realize socialism. Was Russian capitalism insufficiently developed? Certainly it was. Well then, it would be necessary to pass through a phase of state capitalism: the ultimate centralization and concentration that such a process involves would allow the necessary effort of accumulation to take place and so would serve as a sort of antechamber of socialism.

At the beginning of the 1920s all the Bolshevik leaders felt the necessity of making significant concessions to the peasantry. The NEP was devised; its political objective was to consolidate the worker-peasant alliance, and it led to a large increase in agricultural production.[31] Though the leaders as a whole agreed about resorting to the NEP, there was disagreement about the place of agriculture within the national accumulation effort. Toward the middle of the 1930s, Bukharin and Preobrazhensky clashed.

Bukharin had said to the peasants: "Enrich yourselves." In a 1925 pamphlet on *The Road to Socialism and the Worker-Peasant Alliance*, he advocated harmonious development:

> In order for industry to enjoy increasing opportunities for development it is also necessary for the peasant economy itself to develop. . . . [The] basic and most fundamental interest of the working class and peasantry finds expression in the need for mutual help between industry and agriculture, each of which is fundamentally dependent on the other. . . . The more quickly accumulation occurs in our peasant economy, the more quickly will it occur in our industry. . . . Thus, industry requires successes in agriculture for its own development; and agriculture, in order to succeed, requires the development of industry. (Bukharin [1925–27] 1974, 233, 241, 242)

Preobrazhensky, for his part, emphasized accumulation and distinguished socialist accumulation from primitive socialist accumulation. He defined "socialist accumulation" as "the link between the operating means of production and the surplus product created within the socialist economy once formed. . . . It is used for expanded reproduction." He defined "primitive socialist accumulation" by contrast as "accumulation in state hands of vital resources drawn mainly or simultaneously from sources situated outside the state economy complex." There were to be no illusions:

> The problem of the socialist state does not consist in extracting less from the petty-bourgeois producers than does capitalism, but in extracting more, out of an even greater income that will be guaranteed to small-scale production by the rationalization of all things and in particular the rationalization of small-scale exploitation of the country. (Preobrazhensky [1926] 1966, 140)[32]

Through taxation and through the relative drop in agricultural prices in relation to industrial prices, part of the value produced in agriculture was transferred, either directly to industry or else to the state, which reinvested it in industry.[33]

In a parallel movement, by trial and error and often under the pressure of immediate necessity, the means for managing and directing the economy were invented and put into operation.

Of course, in November and December 1917 the first plans for industrial reconversion had been drawn up, and the Supreme Soviet of the National Economy had been created on 2 December 1917. But under "war communism" economic decisions were centralized; this was unplanned centralization.[34]

The first general plan had to do with a domain considered to be decisive: electrification. This was the Goelro Plan for the electrification of Russia, which was presented in December 1921. It already made use of the system of balancing needs to resources for each product, by taking into account both sectoral and regional dimensions. The Gosplan (July 1922) was formed for the most part by the team that had prepared the Goelro Plan. It still remained, however, an organ of economic and industrial policy, even though it prepared annual and semiannual "plans."

The First Five-Year Plan was elaborated within the framework of the central administration of the iron and steel industries, and covered this industry for the period from 1923 to 1928. An engineer directing the Gosplan at the end of 1924 proposed a five-year plan to deal particularly with transports and agriculture.

The decision to launch a general five-year plan was taken in 1925. Preparatory work took several years and produced the First Five-Year Plan (1928–29 to 1932–33), which was officially adopted in April–May 1929. The plan for investment was the key point of the plan, since the allotment of financial and equipment resources depended on investment; accumulation was at this time very much the major problem of the Soviet economy. And when Stalin defended the First Five-Year Plan against Rykov, supporter of a biannual plan,[35] he intended to impose his objectives, priorities, and approach upon the planners. On the occasion of the twelfth anniversary of the October Revolution, Stalin evaluated current progress by emphasizing that the previous year had permitted "a favorable solution, essentially, to *the problem of accumulation* [Stalin's emphasis] for the major public-works projects of heavy industry" by creating "the necessary conditions for the transformation of our country into a steel-producing country" (Stalin [1929a] 1977, 441).

But here, the stumbling block was low industrial production, one factor of which was low worker productivity. This problem had already been encountered by Lenin, who had put his hopes in raising the consciousness of the workers during the period of building socialism as well as in recourse to Taylorism. This was the same Taylorism, after all, that he had denounced a few years earlier, in 1913, as a scientific system "for pressuring workers" and intensifying exploitation, leading to worker exhaustion and aggravated unemployment (Lenin [1913] n.d., 18:618–19).[36]

Eugene Varga, responsible for the economy at the time of the Hungarian Revolution, encountered the same problems, which he analyzed with great clarity and frankness:

> Due to a lack of revolutionary education and lacking an organized Communist party, the Hungarian workers did not want to deprive themselves of anything for the regime, for the future of socialism. They called for an immediate improvement in their standard of living, and because it was impossible to accord them this, they turned away from the ideal of the dictatorship of the proletariat. (Varga [1920] 1922, 49)

The workers rejected the previous system of industrial discipline; they obtained the replacement of piecework wages by hourly wages, and hourly production rates fell sharply. To deal with this situation, the Superior Economic Council drew up a sort of "disciplinary code" whose "essential points" Varga describes:

> If a worker is guilty of a disciplinary fault, such as arriving late, arbitrarily interrupting his work, going against the instruction of qualified personnel, etc., he will incur the following sanctions:
>   1. reprimand from the operations council;
>   2. posting of his name, with an explanation, on the factory blackboard;
>   3. change in position in the factory;
>   4. reduction in wages corresponding to the work deficiency;
>   5. discharge from the factory and possible exclusion from all the factories of the collective, with or without cancellation of unemployment assistance;
>   6. exclusion from the union, which means that the worker will have to change his line of work.

The last two stated penalties, which are very serious, can be pronounced by the operations council only when the trade union concerned is in agreement. All of the sanctions are made known to the entire factory workforce as an example. In order to increase worker productivity, in each factory a suitable minimum output must be fixed, equal to the preexisting level. Workers who do not attain this minimum will be subject to the above sanctions. For output surpassing what is expected, public praise was foreseen, and possibly even a material reward. (Ibid., 95–96)

Varga returned to this fundamental problem in describing the USSR's own situation:

The question of work discipline and of increasing labor output is today still one of the most important and ardently discussed problems in Russia, especially in connection with the question of the role of trade unions in the proletarian state. The war, which kept at the front more than half, and the better half at that, of the members of the Communist party, has held up the definitive solution. This solution is found in the transformation of the ideology of the working masses, the establishment of a communist spirit in accordance with the foundations of the communist economy and the establishment of a new work discipline based on this spirit. All the rest—contract work, normalization of the labor of the worker, bonuses in money or in kind, and militarization of labor—can only be temporary measures allowing the level of production to be maintained during the period necessary for the transformation of ideologies. (Ibid., xiv–xv)

In the USSR, under war communism and in order to combat the extreme disorganization of economic life, obligatory work was established for all citizens from sixteen to fifty years of age, while at the same time Communist Saturdays symbolized the new attitude toward work and crystallized enthusiasm and competition.[37] Under the NEP more traditional methods for compelling labor reappeared. Relying often on forced hiring, the rate of growth in the number of workers increased from around 3 percent per year on average from 1899 to 1913 and reached 14 percent per year on average from 1922–23 to 1927–28.

But even this rate of growth was not sufficient for Stalin's ambitious modernization and industrialization plans. After 1928, it was a forced march involving the collectivization of agriculture, deliberate planning, the prioritization of heavy industry, and mass repression.

The percentage of land cultivated by the kolkhozes grew from 2 percent in 1928 to 34 percent in 1930 and 78 percent in 1932 (Zaleski 1962). Such rapid collectivization opened a profound and lasting crisis in Soviet agriculture: though agricultural production had risen 8 percent to

12 percent per year in the period from 1921 to 1927–28, it stagnated or regressed from 1928 to 1938 (Lavigne 1970).

The forced requisitions extracted from the agricultural sector sharply affected the producers, provoking deep-seated resistance, and, in turn, heavy repression.

The number of workers increased rapidly: more than 23 percent per year from 1927–28 to 1932 (though only 4 percent per year from 1932 to 1940). Thus the number of industrial workers, which had fallen to 1 million during the period when the economic situation was extremely disorganized, picked up from 1921 onward, and reached 3 million in 1925–26, 3.7 million in 1928–29, and then rose even more steeply to reach 8 million in 1932 and 10 million in 1937.

Never has there been such a rapid and intense push toward industrialization, and, at the same time, the creation of a working class from a primarily rural source of manpower. In this process, collectivization played in the USSR the role that the enclosures had played in England: there is a terrible similarity here between "primitive statist/collectivist accumulation" and the "primitive capitalist accumulation" whose brutality and cruelty had been so thoroughly denounced by Marx.

But it was not enough to pull the peasants away from their plots of land, their fields, in order to form a working class. These new workers still had to learn about industrial work and the special sort of discipline it required. In 1929 Stalin proclaimed that there had taken place "a *decisive turn* in the domain of labor productivity. This change is evident through an increase in *creative initiative* and a powerful *enthusiasm for work* among vast numbers of the working class involved in building socialism." Stalin then expanded on the ways in which such progress had already been—and still remained to be—accomplished: (1) by fighting against bureaucratism, which slowed down initiative and the activity of the masses in their work—by *self-criticism*; (2) by fighting against shirkers and the elements that reduced proletarian work discipline; (3) by fighting against routine and inertia in production—by organizing the *uninterrupted work week* (Stalin [1929a] 1977, 439, 440).

Throughout the 1930s measures were taken to limit workers' freedom of choice by strengthening work discipline, even if this meant relying on severely repressive methods: the limitation and then the prohibition of workers' repudiation of their work agreements; the systematic and authoritarian allocation of manpower (starting in 1930); discriminatory measures against "production disorganizers"; a mandatory passport for all of the USSR; a mandatory work-license and the stiffening of work rules (1938).

At the same time, piecework wages, the most primitive form of payment by output, spread from 58 percent of industrial workers in 1928 to 73 percent in 1940 and 77 percent in 1950. Thus the "principle of socialism" contained in the 1936 Constitution, "From each according to his capacities, to each according to his work," was taken in the strictest possible sense. And Article 12 of this Constitution took on in this context an unsettling air: "Labor in the USSR is, for each citizen able to work, a duty and a question of honor, according to the principle: 'whoever does not work, does not eat'" (Desobre 1977, 52).

Extraction of surplus labor from the peasant and craft sectors of society; formation of a working class out of manpower torn away from traditional small-scale production; learning the hard discipline of industrial labor: these were the three bases upon which British industrial capitalism had been established in the eighteenth and nineteenth centuries. It was on these same three bases, using different methods, that statist Russian industrialization was carried out in the decades following the October 1917 Revolution.

2. A NEW DOMINANT MODE OF PRODUCTION

In Marx's thought, capitalist society was to be the final class society, the last society based on oppression and exploitation. Socialist society was to follow capitalist society and was to be characterized, we recall, by the end of exploitation of man by man. Within this society two movements were to have begun: one leading toward the disappearance of class differentiations, and the other leading toward the withering away, not only of the state, but of all political power.

The coherence of Marx's thinking resides in the idea that the socialist revolution was supposed to follow as a consequence of developments within capitalist society itself. The socialist revolution supposedly was to take place, then, within a social formation that had attained highly developed productive forces and that had accomplished a high degree of socialization. Yet it was in Russia, which, in point of fact, had experienced only minimal capitalist industrialization, that the powerful movement of the 1917 Revolution broke out, permitting a small nucleus of Bolshevik militants to seize the state apparatus.

They used this state apparatus against their opponents—foreign armies and then internal enemies; it was a remarkably effective tool when directed by a political will.

And then, very quickly, the problem of production posed itself: produce in order to survive and fight; produce, as well, in order to accumulate and produce even more. The Bolshevik leaders discovered that individualism, selfishness, and laziness—or very simply a preference for rest—did not disappear in a single day. More concretely, they had to deal with absenteeism, tardiness, work stoppages, and low work productivity, all in a context of extreme scarcity, urgency, unending necessity, tension, and struggle.

Fighting capitalism, they had only temporarily accepted the survival of its logic (the NEP) and did not succeed in obtaining from foreign investors the resources they badly needed. As for small-scale commodity production, it was incapable of supplying the efforts planned for heavy industry and equipment, and later on, weaponry. There remained statist production. This, of course, the Bolsheviks did not invent. We don't need to look as far back as the ancient societies of Egypt, Asia, or pre-Columbian America; we can see that statist production developed along with capitalist production: royal manufacturing in the sixteenth and seventeenth centuries, large-scale equipping of infrastructures, arsenals, postal systems.

As rulers of the state, the Bolsheviks attempted the major part of their industrialization effort through statist production. And this was all the easier since the passage from "socialization" or "collectivization" of the means of production to the reality of state property could be made to seem to be only a lengthy shift, and clever speech could make what was only "state property" seem to be "socialization."

State collectivism was no more born fully clothed straight out of the brains of a few history-making demiurges than was capitalism.

Capitalism was formed in the same movement in which the bourgeoisies were formed; in which the relations of exchange and production on national *and* world scales specific to capitalism were established; in which the first mills and factories were established, and with them, the working classes, the exploited proletarians. Turgot, Quesnay, and Adam Smith were the first to see the logic of surplus production as the fundamental condition for accumulation. Symmetrically, Linguet, Godwin, and many others denounced the exploitation and unbearable conditions imposed upon the proletarians. A few decades later, Marx constructed the theoretical tool that provided an interpretation of capitalism as well as a vantage point from which to critique political economy. This tool was the idea of the capitalist mode of production. Yet by this time capitalist logic had already been at work in the world for several centuries (see Beaud [1981] 1983a).

What is of interest to us is that in a world dominated for the most part by capitalism, state collectivism developed in order to escape capitalist domination and at the same time to respond to the blockade that the capitalist world set up. It also involved the formation of a new ruling class and the improvisation and organization of new methods for production, extraction, appropriation, and allocation of surplus product.

To those who, relying on arguments from "authorities," tell us that state collectivism "does not exist," we reply "no more than the giraffe."[38]

For those who agree to accept the hypothesis that we are proposing, we will attempt to continue further.

First of all, our hypothesis signifies that capitalism is not the last class society; that another class society coexists with it at present and will perhaps succeed it. Further: other class societies are possible, of which we are unable at present even to conceive. Finally: the arrival of socialism is not ineluctable. Socialism can only be a project of society for which one works and fights. No one is any more sheltered from this risk—the risk of fighting for socialism and ending up finally at a quite different society—than were the Russian Bolsheviks. But to know that this risk exists should allow one to reduce it.

In addition, state collectivism resembles capitalism in certain aspects (like capitalism, it allows an increased pace of accumulation), while in other aspects it differs profoundly from capitalism (the methods utilized are principally statist).

In many respects the state-collectivist mode of production (SCMP) bears the same relation to the capitalist mode of production (CMP) as the Asiatic mode of production did to the feudal mode of production. Like the CMP, the SCMP corresponds to a period of strong development of productive forces, especially in the form of industrialization and scientific and technical progress; it requires, then, that a considerable amount of surplus labor be extracted, first from agricultural and then from industrial production, which will allow the accumulation of dead labor in equipment and infrastructure (mines, transport, industries, social installations) and the qualitative improvement of living labor (teaching, health). At the same time, this implies the maintenance of a class society (the importance of the peasantry at first, the formation of a working class, pressure on this working class) and the continuing domination over the producing classes by the dominant class, which organizes and directs this accumulation effort.

But in contrast to the CMP, which originally was based mainly on decentralized domination and exploitation (merchant capital becoming transformed into industrial capital; poor and proletarianized small-scale producers forced to sell their labor power; wage labor), the SCMP is based on the centralized organization of three linked efforts: (1) the industrialization/accumulation/development of productive forces; (2) the creation of an industrial working class/proletariat, arising primarily from the peasantry; and (3) the extraction of the necessary surplus labor for accumulation, first from the peasantry and from traditional small-scale production and then from the working class. In each of these three domains the role of the state is decisive. The state, with the party as its nervous system, is also the basis and location for the reproduction of the ruling class: the "state techno-bureoisie."[39] And the domination of the state, its omnipresence, its compulsions and controls, its giving and taking away, its protection and its repression, in a way structures and "corsets" the whole of the society.

3. THE STEEL GRIP OF THE STATE

During the present phase of transition, the fundamental task of the Constitution of the Soviet Socialist Federative Republic of Russia (SSFRR) lies in establishing, under the form of a strong Soviet pan-Russian power, the dictatorship of the proletariat over the cities and the countryside, as well as over the poorest peasantry, with the objective of totally crushing the bourgeoisie, of abolishing the exploitation of man by man, and of establishing socialism under which there will be neither class division, nor state power. (Cited in Desobre 1977, 20)

This appeared in 1918, in Article 9 of the Constitution of the SSFRR. A strong power . . . with the objective of a society without classes or state: socialism.

"The Union of Soviet Socialist Republics is a socialist state of workers and peasants" (cited in Desobre 1977, 51). This appeared in 1936, in Article 1 of the Constitution of the USSR: the state is proclaimed to be powerful without further ado, but all danger is avoided—is it not?—since the state belongs to the two producing classes, the workers and the peasants. From then on, the Constitution can emphasize state ownership (ownership by all the people, Article 5) and state plan (taking care of the management of economic life, Article 11) before considering the higher organs of the state plan (Chapter 4), the administrative organs of the state administration (Chapter 5) and the local organs of state power (Chapter 8).

A diligent pedagogue who never left room for doubt, Stalin made sure to explain matters to anyone confused by the rapid turnaround. So far as classes were concerned:

The class of major landed property owners had already been eliminated. . . . The other exploiting classes meet the same fate. No more capitalist class in industry. No more class of kulaks in agriculture. No more merchants or speculators in commerce. All this with the result that all exploiting classes have been eliminated.

There remains the working class.
There remains the class of peasants.
There remain the intellectuals.
. . . [But] the distance between these social groups becomes smaller and smaller. . . . The contradictions between these social groups fall away and disappear. (Stalin [1936] 1977, 813, 816)

Regarding the state: to those who—because there are no more exploiting classes, no more classes inimical to each other—said, "The state is no longer necessary; it should disappear. Why then are we not contributing to making our socialist state disappear? . . . Isn't it time to put the state into the antiquities museum?" Stalin responded:

These questions show that their authors have conscientiously learned certain theses of Marx's and Engels's doctrine of the state. But . . . [they] have not understood the essence of this doctrine. . . . They have forgotten the capitalist encirclement and the accompanying dangers thus presented to the socialist country. . . . One must not extend the general formula of Engels about the destiny of the socialist state in general to the particular and concrete case of the victory of socialism in a single isolated country, circled by capitalist countries and threatened by military agression from outside. (Stalin [1939] 1977, 944–45, 948)

In 1977, de-Stalinization complete, Stalin's ideas had been perfectly assimilated: "The Union of Soviet Socialist Republics is the socialist state of the whole people, which expresses the will and interests of the working class, the peasantry, and the intelligentsia" (cited in Desobre 1977, 75). So reads Article 1 of the 1977 Constitution. Far from being summoned to wither away, the state was charged with a heavy burden:

The supreme goal of the Soviet state is to construct a communist society without classes. The following are the essential tasks of the state: create a material and technical base for communism, perfect the socialist social relations and transform them into communist relations, form the man of communist society, raise the level of living and culture of the workers, assure the safety of the country, and contribute to the strengthening of international peace, development, and cooperation. (Cited in Desobre 1977, 74–75)

The Constitution examined "the higher organs of state power" (Section 5), "the statist and national structure of the USSR" (Section 4), and "the state and personality" (Section 2).
Rudolph Bahro has expressed the matter concisely:

Instead of the state being taken back into society, we witness a desperate effort to integrate living society as a whole into the crystalline structure of the state. State-ization instead of socialization: this signifies *socialization under a totally alienated form*. (Bahro [1977] 1978)

No one denies the existence, the weight, or the power of the Soviet state. For not only does it assure international relations and defense, it also organizes social life as a whole: it educates, cares for, punishes, directs, pays, produces, accumulates, divides up, deducts, informs, cultivates; it proclaims the True, the Beautiful, and the Good, and, if one believes the 1977 Constitution, it fashions the man of tomorrow and transforms social relations: in brief, it produces society.

Yet this state is not an abstract, disincarnate power. Is it a state of the workers and peasants? Let us accept the hypothesis; the only way to support the hypothesis is to show that the decision-making processes are dominated by workers and peasants; this is, after all, what Article 3 of the 1936 Constitution suggests: "All power in the USSR belongs to the workers in the cities and the countryside in the person of the soviets of workers' deputies" (cited in Desobre 1977, 51). But has it ever happened that even one of these—unopposed—candidates has not been elected? And who would deny that in fact these candidates are selected ahead of time, chosen by the party apparatus?

From this point, in order for the state to belong to the working class and to the peasantry, it would be sufficient to show that the party is in fact the party of the working class and the peasantry.

To do this, the Communist party of the USSR could only depend on the sixteen million people who were party members in early 1977:

13.5%   were kolkhozians
42%   were workers (in the large sense)
44.5%   were "intellectuals and white-collar workers"[40]

Seen in another way: if one considers that in the USSR there are around 170 million men and women of voting age, one may estimate that the following percentages of the indicated groups were party members:

<10%   of the electors
 3.3%   of women
 8%   of the peasants
12%   of the workers
65%   of the Ph.D. scientists
90%   of higher officials
99.9%   of the "upper echelon directors of the state apparatus"[41]

Thus the figures indicate, and what we know of the concrete functioning of institutions and power in the USSR demonstrates sufficiently, that there exists, in the spheres of power within the Soviet state apparatus, an organic imbrication between this apparatus and the party. In addition, and inseparable from this first statement, there exists mutual interpenetration between the ruling personnel of the state and the ruling personnel of the party. This situation—which was supposed to be only temporary, in response to revolutionary imperatives, in response to internal and external enemies and the imperialist threat, in response to the many tasks that had to be immediately undertaken—became established and has reproduced itself from decade to decade. This occurred under Stalin, who, brutally, through purges, trials, and liquidations, guaranteed a certain renewal from below of the ruling strata; and then after Stalin, in a situation that in fact could only lead to the autoreproduction of these strata and to their forming a ruling class.

The base of reproduction for this ruling class is the simultaneous mastery of the state apparatus and the party apparatus, which is responsible for the direction of all domains of economic and social life.

And it is increasingly a class that acts for itself, that defends its own interests: power first of all, privileges, various positions in society, material advantages, access to another way of life. It is a class that reproduces itself through modalities that have much in common with the means of reproduction of the ruling classes in the capitalist countries (even though, in the capitalist countries, the means for reproducing the ruling classes are associated with inheritance transmission). M. Rakowski describes the "reproduction of the ruling class" in the Eastern bloc:

> It is obvious that not just anyone may achieve a given level in the hierarchy. The selection of members of the dominant class takes place essentially through three filters: higher education, activity within the interior of an organization, and the system of relations within the ruling class. (Rakowski 1977, 55)

Within the framework of the *Nomenklatura*, lists of responsible positions by organizations, domains, or administrations, with the names of the office holders, increasingly become tools for recognition and identification within the higher spheres, and through this an instrument for the reproduction of the new ruling class.[42]

Here again, many socialists from the nineteenth century would be pushed off their clouds. Most of them believed that once the exploiters were eliminated, once the private ownership of the means of production was overcome, the conditions for a free, egalitarian society would be created. Yet in the case of the USSR a new ruling class has been formed, along with new relations of domination, new chains, new forms of repression.

The subtle distinctions about state ownership, socialist ownership, social ownership, and collective ownership, or overarching ownership, holding, and possession: all these change nothing. Here lies a significant problem for anyone wishing to work toward socialism: under what conditions may the overthrow of the former ruling class open the way toward a real liberation of the former dominated classes?

4. THE BALM OF IDEOLOGY

Oppression, repression, and even terror are not sufficient to hold a society and keep it functioning over a period of decades. Ideology and the conditioning of behavior by a system of ideas and values are indispensable auxiliaries.

In Russia, there was first the idea that socialism had to be constructed, then that socialism was under construction, then that it was passing from the lower stage to the higher stage, then that there were gains to be consolidated and developed.

Following this came the idea that socialism had to be defended, against external encirclement, against the internal enemy; an idea constantly being reborn since it was constantly created by the system and necessary to it.

Finally there appeared the idea that the superiority of socialism had to be concretized in technical, industrial, economic, and military superiority as well as in the claim to a superior way of life.

Stalin, 1929:

We are progressing at the greatest possible speed on the road to industrialization, toward socialism, leaving behind us our ingrained "Russian" backwardness. We are becoming a country producing metals, automobiles, tractors. And once we have placed the USSR in the automobile, and the muzhik on the tractor, let the respectable capitalists who boast of their "civilization" try to catch up to us. Then we will see which countries may be called backward, and which ones advanced. (Stalin [1929a] 1977, 455)

Stalin, 1936:

Today we have a new economy, a socialist economy, which is unaffected by crises and unemployment, suffering or collapse, and which offers to citizens all possibilities for a comfortable and cultured life. (Stalin [1936] 1977, 813)

Stalin, 1939:

The role of our socialist state has changed. The role of military repression within the country has become superfluous; it has disappeared, since exploitation has been eliminated . . . ; [it] has given way to the role of protecting socialist property against the thieves and squanderers of public possessions. . . . The essential task now facing our state, within the country, is to work calmly toward economic organization, culture, and education. So far as our army and our information service are concerned, they are directed against external enemies. (Stalin [1939] 1977, 957)

From Lenin to Stalin, Khrushchev, and Brezhnev, from congress to congress, from May Day celebrations to commemorations of the October Revolution, it would be easy to compile an anthology of these statements, watchwords, and official truths that, from decade to decade, have served as ideological cement for Soviet society.

It is an ideology constructed out of concrete. This point is taken up by Alexander Zinoviev in the story *The Radiant Future*, in which the slogan, "Long live Communism, the radiant future of all humanity!" is permanently written in concrete and steel at Cosmonaut Square, at the entrance to Marxism-Leninism Avenue.

As the *Testament of Varga* explains,

in the Soviet state ideology is created and spread among the population only by the bureaucratic leadership of the party. . . . It is thus ideological centralism that dominates in the country; a single ideology excludes and suppresses all others. . . . The time of political discussions in the 1920s appears incredible. All this transforms the dominant ideology into an infallible official dogma, to a large degree verbal and explicit, founded on an obsession with citations and references to the authorities. . . . This dogmatized ideology is imposed on the masses, through the press and the public declarations of the leaders. It is imposed on young people in the institutions of higher learning, in the party's system of political education, and the party's schools. . . . This official ideological propaganda inevitably produces in many citizens indifference, ideological deterioration, skepticism, and sometimes even cynicism. (Varga 1970, 79, 80, 81)

A former Soviet worker, Victor Feinberg, who was put in a psychiatric hospital for having demonstrated in Red Square in 1968, with several intellectuals, against the invasion of Czechoslovakia, stated:

The Soviet citizen lives through double-think. This is the only form of thinking that allows him to exist. On the one hand he must blindly believe the propaganda, for, if he doesn't, he is declared crazy or he is imprisoned. On the other hand he cannot completely believe in this myth because he lives in a reality different from that presented in the propaganda. This is to say that, in one way or another, he must deceive the ruling power and in addition lie to himself. (Feinberg 1978)

But at the same time an ideology must, in certain ways, be connected to reality: jobs and food had to be provided, more or less well, to most people in the 1930s; the Red Army participated in the victory over Nazi Germany, requiring tremendous sacrifices by the Russian people;

Sputnik was launched and a military force was established; a wider section of the population has increasing access to new consumer goods; working conditions improve. All these show that the ideology does continue to operate, despite the time lag.

For in the final analysis, the Soviet system of domination, as with any system of class domination, is not pure domination. It is also compromise. And the origin of the USSR itself, the reference to socialism, and the official ideology force such a compromise to occur when these factors do not themselves turn against the system.

Consider the following statement by a Polish worker in 1971: "First they told us we had to work hard so that our children might live better, and we accepted that. Then they told us that even our children would not see better times. And that was too much." Consider as well the terrible words of Edward Gierek, named to the head of the Polish Communist party after Wladyslaw Gomulka's resignation. The recent events, he said, "have painfully reminded us of this fundamental truth: the party must always remain closely connected with the working class and the nation as a whole; it cannot allow itself to lose contact with the workers" (Gierek 1970).

This is one way of recognizing, if such recognition were required, the distinctness of the party from the working class, with the implied risk that the party might be cut off or even that there could be a rupture between the two.

For ultimately the ideology of socialism—of the state belonging to workers and peasants—is a boomerang ideology, and in the same way Marxism-Leninism may one day again become a weapon for criticizing society. Without repeating points already made (regarding progress toward a classless society, the withering away of the state, liberation, the abolition of all political power), is it not disturbing that the central formula arrived at by Marx for criticizing political economy and for condemning capitalism,

CONSTANT CAPITAL + VARIABLE CAPITAL + SURPLUS VALUE

has become the formula supporting "the political economy of socialism," or, if one prefers, the political economy of "socialism"?

There remain other ideological weapons, perhaps less subversive in the long term, yet not without danger: nationalism, chauvinism, xenophobia, and, as a last resort, mobilization against a foreign enemy, and expansion on a world scale.

This is a terrible constellation of forces. At just the moment when the capitalist countries are going through the third major world crisis of capitalism and threaten to base an economic upturn on increased armaments production, everything is coming together in the USSR as well to increase militarization. Some factors tending in this direction in the USSR include the following:

• the composition of the ruling class, in which military personnel have a strong position and in which, as in the United States, a military industrial complex has formed (see Ferro 1980);
• the logic itself of the state collectivist mode of production, better adapted to massive and systematic effort (heavy industry, weaponry, space travel) than to diversified production adapted to consumption which has surpassed the satisfaction of elementary needs;
• finally, the impasse resulting from the split between ideological references to socialism and the reality of a state-collectivist society, which runs the risk of necessitating heightened tension with a foreign enemy.

COMMENTS ON CHAPTER 7

They carried out the Revolution. They brought down czarism and capitalism. They believed they were building socialism.

But they accomplished something quite different. Some called it "statist socialism," or "bureaucratic socialism," or . . . "actually existing socialism," or "a bureaucratic system," or "bureaucratic collectivism." We call it "state collectivism" with the intention, shared by many others, of pointing out: (1) that state collectivism is neither the socialism that was hoped for in the nineteenth century and that can still be hoped for, nor capitalism such as it has existed or exists today; (2) that state collectivism is a specific system, based on collectivization of the means of production and the essential, central, and decisive role of an omnipresent and omnipotent state.

State collectivism has certain aspects in common with capitalism:

• a class society in which the productive classes are subject to a ruling class;
• an economy organized in order to clear a surplus, in particular for industrialization and technological development;
• a system capable of imposing the necessary constraints during the period of rapid accumulation, and which must evolve, once this first phase is over, toward a "national compromise."

There are certain aspects, too, which differentiate state collectivism from capitalism:

• the absolute predominance of the state, which provides greater potential for certain large undertakings (basic industrialization, militarization, space travel), but at the same time less flexibility and capacity for diversification and adaptation;

• a ruling class, the upper state techno-bureoisie, which, once collectivization of the means of production has been carried out, reproduces itself mainly on the basis of the mastery it has achieved over state and party;

• the ideological references to Marxism-Leninism, to the construction of socialism, to the state of the working class; an ideology that has been able to contribute to establishing consensus, but whose boomerang effects can only increase with time.

If one had to situate state collectivization within the widest possible perspective, one might say that this system is very close to present-day capitalism, and, like actual capitalism, is very far from the socialism that had nurtured such great hopes in the nineteenth century.

Nonetheless, this system has spread around the world in recent decades: if it has done so it must have its own effectiveness, an effectiveness we must consider more closely.

8

PEOPLES' LIBERATION, SOCIALISM, AND STATE COLLECTIVISM

"Socialism" in China, in Vietnam, in Cambodia, and in Korea; Arab "socialisms," African "socialisms," "socialism" in Cuba: "socialisms" have proliferated in what we today call the Third World.

What nineteenth-century socialist would have been daring—or crazy—enough to imagine the current situation? Of course, Marx had discussed the possibility of a socialist revolution in Russia. Beyond that, however? Among the "peoples of the Orient"? Among "peoples of color"?

Formed in Europe by the very movement within which capitalism developed—the same capitalism it fought against—socialism was, from the start, tinted and sometimes heavily colored by many of the prejudices of the European middle classes. Socialism put its hopes for the emancipation of the oppressed classes (1) in the working classes produced by the development of national capitalisms of old Europe, and (2) in organized workers' movements, on a national as much as an international basis.

However, since the Second World War "socialist" revolutions have succeeded, and "socialist" regimes have been installed, primarily in regions freeing themselves from the yoke of imperialism and in countries having predominantly peasant populations. Though this has not been the same "socialism" proclaimed in the nineteenth century, still we must deal with the substantial fact that a great number of the national liberation movements and movements struggling against colonization or oligarchic regimes have taken up the flag of socialism. Once this point is established, how can one avoid studying the relations between these "national socialisms," the anti-imperialist movement as a whole, and the principal "rival" of the United States, the USSR?

Beyond this, once independence has been obtained, or once the revolution has been carried out, the problems of economic development, of modernization, and of industrialization present themselves. For those who refuse dependent capitalist development, does there exist some other road than state collectivism, formed, as we have seen, in the great Soviet experiment of the 1920s and 1930s? Is there a socialist road toward development? Or, in the same way that the balance of forces imposed by workers in several developed capitalist countries established a "social capitalism," have the conditions of struggle permitted the growth, here and there, of a "social collectivism"?

It would be easy, certainly, by invoking spilled blood, repression, torture, and sacrificed freedoms, to deny to an intellectual of Western Europe the right to take up these questions. Yet these are the questions that must be asked by anyone who, at the end of the twentieth century, still sees in socialism the possibility of a free, just, and fraternal society. These are questions that many young people from all continents ask themselves and have asked us.

1. STRUGGLE FOR SOCIALISM: FROM ONE DEPENDENCE TO ANOTHER

Socialist ideas on the other continents originated in Europe, as did capitalism. And the first organizational cells were made in the image of this or that component of the European socialist movement.

Phalansteries and "socialist colonies" in Latin America during the latter half of the nineteenth century and in the first half of the twentieth century were inspired by the writings of the great European utopians, especially Fourier, and were often established by people from Europe: socialists, Communists, Christians, anarchists. Discussion groups organized around disciples of Saint-Simon, Lamennais, or Proudhon. Forced to flee by the successive waves of repression, the banished and the exiled came with their ideas, ideals, and experiences. Workers, craftsmen, and immigrants brought with them their ways of thinking as well as their specific traditions of struggle and organization: mutualism and trade unionism, social democracy, and various conceptions of socialism and anarchism took root in the various immigration zones.

For several decades, then, socialist thinking and action developed from people of European origin, on the one hand among the middle classes and the intelligentsia, and on the other hand among the working classes.

During his travels in Argentina in 1908, the Italian socialist representative Enrico Ferri emphasized this problem:

> The Socialist party is, or should be, the natural product of the country in which it develops. Here, by contrast, it seems to me that the Socialist party is imported by European socialists who have emigrated to Argentina, and that it is imitated by the Argentines who translate socialist books and brochures coming from Europe. But the economic conditions of Argentina, which is going through the agro-pastoral phase (however technical), would certainly not have allowed Karl Marx to write the book *Capital*—which his genius was able to draw from English industrialization—in this country. (Cited in Droz 1972–78, 4:165)

This is to say that for many years in Latin America a gulf—whose depth varied from one country to the next—separated the socialist movement and the trade unionism of the broad masses from the often native or crossbred peasantry. One tragic sign of this opposition is found during and directly following the Mexican Revolution (1910–1911), in the divergences and then the opposition and clashes between worker trade unionism and the peasant movement.

Elsewhere in the world, the European origin of socialism and of trade unionism was, in the first quarter of the twentieth century, particularly evident in the populated colonies.

For example, in South Africa: composed exclusively of whites, who were for the most part English speaking, the South African Labour party took positions similar to the workers' movement in general when it fought against the exploitation practiced by the large mining companies, though the only workers it defended were white workers. In addition this party defended the privileges of white workers relative to black workers by means of decrees that forbade access by blacks to certain trades, or gave access only within quotas, or established lower wages for blacks.

For example, in North Africa: among the European communities, especially among dockworkers and railroad workers, as well as among civil servants and teachers, there existed deep-rooted socialist beliefs. Before 1914 there were socialist groups in Algeria and Tunisia, with a few anarchist groups in Tunisia and Morocco. Confronted with the nationalist claims of colonized peoples, this "colonial socialism" responded either with a sickly internationalism or with a virulent nationalism (French or Italian). These were two ways of denying and stifling nascent national consciousness.

For example, in Palestine: in the multiple waves of Jewish immigration the dominant ideology was a "socializing Zionism"; possessing various origins and tendencies, these socialist ideas were concretized in the cooperative *mochavik* villages, in the collectivist villages (the kibbutzim), and, in another way, in the general confederation of Jewish workers (the Histradruth, founded in 1920). In 1930 the Histradruth represented nearly all of the Jewish workers in Palestine, and its 26,000 members were nearly all Jewish.

We see, then, at the end of the nineteenth century and the beginning of the twentieth century, when the European powers dominated and divided up the world, when European capitalisms sought, in new lands, new possibilities for expansion, that the socialist movement throughout the world developed under the influence of European socialists and sometimes within the movement of colonization itself. This was a contradiction that was present at the very beginning of the diffusion of socialist ideas beyond Europe, and which has given rise to tragic and painful divisions.

The October Revolution created a new pole of attraction, providing the worldwide socialist movement with new momentum. Yet when Lenin exclaimed to the Petrograd soviet, in the night of 6–7 November 1917, "Long live the world socialist revolution!" he was thinking above all of the revolutions in Germany and old Europe. And the manifesto of the First Congress of the Communist International (1919) remained in line with the dominant tradition of European socialism regarding the colonial question:

> Emancipation of the colonies is conceivable only if it is accomplished at the same time as emancipation of the working class in the homelands. The workers and peasants, not only in Annam, Algeria, and Bengal, but in Persia and Armenia as well, will not be able to enjoy an independent existence until the workers in England have overthrown Lloyd George and Clemenceau and have taken government power into their hands. (Cited in Droz 1972–78)

In the spring of 1920 however, at the time of the Second Congress of the Communist International, a new direction began to emerge, as indicated by the eighth of the twenty-one terms of membership:

> Any party belonging to the Third International has the duty to expose mercilessly the exploits of "its" imperialists in the colonies, to support, not in words but in deeds, all emancipatory movements in the colonies, to demand the expulsion of the imperialists from the colonies, and to nurture in the hearts of workers in the home country truly fraternal feelings toward the working population of the colonies and toward oppressed nationalities. A further duty is to maintain continuous agitation among workers in the home country against all oppression of colonial peoples.

The *Theses and Additions on the National and Colonial Questions*, adopted by this same Second Congress, clearly defined the objective: "To create a tight link between the European Communist proletariat and the peasant revolutionary movement of the Orient, the colonies, and backwards countries in general." Acting in this spirit, the Congress of the Communist International decided to call for a congress of peoples of the Orient, which met in September 1920 in Baku with nearly two thousand delegates present.

The Indian Communist, Manabendra Nath Roy—no doubt too far ahead of his time—proposed a radical change in the still-dominant view within the socialist and Communist movements: "It is essential to transfer our energy to the development of the revolutionary movement in the Orient and to take as our fundamental thesis the idea that the destiny of world Communism depends on the victory of Communism in the Orient." Lenin thought Roy went too far; Lenin advocated struggle against imperialism—especially British imperialism—involving an alliance with bourgeois nationalist movements.

Representatives of the Communist International traveled throughout Latin America and Asia; year after year Communist parties were created, either on the basis of formerly existing socialist organizations, or else on new bases.

For example, M. N. Roy and Sen Katayama stayed in Latin America between 1920 and 1922. In September 1920 the Uruguayan Socialist party decided by a very large majority to join the Communist International. In Argentina in 1921 the Socialist party refused the twenty-one conditions for joining the International by a 3 to 2 majority; the dissident minority then founded the Argentinian Communist party. In Brazil, on the contrary, the majority of the Socialist party decided to join the Third International, and in January 1922 the Chilean Socialist party made a similar decision. In Mexico the same year M. N. Roy, Sen Katayama, and Bertram Wolfe—a Hindu, a Japanese, and a North American—supervised the founding of the Mexican Communist party.

In North Africa, as well, the Communist movement established itself. The socialist groups in Algeria and Tunisia chose by a clear majority, at the time of the Congress of Tours, to join the Communist International. In Egypt, in July 1922, the Socialist party that had been founded in August 1921 also decided to join the Third International.

In immense India, five small Communist groups were active in 1922. In sprawling China, a few Marxist study groups led by radical intellectuals transformed themselves into groups for Communist action before federating themselves, in July 1921, in order to found the Chinese

Communist party. At the Congress of Tours, the representative from Indochina, Nguyen Ai Quoc, issued a moving appeal:

> French imperialism penetrated Indochina fifty years ago. . . . Since that time we have been not only shamefully oppressed and exploited but also tortured and imprisoned without pity. . . . The Socialist party must act concretely in support of oppressed indigenous populations. . . . The party must spread socialism throughout all colonial countries. . . . We realized that the entry of the Socialist party into the Third International signified the implicit promise to devote to the colonial question the true importance due it. . . . We call out to you to help! Comrades, help us! (Ho Chi Minh [1956] 1968, 13, 14, 15)

Thus spoke the young Ho Chi Minh.

The Communist movement became organized in each country and region of the world, dealing with local situations in all their specificity, though acting with the support and within the framework established by the Communist International. This was not accomplished, of course, without frictions and contradictions.

An example of such a contradiction may be seen in the appeal issued in 1922 by the Executive Committee of the Communist International for the liberation of Algeria and Tunisia. Following this appeal the Sidi-bel-Abbès section of the Communist party denounced

> the project of an uprising of the Algerian Islamic masses as dangerous madness for which the Algerian federation of the Communist party, possessing above all a Marxist sense of situations, does not want itself to be held responsible before the judgment of Communist history.

At this time many European militants in Algeria left the Communist party sections and came to join the Socialist party sections then being reformed. For several decades the problem was discussed of the connections and contradictions between the struggles of metropolitan workers and the struggles of colonial peoples. This same problem still exists today, in another form, in the contradictions—too often evaded or denied—between the producing classes in the imperialist countries and the peoples and countries suffering imperial domination.

Another problem was that of the alliance between the Communists and bourgeois nationalist forces, which could of course carry out a real struggle against imperialism but which at the same time fought against communism from the inside. This was the case, starting in the 1920s, in Turkey and Persia, where the USSR chose to support the nationalist forces, with the objective of weakening British imperialism. It was also the case in China between 1924 and 1927, where the Communists, after aiding the fight of the Kuomintang, were afterwards fiercely repressed. The defeat of the Chinese Communists in 1927 drew attention to two related problems:

• the inadequacy of the model for revolution carried out and led by the industrial proletariat of the cities within an overwhelmingly peasant country;
• the divergences between the line defined in the "center," that is to say, in the USSR, for the international Communist movement and the program for action that the Communists of a given country believed was called for by the situation of that country.

This second problem was made more pressing by Stalin's ideas, in which pragmatism and dogmatism were closely linked. Stalin wrote in 1927:

A revolutionary is he who is ready to defend the USSR without hesitation, without second thoughts, openly and honestly, without military discussions, because the USSR is the leading proletarian and revolutionary state in the world, a state building socialism. . . . Whoever calls for defending the international revolutionary movement without wanting at the same time to defend the USSR, or who rebels against the USSR, rebels in fact against the revolution and slides irrevocably into the camp of enemies of the revolution. (Stalin, cited by Levesque 1980)

The program of the Communist International, adopted in September 1928, was even more to the point:

The international proletariat, of which the USSR is the only homeland, the safeguard of its victories, the essential factor in its international emancipation, has the duty to contribute to the success of building socialism in the USSR and to defend the USSR by all means against attacks by capitalist powers.

European socialism had for a long time seen victory by the metropolitan workers' movement as the condition for freeing colonized peoples. After 1927–1928, Communists throughout the world were supposed to see the strengthening of the USSR as the condition for freeing dominated people and countries.

The reversals in policy—from the strategy of class against class to the strategy of popular fronts; from antifascist mobilization to the call against the "spoliatory, unjust, imperialist" war following the German-Soviet pact—were not always easy to undertake or to explain. In particular the appeal to the world antifascist front, issued in 1935 by the Seventh Congress of the Communist International, put those engaged in the world anti-imperialist struggle in a difficult position:

[it] marked the end, in Latin America, of the anti-imperialist League of the Americas, which had been founded to fight "against the growing penetration by Yankee imperialism" and which the Communists had actively supported since 1929. (Rebérioux, in Droz 1972–1978)

In southeast Asia, this antifascist position of 1935 was applied, though hesitantly and unequally, depending on local conditions.

There is no doubt that first socialism and then communism brought ideals, analytic tools, ideological weapons, and methods of organizing to the dominated countries and peoples throughout the world. But at the same time the model was not well adapted to primarily agrarian countries, especially regarding the role attributed to the working class. And a world movement directed from a center—first by European workers' movements, and then by Soviet leaders—could hardly take into account all the possibilities concealed within the three huge continents—Latin America, Africa, and Asia—that remained under domination in one form or another.

To get beyond this impasse required many simultaneous factors: the intensification of imperialist exploitation and the destabilization of colonial empires; the Second World War; the invention of strategies better adapted to individual situations; the recognition of and reliance on peasant masses; an analysis linking the struggle against occupation, colonization, and imperialism with the process of social transformation; and finally, dependence on indigenous resources while remaining open to foreign support.

The Chinese Communists were the first to open up a new path.

2. THE CHINESE ROAD

After their defeat in 1927, after the failure of various attempts at insurrection in the years 1929–1931, after the Long March (October 1934 to October 1935), which, at the price of great losses, alone allowed them to escape from the campaign of encirclement and from being wiped out, the Chinese Communists regrouped their remaining forces in the Yenan region.

For many years Mao Tse-tung had fought, without being able to impose his point of view, against decisions based on a conception of revolution too dependent on the determining role of the working class and urban insurrection. He advocated, for China, a different strategy:

- to rely on the peasantry first of all;
- to take root in backward regions, far from cities, in order to develop centers of revolution;

• to organize for armed struggle, with a Red Army;
• to carry out a long-term struggle, to be progressively extended to the whole country.

This strategy was put into action marginally, in parallel with the main strategy, after 1928. In 1931 a dozen "red districts" represented three million inhabitants. These districts became the principal axis for action by the Chinese Communist party in its struggle against the Japanese occupiers. In 1945, when the Japanese capitulated, the liberated zone represented a hundred million inhabitants, the Red Army claimed more than a million soldiers, and the Chinese Communist party 1,200,000 members.

Then began the last phase of the conflict between the Communist forces and the Kuomintang: a conflict that was at first political but that gave rise to armed confrontation. Eventually the crumbling of the nationalist forces opened the way for Mao to take power.

Stalin, who had shown himself to be more than hesitant toward Mao's conceptions of the military and the peasants;[43] Stalin, who had pushed toward high posts in the Kuomintang Chinese leaders forced out of their positions of responsibility in the Chinese Communist party after 1935; Stalin, who had given hardly any aid to the struggle of the Chinese Communists and who had kept up relations with Chiang Kai-shek right to the end—this same Stalin attempted, by finally helping China, to profit from some of the momentum of the Chinese Revolution, and, if possible, to guide it. Mao himself declared in 1938: "There exists no abstract Marxism, only concrete Marxism, which has taken on a national form, and which has been applied to concrete struggle under the concrete conditions of China." Mao, in 1942: "We must get rid of pre-formed dogmatic schema borrowed from other countries." Mao, in 1945: "One must depend first of all on one's own strengths." Yet Mao was enough of a realist not to refuse Soviet aid; on 16 December 1949 he arrived in Moscow for the first time.

Soviet aid took the form at first of a 300-million-dollar loan; it was given at the beginning of the Second Five-Year Plan (1953–1957), which emphasized heavy industry. The aid package also included sending Soviet technicians to China, especially for carrying out major industrial projects. The Soviet influence was so overwhelming that Mao stated in 1958:

In the period following the country's liberation [from 1950 to 1957], dogmatism appeared in the domains of economy, culture, and education. . . . I was unable to eat eggs and chicken bouillon for three years because an article had appeared in the USSR that forbade eating eggs and chicken bouillon. . . . The Chinese obeyed everything; they applied everything. In a word, the USSR directed everything. (Mao Tse-tung [1958a] 1975b, 480)

Let us not forget nonetheless that agrarian reform had begun by 1950, and that after the start of the agricultural mutual-assistance brigades (1953), collectivization in the countryside increased with the socialist cooperatives (1955) and the people's communes (1958): in the same way that he anchored himself in the countryside at the time of the fight against the Japanese and against the Kuomintang, it was in the country-side that Mao rooted the fundamental transformations that he believed the construction of socialism demanded. And it is difficult to imagine that pressure from Soviet advisors pushed Mao to launch, in 1951, the "three anti-" campaign: anticorruption, antiwastefulness, and anti-bureaucratism.

Beyond these original frictions, there were territorial, political, and ideological disagreements, and ultimately the rivalries of two great pow-ers, both wishing to play a role in the world—especially toward and with the Third World—that together explain the divergences, polemics, and rupture of 1960, when the Soviet advisors departed and opposition between the two countries become ever more shrill.

Yet, well before the break, Mao judged the direction of Soviet choices to be wrong, especially the prioritization of heavy industry, which Mao believed would be accomplished at the expense of agriculture and the peasants. In a text written in April 1956, "On the Ten Chief Rela-tionships" (a text made public only after his death in 1976), Mao ana-lyzed the conditions for an accumulation simultaneously bearable economically, politically, and socially. In certain ways we find in this text, reformulated in a "Mao Tse-tung style," some elements of the debate that thirty years earlier had pitted Bukharin against Preo-brazhensky in the USSR.

For example, on the relation between the state, the units of produc-tion, and individual producers, Mao wrote:

The state needs accumulation, the collective needs accumulation as well, though there must not be an excess of accumulation. . . . It is necessary to concern oneself, simultaneously, with the state and the factories; the state and the workers; the state, the collective economic organizations, and the peasants. One cannot concern oneself with only a single element. . . . This is an important problem, important to six hundred million people: the whole party should devote full atten-tion to it. (Mao Tse-tung [1956] 1975a, 179)

Though this is neither very brilliant nor very original, it gives the impression of solid good sense, which certainly allowed many errors and dangers to be avoided.

On the relation between agriculture and industry, and between light and heavy industry, Mao wrote:

> To develop heavy industry, capital accumulation is necessary. Where does this capital accumulation come from? It could come from heavy industry itself, but it could also come from light industry and from agriculture. Now there is more accumulation possible from light industry and from agriculture, and more quickly, too. (Mao Tse-tung [1956] 1975a, 171)

More exactly: if in order to develop heavy industry, the development of the two other activities is reduced, then the living conditions of the people are impaired, discontent rises, and in the end "a development of heavy industry is obtained which is slower and less beneficial." On the other hand, if "heavy industry [is developed] by satisfying people's needs, then heavy industry is built on more solid bases, which assures it better and more rapid development" (Mao Tse-tung [1956] 1975a, 172–73).

Mao, who in 1958 declared his intention to leave the presidency of the Republic (which he in fact did in 1959), continued these basic reflections in his reading of Stalin's *Economic Problems of Socialism in the USSR*. He observed:

> As for problems of heavy industry, light industry, and agriculture, the Soviet Union has hardly paid any attention to the second two. And the USSR has had to suffer the consequences of this. In addition, relations between immediate and long-term interests of the people in Soviet society are poorly established: basically they are walking on one leg. (Mao Tse-tung [1958b] 1975b, 32)

Mao came back to this problem again in discussing his 1960 reading of the USSR's *Manual of Political Economy*: "We advocate the simultaneous development of industry and agriculture while giving priority to development of heavy industry" (Mao Tse-tung [1960] 1975b, 146).

In this same year, 1960, the following idea was put forth as a "general principle for the development of the economy": "*Take agriculture as the base and industry as the dominant factor*" (see Tsien Tche-hao 1979, 197).

So, once they gained power, Mao and the Chinese Communist party began to carry out two major transformations.

• The first, no doubt fundamental in Mao's eyes, sought to establish new social relations in the countryside, in order to increase agricultural production while improving conditions for the great majority of the peasants; for this effort, the experience gained since 1928 helped provide a guide for action.

• The second, essential for the future, aimed at developing industry, and especially heavy industry; Mao accepted the use of Soviet ideas at least temporarily in this domain, for he needed their techniques, equipment, and credit.

In this framework, and with the effort of the Chinese people as a whole, reconstruction took place under favorable conditions: from 1949 to 1952 agricultural production increased by 50 percent, and industrial production and coal production both doubled. During the First Five-Year Plan, agricultural production rose again by 20 percent, and industrial production doubled once again, with the result—the first symbolic result of the continuous effort—that steel production reached several million tons.

However, no matter how much one may admire these advances, one must not idealize them. First of all, during this period the population grew by a hundred million, nearly 20 percent, and this increase slowed the growth of products available per person. Second, the accumulation effort necessarily consumed a significant share of national production; Mao estimated this share to be 27 percent in 1957 (Mao Tse-tung [1960] 1975b, 148). This implies, in China as elsewhere, the formation of a working class: a process that took place at the time progressively. There were three million industrial workers in 1949, five million in 1952, nine million in 1957. Finally this process implied, in one form or another— material, political, or ideological incentives; individual benefits; or collective pressure—an incitement, and no doubt in some cases, a compulsion, to work. Such compulsion was tempered, though, by the experience of previous decades:

We have two basic principles:
1. don't work men to the point where they die; and
2. don't make them work to the point where their bodies are weakened; on the contrary they must be strengthened bit by bit.
When these two principles are followed, all the rest has hardly any importance. (Mao Tse-tung [1960] 1975b, 127)

The peasants were put to work, a new working class was formed, and roles were filled by the party, the state, managers, directors, and bureaucrats. How many of these managers, these bureaucrats, were there among the nonagricultural workers in the modern economic sectors, which grew from eight million in 1949 to sixteen million in 1952 and twenty-four million in 1957? And who could deny their existence—and their faults—when in 1951 Mao and the Chinese Communist party launched the "three anti-" campaign against corruption, bureaucratism, and wastefulness, and when in 1957 the party published "instructions concerning the participation of managers in manual work" (Tsien Tche-hao 1979, 104).

The whole evolution, with all its upheavals, of China since 1949, can be understood only by taking into consideration the contradiction in this period between

• the desire to develop and modernize the economy, "to advance production," and thus to accumulate by compelling the extraction of surplus labor within the framework of a collectivist mode of production, with economic development leading simultaneously to class differentiation and to the establishment between classes of relations characterized by domination/dependence/resistance; and
• the desire to transform social relations, to "make the revolution"; for some, this meant preventing the formation of a new ruling class or, at the very least, avoiding the excesses, abuses, and mistakes brought about through domination by managerial groups and officials over the producing classes and strata.

The break with the USSR only emphasized the importance of this contradiction while giving the Chinese leaders more room to maneuver.

The Great Leap Forward (1958–1960) was supposed to allow this contradiction to be surpassed, through the grass-roots communes, through the movement to create craft and industrial workshops in the countryside, through the slogan: "Construct socialism according to these principles: Extend all possible effort; Always go forward; Quantity, speed, quality, economy." The transformation of the units and relations of production was supposed to permit rapid economic progress. But the harvests in 1959, 1960, and 1961 were disastrous; in addition China had to contend with the consequences of the departure of the Soviet technical advisors and the sudden end of Soviet aid. It became easy, for its adversaries, to emphasize the failures of the Great Leap Forward.

There remained—and this is one of the tasks of any collectivist system during its period of development—a sharp increase in nonagricultural employment, especially industrial employment; this is to say that the stage of rural industries represented a step forward in the formation and development of the Chinese working class.

However in 1961 the urgent task was to make up what had been lost during the "black years": private business remained an active incentive, and the expanded role for family plots of land and for "private markets" contributed to rekindling production. In addition, the financial responsibility of businesses was increased.

With the Great Proletarian Cultural Revolution (1964–1971), several struggles were undertaken at once: supporters of the "Chinese Road" fought managers and methods associated with the USSR; partisans of a tightly administered economy fought economists who advocated capitalist-inspired methods; young people rose up against the swollen and bureaucratized state apparatus; the workers and peasants were called upon to criticize and combat inept management; and Mao, relying on the army, reestablished his power. In the economic domain, the Great Proletarian Cultural Revolution represented a strengthening of leadership by state and party, with campaigns highlighting specific examples to be followed: Taking for industry, Tatchaï for agriculture.

After Mao's death, and especially after the defeat of the Gang of Four (1977), the pendulum seemed to swing back toward granting more room to the market, greater industrial decentralization, and, probably, an increased use of material incentives.

Overall, the policy advocated by Teng Hsiao-p'ing in his 1975 "Document of Twenty Points" was put into effect. This document had been heavily criticized in the journal *Studies and Critique* as the "sinister flag of capitalist restoration on the industrial front." In order to "decipher" this document and its critique more easily, we shall place certain propositions from the document, formulated with great prudence, next to the article's blistering critique:

"DOCUMENT OF TWENTY POINTS"	ARTICLE FROM STUDIES AND CRITIQUE
If one pays attention only to production . . . one can no longer speak of building socialism. But it is equally wrong not to pay attention to production. . . . One absolutely cannot criticize as a theory of productive forces [the fact that], guided by the revolution, production is being carried out well.	It [the "Document of Twenty Points"] praises with frenzy the theory of productive forces and the end of class struggle.
Regarding wages, the unswerving policy of our Party has been to oppose imbalance as much as egalitarianism. . . . To put everything on the same level, when sharing out our resources, discourages the dynamism of the masses for socialism.	The "Document" peddles material incentives and profits for the managers.
Decentralization of operations implies management at different levels, but absolutely must not weaken centralization and unification of the central organs. That which should be centralized should be centralized, and should not be dispersed.	The "Document" . . . peddles top-down dictatorship [of the minister over the base units].

"DOCUMENT OF TWENTY POINTS"	ARTICLE FROM STUDIES AND CRITIQUE
In all undertakings, one must rely on the masses. . . . Without a rigorous system of responsibility, production is carried out in chaos. . . . Every worker, manager, and technician should have explicitly specified responsibilities.	The "Document" . . . peddles management of the factory by experts.
We must continue studying and innovating. We must carefully consider advanced techniques and useful things from foreign countries, and import them for our use, following our planned priorities, so as to speed up development of our national economy.[44]	The "Document" . . . peddles a policy of servility toward foreign countries.

In China the alternative is not now, and has not been in recent decades, between socialism and capitalism. Rather, the alternative, within a system founded on and determined by the collectivist mode of production, is

• between a path in which state management and centralization predominate, and a path that increases autonomy for commercial enterprises linked together by one form or another of market and judged on their overall performance;[45]
• between a path in which widespread political mobilization of the people provides energy and direction and allows obstacles to be overcome, and a path in which economic development results from firm, decisive leadership by managers and technicians having the confidence—and following the directives—of the party;
• and probably between a path that is more attentive to the needs and hardships of the workers (especially the peasants) and a path prescribing increased sacrifices in the present in order to attain a stronger position in the future.

Put another way, a society may "break with capitalism"—as China, following the USSR, has done, collectivizing the essential means of production, reducing the former classes of landed property owners and capitalists, and seeking to advance national economic development on the basis of autonomy so far as the world capitalist market is concerned. Yet socialism is not necessarily realized because such steps are carried out. And the mode of production that allows the accumulation necessary for significant economic development to take place has hardly anything in common with the "free association of producers" dreamed of by the socialists of the nineteenth century. This is what we have called the "state-collectivist mode of production," that is to say, accumulation organized on the basis of collective appropriation of the means of production, under the direction of the state and, if needed, under compulsion exercised by the state and by the new ruling class (the techno-bureoisie of the party, administrations, and business operations) relying on state authority.

State-collectivist society may be authoritarian (up to and including totalitarian) or democratic, centralized or decentralized, severely exploitative or generous. These characteristics are not necessarily linked. Nonetheless it appears that there is a broad tendency among regimes calling themselves socialist since the Second World War—confronted by the collectivist, centralized, harshly exploitative and yet not always efficient, authoritarian, and in many respects totalitarian Soviet/Stalinist state—to seek another path for state-collectivist development. This path seeks to be more decentralized, moderating the rate of accumulation in order to avoid overwhelming the producing classes, accepting the legitimacy of opposition forces, and acting democratically so far as this is possible.

3. THE FLOURISHING OF "THIRD-WORLD SOCIALISMS"

During the 1960s socialism appeared to make several breakthroughs in the Third World.

In 1954, after a lengthy struggle against the armed forces of a France incapable—and this was true of large sections of the left—of accepting the break with France's colonial past, the Vietnamese revolutionary leaders forced the recognition of their right to govern the northern half of the country, while the reunification of all of Vietnam, by means of free elections, was to take place within two years. The United States, however, acted to maintain, in the southern half of the country, a "domino" that was hostile to socialist North Vietnam.

In 1959 Fidel Castro and the revolutionary forces entered Havana; in the following two years the socialist character of the new Cuban regime was proclaimed, and during these years Cuban connections with the USSR also developed.

In 1962, after a seven-year war against the armed forces of a France— including large groups claiming to support democracy, peoples' right to self-determination, and socialism—once again incapable of renouncing this specific form of colonial domination inherited from a past age, the FLN and the Algerian people forced the French to recognize Algerian independence. Two years later the Charter of Algiers confirmed the country's socialist orientation. During the entire period, the Vietnamese people carried on a heroic, relentless battle against American troops, who were supplied with the most powerful and modern weapons and material.

There were advances and victories by forces calling themselves socialist in Cambodia and Laos; socialist references and neutralist positions in Nehru's India; progressive currents and socialist tendencies in certain of the national-populist endeavors in Latin America. Above all there was great activity in Africa and in the movement toward "African socialisms."[46] The map of the world seemed to be covering over with pink and red.[47]

New "national roads" toward socialism seemed to be opening. New "models" were praised to the skies by unquestioning propagandists. And intellectuals from the developed countries found new sites for summer pilgrimages, allowing them to mix politics and tourism, all without spending too much money.

So many illusions have been lost, so many bitter deceptions have degenerated into fierce denunciations, since that time. Where socialism was flourishing, suddenly one discovered state capitalism, or just plain capitalism, or bureaucracy, inefficiency, oppression, chaos, corruption, or even, as in Cambodia, absolute terror.

The error—there have been many who have committed it, and we ourselves have taken years to describe and analyze it—has been to confuse anti-imperialist revolution with socialist revolution, to confound emancipation from colonial power with the opening stages of building socialism. Fidel Castro gave powerful expression to such thinking in 1961, a few months after the counterrevolutionary attack at the Bay of Pigs was repelled by worker and peasant militia:

> It was necessary to carry out an anti-imperialist revolution, a socialist revolution. Now this was a single revolution, for there can be only one. Such is the great dialectic truth of humanity: imperialism confronts only socialism. And the result is that socialism triumphs, that the epoch of socialism succeeds the epoch of capitalism and imperialism, that the era of socialism is established and will be followed by the era of communism. (Castro, cited in Löwy 1980, 274)

This conviction is founded on the following straightforward idea: "There is no middle term between capitalism and socialism" (ibid., 269).

Despite this, alongside capitalism, and with socialism not yet having been brought into existence anywhere, another reality, which we call state collectivism, has developed. This process has occurred in places where, capitalism not being developed, a collective effort has been undertaken—organized by and around the state—to develop, accumulate, and modernize.

Once this is recognized, in our eyes it is hardly possible—except for purposes of mobilization and political exhortation—to continue to affirm the socialist character of anti-imperialist revolutions. It is important to note the following.

• The anti-imperialist revolutions, the movements and the wars of national liberation, the struggles of various peoples to determine their own future, have all definitely taken place within the "general trajectory" of liberation and freedom movements, and in this sense they are one moment in the advance toward socialism.

• Victorious, these revolutions, wars, and struggles do not allow the stage of building socialism to be reached easily; as in the case of the Soviet and Chinese revolutions, they come up against the two central—and connected—problems of power and the necessity to produce.

Put bluntly, these movements oppose capitalism, but they are not, for that reason alone, socialism.

And it is because they have seen only one side and then, after discovering the second, forgotten the first, that many who have lauded the socialism supposedly realized here or there become pitiless accusers a few years later. This is all the more so since, once the celebration of the liberation has passed, the effort to produce, accumulate, construct, modernize, and equip must be carried out each year, each month, each day, often relying on compulsion to accomplish needed tasks.

Thus, the historic movement occurring before, during, and after the 1960s was principally a movement of decolonization and emancipation for dominated peoples. The flag of socialism may have been raised in the forefront of battle, as it had been in 1848, in 1871, and during workers' struggles at the end of the nineteenth and in the twentieth centuries: for all this, socialism—in all its richness and depth—remains yet to be developed.

Now this movement does not take place in an aseptic and favorable world. Imperialist domination remains powerful and stubborn—as the war carried out by the United States in Vietnam demonstrates—and pitiless, as the recapture of the South American continent as a whole by the might of the North daily demonstrates. Any people, any national community, that, once having won political independence, seeks to consolidate such independence by constructing an economy centered within the new nation itself—out of reach of the dictates of industrial and financial companies and the world market—finds itself exposed to the threats, reprisals, and even the outright attacks of imperialism.

But the principal force confronting Western imperialism, led by the United States, remains the USSR, which has at its disposal not only economic and military strength, but also the prestige of the Soviet Revolution, and the discourse and ideology of socialism. The USSR can call upon its know-how regarding domination and production under statist management (with the single party and the various means of political and police control, collectivization of the means of production, and planning). Any country that has started down the road of significant social transformations on the basis of national independence, and that is threatened by imperialist forces, then has only to ask for help and protection from the USSR. The USSR in its turn finds itself able to exert pressure so that the social transformations in countries receiving its aid are patterned after the Soviet model.[48]

Once again, for anyone who wishes to reopen or widen the paths toward a socialism guaranteeing full development of freedom and democracy, it is obviously necessary to open up a space in the world, in between the Soviet Union and the United States, where all the forces working and struggling for socialism and democracy may associate with, support, and strengthen one another.

To sum up, the period centered around the 1960s was marked, for many countries in the Third World, by the beginnings and development of a process rich in lessons for each country, at each of the following stages.

1. There is a war of national liberation or a struggle for independence.[49]

2. Independence is forced or obtained in many different ways: for some countries, by an uprising against a regime itself rigidly under the sway of imperialism.[50] In every case the importance and strength of the peasantry make themselves quickly apparent.[51]

3. A movement of social transformation and economic development begins with extremely diverse references to socialism serving as ideological cement:[52] Soviet- or Chinese-inspired Marxism-Leninism, Christian humanist socialism, socialism relying on Islamic references, African socialisms.

4. As in the USSR after 1917 or China after 1949, the new leaders are confronted with the necessity of ensuring production, clearing a surplus, and accumulating: this means imposing tasks and sacrifices upon the peasantry and the mine and factory workers.[53]

5. Important choices are now made within the following two broad domains:

ECONOMIC AND SOCIAL TRANSFORMATIONS	RELATIONS WITH THE WORLD MARKET
Agrarian reform or not; development of a cooperative or communal form of agriculture; collectivization or not of the other means of production; lastly, choices among quite different directions:	Attempt or not at development centered within the country; privileged relations with the capitalist world or with the collectivist world, or the maintenance of relations with both camps; lastly, choices among differing directions:
a. liberal capitalism (especially in the manufacturing and mining sector);	A. submission to the capitalist market and to multinational companies;
b. capitalism with strong statist intervention;	B. dependence, in part negotiated by the state, regarding the capitalist market;
c. mixed capitalist/collectivist system under statist domination;	C. an effort to maintain balanced relations with both camps;
d. state-collectivist system with a large variety of forms in the countryside.	D. privileged ties to the USSR and the collectivist countries.

Frequently there exists a certain coherence in the choices made in the two domains, such as *a* being linked to *A* and *d* to *D*. A country dominated by liberal capitalism *a* may, however, following a disagreement or misunderstanding with the American government, develop relations with the USSR (*C* or *D*); and a country following the state-collectivist road *d* may, following a change in direction, seek to depend less on the USSR and opt for foreign relations of the sort summarized by *B* or *C*.

6. In recent years, then, one observes a tremendous variety in national situations, situations which are often themselves in the process of evolving. And since the references to socialism are in some cases abandoned or toned down and in other cases maintained or increased, without an evident link to the real evolution of the country, it is understandable that people become disoriented and confused.[54]

In order to advance further, it is useful to study, case by case—that is to say, country by country—how the historical movement has occurred, and what sort of situation it has led to in each case.

More generally, even if there has been no more socialism realized in the Third World than elsewhere, it is significant that the powerful postwar movement toward liberation as well as many other attempts at national development have taken place under the sign of socialism.

• First of all, because—and we stress this once again—this movement for the emancipation of dominated peoples and countries takes place within the historical trajectory whose ideal endpoint is socialism.

• Second, because many achievements, and many attempts, especially having to do with the development on a communual or cooperative basis of solidarity, equality, social progress, etc., have occurred within a socialist perspective and contribute to the advance toward socialism.

• Third, because socialism, which until this time had been a primarily European effort deeply influenced by Judeo-Christian culture, has since been reappropriated by the common people, intellectuals, and progressive forces on all continents.[55]

• Finally, because out of this process of becoming worldwide, out of this reappropriation by social formations in Asia, in Africa, and in the Americas, the socialist project will emerge—whatever disappointments there may have been in the immediate present—revitalized, enriched, diversified, and ultimately strengthened.

Beyond the great founders—utopians, thinkers, political men—of European socialism, socialism must from now on take into account the analyses, the vision, the generosity of spirit, and the daring, along with the errors and the failures, of socialists from the three huge continents of the Third World: forerunners such as José Martí or José Carlos Mariátegui; contemporary fighters for socialism assassinated or killed in the course of the struggle: Salvador Allende, Mehdi Ben Barka, Amilcar Cabral, Ernesto "Che" Guevara, Patrice Lumumba, Carlos Marighella, Camilo Torrès . . . ; combatants in the anti-imperialist struggle, who worked or attempted to work in the direction of socialism all or part of their lives: Mao Tse-tung and Chou En-lai, Ho Chi Minh and Vo Nguyen Giap, and in another way, Jawaharlal Nehru; Fidel Castro of course, but also Raúl Sendic and many others; and in various ways—and judged variably as well—Ben Bella, Ben Salah, Mamadou Dia and Léopold Sédar Senghor, Gamal Abdel Nasser, Kwame Nkrumah, Julius Nyerere, Sékou Touré. . . .

In this list, purposefully left incomplete and unorganized, we wish to stress the diversity of intentions, inspirations, and accomplishments. Time and history will sort them out.

COMMENTS ON CHAPTER 8

In the regions of the world at one time conquered by Europe and swept along one way or another by the development of capitalism on a world scale, the process of decolonization accelerated after the Second World War. There were independences negotiated or won after long wars of liberation, anti-imperialist revolutions, and revolts against "puppet regimes."

There have been many movements carried out in the name of socialism, and many "socialist" revolutions and "socialist" regimes have blossomed in the recent past.

Yet contemporary history forces us, and will continue to force us more and more, to open our eyes to this point: *there exists no identity between anti-imperialist revolution and socialist revolution.* Anti-imperialist revolution breaks the chains and liberates; it overthrows the regime and the classes that served as the connecting links to the groups, interests, and forces of imperialism. But once this sort of revolution is carried out, socialism is not yet, on the basis of anti-imperialist revolution alone, within reach.

While the peasants and workers who have fought successfully for the revolution hope to benefit from the freedom and dignity for which they have made so many sacrifices, will the movement cadres and party leaders, the technicians and civil servants, fade into the background, sacrifice themselves, and merge back into the people by devoting themselves to the tasks of production? Most of them have no inclination to do this, and it would take heroism to carry out a socialist revolution that questions the role of the leader himself as well as the distinction "leaders/led," when those who might conceive and give energy to this new level of revolution have only very recently won power and are finally—like the bourgeois revolutionaries of the great French Revolution—going to rule in the name of the people, by the people, and for the people.

Beyond this, everything still remains to be done: reconstruct, refashion a society, get production going again, combat enemies within and without the country, develop education, establish health-care delivery systems, improve agricultural production, modernize equipment, industrialize, cope with emergency situations, and prepare for future needs. There is so much to do that, beyond the questions of goodwill or of foot dragging, beyond the interests of the new ruling strata, it remains an open question whether there exist ways to accomplish what needs to be done other than those offered either by capitalism and its state or by state collectivism.

And to start down either of these two roads means accepting the establishment of a society where a ruling class (local bourgeoisie or state techno-bureoisie) takes control of essential matters. Such a class may do this by relying more or less on the popular classes (peasantry and working classes), by being more or less receptive to the people's claims and hopes, and by allowing the people more or less to express themselves and to influence local matters. Nonetheless: the distinction is drawn between those who rule and those who produce; the gap deepens, and one day the workers rise up against "their" party, against "their" leaders, against "their" state.

This observation does not in the least devalue the struggles that have been carried out in Latin America, Asia, and Africa against colonial powers. On the contrary, these struggles have advanced the fight for the emancipation of all oppressed people in essential ways.

Rather, what we have noted above only serves to emphasize that the road toward socialism is longer and more strewn with difficulties than our impatience at first imagined. And the danger today would be to refuse to admit the existence of these delays and difficulties. For in fact it takes time to modify social relations deeply and lastingly; it takes time to transform individual attitudes; it takes time—generations of time—for a new society to emerge and develop out of an old one.

Thus, in our view, the situation and possibilities in the Third World may be analyzed in the following terms.

1. The national liberation struggles, against imperialism as well as the oligarchies linked to imperialism, take place within the broad movement toward freedom, equality, and the abolition of exploitation and domination: in a word, toward socialism.

2. The necessity to produce, reconstruct, and accumulate, in order to create the conditions for a better future, and the necessity to confront foreign threats, lead to the establishment of a class system in which a ruling class inveigles or forces workers and peasants to produce, and then to produce still more.

3. Insofar as imperialism or the former ruling classes refuse to accept the newly chosen direction, threats and outright attacks lead a country that has won its independence to seek alliance with another power, most often the USSR. And the USSR will push for the adoption of the methods it well knows: organization of society by the state, a single party, and state collectivism.

There remains hardly any space in today's world between the imperialist domination perpetuated through local oligarchies and dependence on a state techno-bureoisie more or less tied to the USSR. *To win back, between the two great superpowers, a geopolitical space for socialism and democracy is an essential task for the closing years of this century.*

Finally, we note that even if the anti-imperialist revolutions, the overthrow of oligarchies and dictatorships, do not directly give rise to socialism, their contribution to the struggle for socialism is nonetheless essential, in three respects.

1. First and most simply because by weakening imperialism they

restrict the space in the world open to capitalism. This alone, however, should not serve as a reason for letting forms of tyrannical or totalitarian state collectivism develop that one day may reveal themselves to be as odious as the worst capitalisms of today.

2. Second, because they enrich the very content of the socialist project, by bringing to light the hopes and potential of peasantries, as well as of intellectuals, young people, and women. . . .

3. Third, because they give new life to socialism from the venerable traditions of communal life, openness, and solidarity of African villages, Asian societies, and peoples in Latin America; and they break the socialist perspective out of the Judeo-Christian framework through new encounters with Islam, with Confucianism, and with still other forms of thinking and morality.

This is to say that at the very moment when socialism seemed to be transmuting into the new reality of state collectivism, the socialist movement has found the chance for new life and the possibility for a new dimension.

9

THE WINTER OF SOCIALISM[56]

In some ways, after the Second World War socialism attained greater power and a wider reception than ever before. The workers' movements on the five continents are based upon socialist ideals. A significant portion of the intellectuals have been won over to the ideas and the ideal of socialism. Many straightforward and unpretentious people as well as members of the middle class are intellectually or emotionally committed to socialism.

In many people's eyes, the USSR continues to build socialism, China has begun to follow a similar path, and with the aid of the USSR the countries of Eastern Europe have formed themselves into socialist regimes. Elsewhere in the world political parties of workers, socialists, Social Democrats, and Communists are powerful. In many capitalist countries, socialists (and before 1947, Communists) have taken on governmental responsibilities, either alone, or within the framework of political alliances. In the Third World many movements for liberation and against colonialism and imperialism have rejoined or rediscovered the fundamental project of liberation and emancipation that is at the heart of socialism.

But this extension of socialism that occurred toward the middle of the twentieth century in the developed capitalist countries as well as in the state-collectivist countries has not advanced without passing through torturous and withering circumstances.

What remains of the absolute refusal of injustice and suffering? Of the thirst for the liberation of all people in all aspects of their lives? Of the call for a society without classes, without a state, without political power? Of the vision of a reduction in the differences between manual

166

and intellectual work, between city and country, between leaders and the led? Is hope the only thing that remains in all these countries, in all these states where socialism is constantly referred to, but where political realism, pragmatism, and state ideology are presented, with their terrible reductive force, as the only possible options? Is the idea all that remains?

For the words themselves get used up too. How can one still believe the words when "socialist" government leaders do something other than what their congress's resolutions call for, when their actions are the opposite of the official speeches? How can one continue to conceive of contemporary history using the concepts of a "Marxism-Leninism" that has become a dogmatic, mechanical, immobile, and ultimately content-less state doctrine?

In another way then, and despite its spread and influence, the great socialist hope has entered a difficult period. The flowers have faded; the leaves fall; the sap ceases to flow; the branches harden: this could be called the winter of socialism.

1. IN THE EAST, THE GREAT CLOSING-IN

It is in the East that the winter is most severe.

Within the logic of the Yalta accords, in some cases on the basis of a national movement that developed during resistance to Nazi occupation and in other cases because of the decisive presence of the Red Army, Soviet-type regimes have established themselves throughout Eastern Europe. Though national specificities are far from negligible, we will not consider them here in the brief section that follows; we will, rather, focus on the common logic of production, classes, and power that, based on the Soviet model, has developed in all these countries.

This is a tragic logic of immobilization and enclosure. For social reality is opposed, term for term, by the ideological representation; what actually occurs is opposed by what is said to occur:

WHAT IS SAID: IDEOLOGICAL REPRESENTATION	WHAT ACTUALLY OCCURS: SOCIAL REALITY
the working class as ruling class	a new ruling class, the state techno-bureoisie
the Communist party as the party of the working class, at the service of the working class	the party, controlled by the high-level state techno-bureoisie, as a tool for ruling the country
effort asked of everyone, within the perspective of building socialism, and which should benefit the "whole	a mode of production and accumulation, comparable in many ways to capitalism; an accumulation

WHAT IS SAID: IDEOLOGICAL REPRESENTATION	WHAT ACTUALLY OCCURS: SOCIAL REALITY
people," and first of all the working class	effort sustained mainly by the peasantry and the working class but whose benefits accrue largely to the ruling class
no antagonism between the working class, the peasantry, and the intelligentsia, nor between the workers and their managers	antagonism between the ruling class and, first of all, the peasantry, and then the working class, with the ruling class imposing, and the other classes bearing, the effort of accumulation
for those who rely on the writings of Marx, Engels, and Lenin (mainly the intellectuals), the withering away of the state and of political power, democracy for the greatest number, the reduction of class differences . . .	the strengthening and extension of the state; state-ification of all aspects of social life; omnipresent political power, sometimes taking tyrannical, police, or totalitarian forms; the establishment of clearly differentiated classes . . .

Marx and Engels had warned that "one must not believe straight out what societies say about themselves . . . nor the illusions they create about themselves either" (Marx and Engels [1844] 1947). But they did not foresee that their own writings would serve to elaborate such illusions in class societies calling themselves socialist.

And when the gap is so immense, the opposition so profound between official truth and historical reality, between what the society says about itself and the everyday lived experience of the people, hardly any outlet other than oppression and repression is possible.

It is true that tyranny during Stalin's years in power made political openness exceedingly difficult. Yet, either in the 1920s or during the time of "de-Stalinization," it would not have been shameful to have acknowledged: "We overthrew the old regime; we believed we were carrying out the socialist revolution, but in fact we ran into problems that had been ignored by prior socialist thought; let us, together, analyze these problems, seek solutions, and master the contradictions involved."

In the place of such openness, there appeared the official truth of "socialism being built": the forced march toward collectivization and the creation of a working class; the pressure, oppression, and terror that forced peasants and workers to produce, and that also pressured cadres and managers to get the peasants and workers to produce. Political power on the one hand became concentrated in the hands of a small group and then in the hands of a single man; and on the other hand this power extended itself, branched out, diversified, became more complex: it became power concentrated infinitely. In order to keep its grasp, the established power used police (both official and secret), terror, purges, deportations, trials, censure, daily intimidation, and surveillance.

After all this, the ceremony of de-Stalinization would be laughable if it were not so tragic: Khrushchev reading a secret report, at night, behind closed doors. Laughable, since the crimes and dramas exposed that night, the assassinations, the fixed trials, the torture, the intrigues, the purges, the liquidations, the falsifications, the mass repression, the notion of the "enemy of the people" allowing the physical annihilation of "individuals judged to be undesirable": all these terrible failures to observe the basic rules of a state of law—not to mention of socialism— were explained by two "fundamental" causes: Stalin's brutal character and the cult of personality. Serving as proof here were unadorned arguments relying on authority in the purest Stalinist fashion: Lenin had already denounced Stalin's brutality in 1922 and 1923, and Marx and Engels had already critiqued the tendency to exaggerate the role of individuals (including the role Marx and Engels themselves played).

This was tragically derisory not only for anyone believing in socialism, but for anyone placing confidence in man's intelligence and courage to progress toward a less unjust and oppressive society.

The Soviet ruling class might attempt an exorcism, but they could not hide reality. Were they even capable, though, of analyzing this reality? Were they not enclosed within the logic of power, within relations of compulsion and interpretation that, at their very heart, had formed, developed, and defined this class itself?

There remain two forces able to shatter, or more modestly, to open up, the mantle constricting the state collectivist societies of the East: the critical intellectuals, and the strength of the people.

Through discussions "between friends," with the fear of being listened in on or given away, clandestinely duplicated texts, reviews and publications during the brief "thaw," meetings with foreigners, news passed on by telephone, or texts or books published in the West, some intellectuals have managed to pierce the curtain of prohibition, silence, and taboo. But very quickly the doors reclose: daily persecution or denial of work, arrest, deportation, internment, exclusion from the national community, forced exile.

Still, many problems have been discussed and exposed; the left in Europe and throughout the world has learned of these problems and debated them; and some Communist parties, such as the Italian CP, attacked these problems as issues urgently requiring resolution. No matter how powerful the oppression and how cruel the repression, some individuals have had the courage to seek out the truth and to recapture the freedom to speak.

But without the strength of the people, how might the grip—political, ideological, police—be undermined? The workers have been told that they run the country, that the state is their state and the party their party, and yet they are the ones who have been compelled or incited to produce more and more, who have had to put up with inadequate wages, and deficient housing and food. One day a moment will arrive when the problems facing them will make the gap between the reality and the ideology intolerable any longer: an explosion may break out. The same may occur with students whose ideological training has been based on Marxism-Leninism and who rediscover—if they read, observe, or reflect at all—all of Marxism's critical content. More widely, this may occur with young people and all men and women who keep hoping deep within themselves to live in freedom and dignity. But in the name of what, exactly, might they rise up?

Democracy? But doesn't the USSR have the most democratic Constitution in the world? Socialism then? But is this still possible after sixty years of an oppressive regime calling itself socialist? More fundamentally, isn't there enough discouragement, suspicion, and saturation to defuse any movement attached to a grand ideal? In other words, is not the East totally closed in, since the only forces capable of breaking the enclosure can no longer find inspiration in the powerful ideas that have sustained the great historical movements?

2. "SOCIALIST" STATES AGAINST WORKING CLASSES

And yet, consider what has happened in so many Eastern countries: in the German Democratic Republic, in Hungary, in Czechoslovakia, in Poland, in the USSR itself.

Stalin died on 5 March 1953.

Soviet officials proceeded, especially in the economic domain, with extreme prudence. But in East Germany the leaders decided on and announced at the end of May a 10 percent increase in industrial norms. This measure was criticized by the Soviets, but it was not retracted. On 16 June the construction workers at the Stalin-Allee yards went on strike and demonstrated; the next day all of East Berlin was on strike.

The strikers called for the elimination of productivity minimums, without wage reductions, and for a reduction in the cost of living. The demands rapidly widened to include free elections, the freeing of political prisoners, the dissolution of the police, the resignation of the government ministers, and the elimination of borders between zones.

Soviet tanks occupied East Berlin, but the movement spread to several other cities. The Soviet Army broke the movement, at the cost of three hundred dead, two thousand wounded, and twenty-five thousand arrested.[57]

Fourteen of those arrested in East Berlin were deported to the Soviet camp of Vorkuta, where strike preparation committees had been forming since the end of May. After several weeks of ferment, the strike broke out on 21 July. A tract was distributed:

> Detainees! You have nothing to lose but your chains! Don't wait for a miracle! Don't hope for your liberation from anyone other than yourself! No one will help you, no one will save you; only you can change your fate. Stop working! Our only weapon is the strike! (*Samizdat 1* 1969)

The strike developed and won appreciable concessions; before long, however, the movement was crushed. But a hunger strike took place at Vorkuta in the summer of 1954, and another protest strike broke out in the fall of 1956. Still other strikes occurred at Taïchet at the beginning of 1955 and at Khabarovsk at the end of the same year. With de-Stalinization, a partial dismantling of the camps was decided on in 1956.

At the Twentieth Party Congress, in February 1956, de-Stalinization was launched.

The preceding year, in Poland, production norms had been increased while wages remained low, but the discontent among workers was not heard in high places. After several agitated months, the workers in the locomotive and railroad supplies factory at Poznan— fifteen thousand workers—decided to send a delegation to the minister in Warsaw. This was done on 25 June 1956, but produced no results. On 28 June, all the workers in the factory threw down their tools and formed a procession to the City Hall to demand bread, an increase in wages, and a reduction in prices. On its way the procession grew, becoming a protest march in which new slogans appeared: "Bread and Freedom," "Free Cardinal Wyszynski," "Give us back religion," "Down with the USSR, down with the Soviet occupation," and "Wieslaw, Wieslaw" (see Gallissot, in Droz 1972–78). This last was a reference to Gomulka, whom the demonstrators called by his first name; Gomulka, who, condemned in 1951, had just been freed during the great wave of de-Stalinization, which also pardoned thirty thousand of the least heavily sentenced political prisoners.

The protest swelled; a group penetrated the headquarters of the police and procured weapons there; other groups attacked the courts and the central prison. Polish Army tanks reestablished order the same evening, though at a cost of fifty-four dead, three hundred wounded, and hundreds arrested.

Against a background of intellectual and popular ferment, including the establishment of workers' councils in the factories, Gomulka and other former leaders earlier banished from their posts returned in August to the inner circle of the party. On 19 October a summit discussion took place with the highest Soviet leaders: Khrushchev, Mikoyan, Molotov, Kaganovich, and Marshal Konev, Warsaw commander. Gomulka extracted recognition of the "Polish road toward socialism," but the next day, 20 October, during a long speech in which he both criticized the errors committed by the previous leadership and indicated new possibilities then opening up, Gomulka emphasized that "at the head of the process of democratization stands our party."[58] On 21 October Gomulka once again became first party secretary; soon after Cardinal Wyszynski was freed and a Polish general took the place of the Soviet marshal then in power at the Defense Ministry.

At the same time, but not without interference, a powerful movement was developing in Hungary. By 1953, even before Khrushchev began the process of de-Stalinization, Imre Nagy had begun a policy of reform. This policy was broken off in 1955 and Nagy was replaced by Rákosi. The Petöfi meeting house, created at the end of 1955, became a center for free discussion and debate; on 14 June 1956 more than a thousand persons listened to the philosopher Georg Lukács there. On 19 June Mrs. Rajk asked for the eviction from the government and the party of those responsible for assassinations; on 27 June a debate on freedom of the press took place before six thousand persons.

But the Poznan uprising on 28 June led the authorities to limit freedom of expression. At the same time gestures of appeasement were made: Rákosi was replaced by Gerö; Rajk was rehabilitated with solemn funeral rites; Nagy was brought back into the party. But the political agitation did not calm down, the demonstrations continued, and Soviet troops were required to disperse the crowds. Mikoyan and Suslov arrived from Moscow and attempted to find a solution similar to what had just been negotiated in Poland: Imre Nagy once again became head of the government, and Janos Kadar assumed the post of party chief.

Far from calming down, the demonstrations expanded; hostility to the Communist regime and the USSR deepened: Imre Nagy then announced the formation of a coalition government, the end of censorship, and authorization for previously existing political parties to re-form. Besides this, he denounced the Warsaw Pact and proclaimed Hungary's neutrality.[59]

On 1 November Soviet troops occupied Budapest. Though Imre Nagy issued an appeal to the United Nations, Russian tanks crushed the insurrection: 2,700 dead, 15,000 wounded, and 20,000 in prison. Three hundred thousand persons left their country, which was now controlled by a Soviet Army of 400,000 men. Janos Kadar was installed as head of the government, after which the party was purged: out of a million members, only 100,000 were judged sufficiently trustworthy to be allowed to remain in the party. The Writers' Union was dissolved, its leaders arrested, and censorship reestablished.

On 30 November 1956, at the end of a course in Marxism-Leninism given at the Lomonossov University of Moscow, a student asked the professor:

Lenin rightly declared that the general strike is the weapon of the proletariat, that it can never become the weapon of the bourgeoisie. How is it then that, in a socialist country, that is to say Hungary, a general strike could occur, when it is impossible that it be directed against a worker and peasant government? (*Samizdat 1* 1969)

This marked the beginning of a period of agitation, which the authorities worked to calm down. During one debate another student went so far as to ask

if a similar development might not one day take place here, and if our own workers will not one day rise up, invoking the teachings of Lenin against their now-respectable and bureaucratized exploiters. (*Samizdat 1* 1969)

On 3 December, 150 students were excluded for "hooliganism," and the courses in Marxism-Leninism were suspended. Discussion groups formed: in one of them the idea was put forth of a "socialist revolution against the pseudo-socialist state."

In Leningrad, a similar movement developed: two thousand students were barred from their institutes or faculties. At the beginning of November, at the Kaganovitch factory in Moscow, workers struck for the first time since 1924, and obtained, by striking, some improvement in their working conditions.

We may describe this movement by saying that, following Stalin's death, intellectuals, students, and clear-sighted management-level workers became aware of the intolerable and of the distortion between what existed and what was supposed, officially, to exist. Many people survived by burying themselves in indifference and prudently keeping quiet, though discussions "between friends" became more and more critical and "jokes" exposing this or that defect in society circulated widely, as did texts duplicated on whatever means were at hand.

Journals even appeared: *Literary Moscow* in October 1951; *Kolokol* in Leningrad in November 1956; *Syntaxis*, edited by Alexander Ginzburg, in 1959; *Phoenix 61*, edited by Yuri Galanskov, in 1961. *One Day in the Life of Ivan Denisovitch* was published in *Novy Mir* in 1961.

As this movement developed however, the opposition of intellectuals appeared as a critique that became less and less bearable to the regime. Intimidation and sanctions arose: the cycle of repression began once again. Sinyavsky and Daniel were arrested in 1965 for having published abroad works judged to be anti-Soviet; their trial took place in 1966. Ginzburg, who had distributed in the West the *White Book* concerned with the Sinyavsky and Daniel "affair," was arrested in 1967 along with Galanskov and others. Thus began a frightening series of events:

1968: arrests of Larissa Daniel, Pavel Litvinov, and five other comrades who demonstrated on Red Square against Soviet intervention in Czechoslovakia; arrest and conviction of the worker Martchenko, author of "testimony" about the camps;

1969: arrests of general Grigorenko and of the teacher Gabaï, defenders of the Tatars of Crimea; exclusion from the Writers' Union of Solzhenitsyn, who was eventually expelled from the country in 1974;

1970: arrest and conviction of Andrei Amalrik; internment in a psychiatric hospital of the physicist Zhores Medvedev, who was released after numerous and strong protests by scientists throughout the world;

1971: arrest of Bukovsky, following his appeal against psychiatric internments. . . .

And these arrests and convictions were only the small, visible indications of a repressive, powerful, and diversified system. . . .

In Czechoslovakia, liberalization was limited: Arthur London, freed in July 1955, described the workings of the trial in his book *The Confession*. Other political prisoners were freed, after the Twentieth Congress, in the spring of 1956. With the thaw, more could be expressed and many discussions took place. Novotný held on firmly to power, though he was led in 1962 to abandon the Third Plan, which had just begun. The same year, too, he removed Rudolf Barak from his post as minister of the interior. In 1963 Novotný made concessions to the Slovakian Communists and put into operation certain of the economic reforms proposed by Eugen Loebel and Otto Sik.

But intellectual opposition grew, along with general discontent. Novotný, who wanted to repress the opposition, ceded the position of first party secretary on 5 January 1968 to Alexander Dubcek, a supporter of democratization. Dubcek declared on 1 February:

The party exists for the working people; it should subsist neither above nor outside society, but should be an integrated part of society. Democracy is not only the right and the possibility of expressing one's opinion, but it is also the taking into consideration of such opinions by the governing political powers, the possibility for each person to take a real part in decision making. (Cited in Gallissot, in Droz 1972–78)

Meetings in factories and universities multiplied. Mass organizations and the party cells themselves became sites for free debate.

On 5 March Dubcek announced the end of censorship. The same day five members of the Warsaw Pact meeting in Dresden addressed a warning to the Czech Communists. Still the movement inside Czechoslovakia continued to develop. Novotný, who had remained president of the Republic, was replaced in this post by General Svoboda who, in an initial symbolic gesture, kneeled before the tombs of Masaryk and Beneš. In its program for action, made public on 6 April, the Communist party announced: "We want to commit ourselves to the construction of a new model of socialist society that will be deeply democratic and adapted to Czechoslovakian conditions." Novotný was excluded from the Central Committee and then suspended from the party. A new government was then formed, calling for economic reforms, an increased role for the market, freedom of expression, management councils in the largest production operations, rehabilitation of formerly convicted political offenders, and freedom of the press. A great number of critiques, statements of opposition, and fundamental questions and proposals appeared, culminating in a two-thousand-word manifesto signed by seventy well-known figures, which assured the government "that everyone will support the government, even by force of arms, so long as it does what it is mandated to do."

Pressure from the Warsaw Pact, whose maneuvers were extended through the summer, did not change the line chosen by Dubcek and his government. In addition, Prague warmly welcomed Tito and then Ceauşescu, who symbolized independence and the existence of national roads toward socialism. In the night of 20–21 August, Soviet troops, along with several contingents of the Warsaw Pact, invaded Czechoslovakia: 600,000 men occupied the country, and despite the passive resistance of the country and of a large majority of the party, normalization was imposed. This meant a widespread purge in the army, the news media, and the universities and among public officials, cultural figures, and the unions. There were dismissals from the party, which was purged of 20 percent of its members, a gradual exclusion of Dubcek, elimination of many newspapers, censorship. . . .

This Soviet intervention brought to light serious differences within the international Communist movement. Once again hopes had been stifled.

Citing Marx—"A people who subjugate another people forge their own chains"—Radio Free Prague broadcast on 25 August 1968: "A people who impose their will on another people through force of arms do a disservice, a terrible disservice, to the cause of socialism and Communism" (cited in Bobowicz 1973). And one year later sixteen Soviet citizens published a declaration:

> The entire world followed with hope the development of the "post-January policies" in Czechoslovakia. The tanks of the Warsaw Pact have destroyed this hope. . . . We are not in agreement with a decision that threatens the future of socialism. We stand in solidarity with the people of Czechoslovakia, who wanted to prove that socialism with a human face is possible. (*Samizdat 1* 1969)

In Poland, the process of liberalization that was begun when Gomulka returned was rapidly reined in, and essentially abandoned. The student demonstrations of March 1968 were suppressed. But price increases and then increases in production norms rekindled worker discontent. In December 1970 a new chain of events began; strikes broke out in the shipyards and steel mills of the principal Baltic ports: Gdansk, Gdynia, Szczecin, Sopot. There were protests, repression, and a strengthening of worker discontent and action. On 19 December Edward Gierek replaced Gomulka. The new measures taken—a mixture of concessions and repression—revealed themselves to be insufficient, and on 24 January 1971 the first party secretary, Gierek, the prime minister, the defense minister, and the interior minister all came to the Warski yards at Szczecin to discuss strikers' demands. Just as Gomulka had done fifteen years earlier, Gierek blamed bad management by the former leaders and announced a new direction. And, like Gomulka before him, he also emphasized the fundamental importance of democracy:

> The unbreakable rule of our political economy and our policies in general must always be to take social realities into account, to confer in depth with the working class and the intelligentsia, to respect the principle of collegiality and democracy in the life of the party and in the actions of the highest authorities. Recent events have unfortunately reminded us of this fundamental truth that the party must always maintain tight links with the working class and the entire nation, and that it should not lose contact with the workers. (Gierek 1970)

Is this not—we repeat once again—a striking sign: the leader of a Communist party emphasizes that the party, the party of the working class, should maintain close contact . . . with the working class!

Soon—humor helping to make the situation bearable—this joke was circulating in Poland: "What is the difference between Gierek and Gomulka? None, but Gierek doesn't know it yet."

Gierek held on to power for nearly ten years. But the deeply rooted forces at work within the state-collectivist societies brought about his fall. These forces included the opposition of the working world and of intellectuals confronting the new ruling class, composed of the upper— as well as the middle—techno-bureoisie, who ruled both party and state. In addition there were difficulties with supplies and provisioning: dissatisfaction with everyday affairs served as a detonator once a certain threshold was reached. Finally, there were the ideas underlying the mass movement: religious faith, national feelings, hopes for democracy. All these were present in the groundswell that developed in Poland in 1980.

In September 1980 Gierek was replaced by Stanislaw Kania, who declared soon afterwards: "The process of change [is] . . . irreversible in its very essence." He went so far as to declare that the party

> gave its support to the new [independent] unions, because a segment of the working class considers that they constitute a guarantee against a repetition of past errors and because the unions' founders have declared that they are situated in line with the fundamental principles of socialism. (Kania 1980)

The changes that have begun are certainly important, particularly Solidarity's development as a trade union movement not controlled by the party. In the summer of 1981, three outcomes appear possible:

1. that the movement will once again be broken through armed force;
2. that it will develop and bring about a dismantling of the collectivist system; or
3. that it will contribute—as the trade-union movement in the capitalist countries has done since the end of the nineteenth century—to the transformation of the collectivist system, and to the establishment of a "social compromise" more advantageous to the working world.

The group of events as a whole that we have just outlined—far too hurriedly—brings to light a fundamental reality: the state-collectivist societies are class societies, in which the ruling class—the state techno-bureoisie—imposes the effort of producing on the working class and the peasantry. The working classes and, along with them, the peasants, students, and intellectuals, learn or relearn to defend themselves, to regain their rights, to limit the extraction of surplus labor. This they do under conditions that are at once difficult and contradictory; difficult, because of the huge arsenal of organizational, oppressive, and repressive forces available, first from national sources of domination and then from Soviet domination, in case this latter is required to strengthen the national forces; contradictory, because of the reference to socialism, to "the state of the working class," which can act, depending on individual circumstances, either as a restraint or as a detonator.

For it is obvious that the workers—who hear that they are the rulers of the country and who learn, especially in the party schools, that the working class is supposed to have the role of ruling and managing; who have to put up with the persecution or commands of managerial workers whose competence is not always evident; who suffer the consequences of high-level errors or, more generally, of inefficiency that no one is able to correct—these workers end up rediscovering the actions and language of the workers' movement.

And for the ruling class, which—according to the official texts— draws its legitimacy from the working world, the strikes and the workers' movements can not be dealt with in a purely repressive manner. Vladimir Borissov, founder of the Free Interprofessional Workers' Association (SMOT), explained this following his expulsion from the USSR:

> The Soviet authorities are enormously afraid of organized workers' movements. In general, the authorities give in to them immediately, and when the movement has broad support, often a member of the Political Committee will come at once to the scene to satisfy their demands, and he will stay however long it takes for the movement to cease. Afterwards everything again becomes as it was before, and when the general movement has passed, they begin to strike at the organizers, who are arrested or fired, and since it is illegal not to work, these two amount to the same thing! (Borissov 1980)

Out of such a situation grows the reality of a certain compromise— within which the guaranteed "social protection" of the collectivist countries is certainly a part—which is nonetheless not without tension between ruling classes and the working world.

Alexander Zinoviev, "authorized" to leave the USSR in 1977, saw this compromise as solidly and lastingly established:

> The current regime has grown up naturally and is not the result of violence on the part of a group of criminals. What other regime could offer this population, in return for so little work, the security it enjoys, however minimal this may be? (Zinoviev 1978)

On the other hand, Andre Sinyavsky, in exile in France since 1973, emphasized the tensions: "The Soviet structure is like a bag, filled with sand, which stays upright only because it is tightly tied. If you pierce it, everything falls apart, everything turns into dust" (Sinyavsky 1979).

In any case, once one admits the existence of a class society, within which significant contradictions develop between the ruling class and the producing classes, and where the ruling class draws a large degree of its legitimacy from a politico-ideological construction which teaches that these contradictions are not supposed to exist, then history and analysis demonstrate that three directions for change are possible.

1. A popular movement may develop that overturns the regime and ruling class in place; this may lead either toward capitalism or toward a socialism in which the twin problems of power and production are resolved democratically and collectively.

2. A new "national compromise" may be established between the ruling class and the producing classes on the basis of concessions on living standards and conditions, work intensity and conditions, democracy, and freedoms. In some ways, this would imply the institution of a "social collectivism" comparable in many ways to "social capitalism."

3. Lacking such a compromise, the ruling class may use other bases to form a consensus: nationalism, chauvinism, racism, bellicosity, expansionism, the feeling of encirclement or of the bastion under siege. And if this consensus is unobtainable, there remain repression, the police system, the pressure of armed forces, and, as a last resort, the Red Army.

The possible directions for evolution of the USSR and the countries in the East are found within this "triangle." At the moment the capitalist world is plunged into a third world crisis. The two previous crises led, each in its own way, to major wars. It would be dangerous if the Soviet ruling class were able to resolidify national cohesion solely through planning for war.

3. IN THE WEST, THE LOGIC OF COMPROMISE

In the developed capitalist countries—or, put in other terms, in the industrialized countries of the West—the workers' and socialist movements appear in two ways.

In the countries where the Social Democratic movement is powerful and where, for one reason or another, the Communist party is not very influential (Great Britain, the Scandinavian countries, and, since World War II, West Germany), the "national compromise" has been explicitly taken up by the party and the workers' unions: one can then in this case speak of the "Social Democratic compromise."

In the countries where the workers' movement is divided, the parties and the unions linked to democratic socialism are often weakened by internal divisions and are criticized and "outbid" by the stronger rhetoric of the Communist parties. In these countries, for example France and Italy, the Democratic Socialist parties and unions are not, as a whole, in a position to assume an explicit strategy of compromise, in the sense we are using the word here. Yet a certain compromise has taken place nonetheless, aided by the fact that, following the division at Yalta, Communist groups have renounced openly revolutionary programs. But such a compromise, established piecemeal through a series of unconnected and uncoordinated movements, has not been explicitly taken up and assumed by the workers' movement.

After the war—that is, for the countries occupied at the time of the Liberation—the workers' movement occupied a position of strength and was able to forge new advances within the compromise.

In its 1945 program, the Swedish Social Democrat party reaffirmed the principle of socialization. Similarly, in their 1944 program, "Facing the Future," the British Labourites drew widely from the ideas that the liberal Beveridge had used to deal with the crisis and the war. They called for a broad extension of social services, the control of the major banks' activities, and for significant nationalizations (the Bank of England, coal, gas, electricity, road and rail transport, steel making). In the same way, in West Germany, when the Social Democratic party was re-formed, its program called for the socialization of heavy industry and for the democratic control of the other branches of the economy.

The victory in Britain by Labour in the 1945 elections led, with the widespread application of their program, to the establishment of the welfare state: on the whole the nationalizations were carried out, though not without difficulty regarding road transport and the steel industry; the 1927 law limiting the exercise of union rights and the right to strike was curtailed; an important system of national insurances (unemployment, sickness, accident, retirement, protection for widows and orphans) was put into place; a national health system guaranteeing free medical care for poor and rich was instituted; a broad construction program for transforming unhealthy and unsafe regions was begun; and the largest fortunes were submitted to progressive taxation and to increased estate duties.

At the same time in France, the program of profound social transformations elaborated during the Resistance was for the most part put into effect: the nationalization of the mines, then of energy and credit sources, civil aviation, some of the merchant marine, Renault, Gnome and Rhône, four deposit banks, thirty-two insurance companies, and finally the Bank of France. A national plan for social security and family allowances, with democratic management, was instituted, along with national planning and committees within businesses.

Thus, in both Great Britain and France, in different contexts and on different bases, the workers' movement made significant gains; within this framework the trade unions and the organizations of the workers' movement, including the Communist party and the General Confederation of Workers (CGT), supported the working class in the productive effort. In both cases, if one may so express it, the national compromise made it possible both to start up the capitalist economy again and to make further social gains.

But very quickly, the situation stabilized. In each country, the popular movement ran out of energy and enthusiasm flagged while the ruling classes re-formed their alliances and their networks of power. Besides this, the hardening of the confrontation between the United States and the Soviet Union was felt in the breakup of alliances, including those that the Communist parties had formed in the West, and the departure from governments of Communist ministers. In France the French Section of the Workers' International (SFIO) was induced to compromise first with the center and then with the right. Governments with socialist participation, even with socialist leadership, used armed force to break strikes just as they used armed repression against the initial uprisings in the countries subject to colonial domination. In Great Britain, the Labour party lost government power in 1950.

In 1948 the Socialist International had excluded "the parties wanting to belong to our socialist confederation, while at the same time in fact obeying Moscow's instructions"; this same International, in 1951 at Frankfurt, adopted a new program:

> Socialism is an international movement not requiring strict conceptual uniformity; whether socialists base their convictions on Marxism or on other methods for analyzing society, and whether they are motivated by religious or humanitarian principles, still socialists struggle toward the same goal: a system assuring social justice, a better life, personal freedom, and universal peace.

Even if socialist forces were in retreat, the "national compromises" were not fundamentally called into question, and this for two reasons:

> • on the one hand because the ruling classes of the leading capitalist countries understood that the benefits to be drawn from the consensus engendered by the compromise far outweighed the burden of any concessions granted;
> • and on the other hand, because these very compromises, by developing mass consumption—housing and housing materials, automobile and highway equipment, material for public facilities and operations—contributed significantly to maintaining the strongest and longest-lasting period of growth ever known by the capitalist

world. Such growth then made whatever concessions were granted more "bearable" (see Beaud [1981] 1983a, 185–229).

Within this framework, not only was the compromise not fundamentally brought into question, but in fact the working world and the common people obtained new benefits even during the periods when the right or the right-center held government power. Real wages rose, mass consumption of durable goods (automobiles, household appliances, radios, and then televisions, and so on) expanded, working hours were reduced while paid vacation time increased, and in many cases workers' rights within businesses increased.

There was a twin basis to this expansion of gains by the working world within the "national compromises" of the principal capitalist countries as a whole.

First, there was vigorous economic growth, itself made possible by significant productivity increases: worldwide industrial growth was extremely rapid between 1948 and 1971, averaging 5.6 percent per year. This was clearly greater than any growth rates previously realized during expansionary periods, such as 1900–1913 (4.2 percent), and 1938–1948 (4.1 percent). During the period 1948–1971 labor productivity rose by more than 8 percent per year in Japan, by nearly 5 percent per year in West Germany and in France, by 2.3 percent per year in Great Britain, and by 1.5 percent per year in the United States. Behind these figures one must read an intensification of productivity demands, an increase in the pressure to produce greater quantities of goods: the acceleration of work rhythms, the extension of assembly-line work, work in production groups, and more generally, an increased application of Taylorism and Fordism.

Second, this period, though marked by the great wave of decolonization, remains distinguished by the main capitalist countries' economic domination on a world scale. This domination was manifest in the profits drawn from the preservation of a system of unequal relations. The inequality of the system as a whole increased with each improvement, for the industrialized countries, of the terms of exchange. Such domination could be seen also in directly measurable profits: for example, in the case of the United States, income from foreign investments and royalties or licenses represented more than one hundred billion dollars for the period 1950–1970.

Thus, the "national compromises" were extended and strengthened both from the effort demanded of the producing classes within the nation (the working class and the peasantry) and from the effort imposed on the producing classes of the dominated countries. These compromises took in not only large sections of the working classes, but also significant parts of the wage earners who were not manual workers. Importantly, the compromises placed the trade-union and socialist movements in a fundamentally untenable position regarding the traditional anticapitalist attitude, since maintaining the benefits that had been yielded up to that point depended on the smooth functioning and even the expansion of capitalism. Within this context, organizations of the workers' movement were induced to assume quite explicitly the "social compromise" by expanding it beyond the working class to include the working world as a whole, which at the time was thoroughly diversifying.

The Swedish Socialist party remained within the line of thinking and practice begun in the 1930s by consolidating their system based simultaneously on the welfare state and on negotiations between employers' organizations and workers' unions. Without breaking from their earlier positions, they declared in 1960: "The welfare state follows the society of mass poverty, insecurity, and intense class contradictions"; still, "in the welfare state certain originally capitalist characteristics, such as inequality or authoritarianism, remain" (cited by Buci-Glucksmann and Therborn 1981).

The British Labourites—except for a left wing that preserved its critical stance—placed themselves within the same perspective. For example, C. A. R. Crosland, examining the "composite society" that "in Great Britain at least is in the process of taking the place of capitalism," declared in 1952:

> Most of the causes of unbearable social tension which so distressed socialism are bound to disappear; we will never again see . . . the humiliation of unemployment or hunger marches. The range and the bitterness of social conflicts have been considerably reduced. (Crosland 1952)

And Harold Wilson was able to write:

> Currently political conflict has to do less with rival programs than with the measures able to guarantee an increase in production; such production increases are the only adequate way to support the social spending program without falling into inflation. (Wilson 1961)

And it is true that the Conservatives in power from 1950 to 1964 did not fundamentally question—except in the case of denationalizing the steel industry—the postwar "social compromise." For its part, Labour, which returned to power from 1964 to 1970, managed to advance the compromise only slightly.

In West Germany the Social Democratic party, after witnessing a decline in its membership following the death in 1952 of Kurt

Schumacher, the man who had helped reconstruct the party, adopted a compromise program in 1959 at Bad Godesberg. The program contained a reaffirmation of how essential democracy is to socialism: "Socialism can be realized only through democracy, and democracy can be given meaning only through socialism." There was also a certain fundamental questioning of capitalism:

> The interest of the whole should prevail over individual interest. In an economy and a society dominated by the search for profit and the hunger for power, democracy, social security, and the free flowering of the personality are all threatened. This is why democratic socialism aims at establishing a new economic and social order.

But at the same time,

> the ownership of the means of production deserves protection and encouragement, insofar as this ownership does not hinder the institution of an equitable social order. Efficient small and middle-size businesses deserve consolidation in order to stand up to large companies.

In brief: "competition as much as possible, planning as much as necessary."

The Social Democrats took on governmental responsibilities in 1966 within the framework of a "grand coalition" with the Christian Democrats, and in 1969 in an alliance with the liberals.

In France, while one may interpret the 1972 Common Program of the Left signed between the Socialist and Communist parties as a program of "rupture with capitalism," one may also interpret it as taking place within the perspective of 1960s growth and as directed toward defining, inside this framework, the bases for a new compromise within capitalist society, a compromise to be manifest in new advances for the working class, the working world as a whole, and the common people.

Whether expressed in the Social Democratic form or in other forms, the compromise established in the decade of the 1950s in the principal capitalist countries confronted, in the 1960s, limits inherent to certain basic elements of the compromise itself. On the one hand, the increase in production speeds and intensities could not be indefinitely prolonged: there were protests against "hellish production rates," strikes, absenteeism, increased turnover, control by the workers of production rates. . . . On the other hand, the countries of the Third World, once they won their political independence, disputed the dividing-up of value on a world scale: the two increases in the price of oil symbolized, for a strategically valuable product, a fundamental demand whose consequences are still far from having fully unfolded.

In a process similar to what occurred in Great Britain after the First World War, the ruling classes sought, particularly in France with

Giscard d'Estaing and Barre, in Great Britain with Margaret Thatcher, and in the United States with Ronald Reagan, to go back on concessions formerly made to the working world and to exert pressure on workers' buying power both through unemployment and through the inflationary game.

For the Social Democratic leaders exercising governmental responsibilities, the situation is delicate. Olaf Palme, during a discussion with Bruno Kreisky and Willy Brandt in Vienna in 1975, observed:

> We who are socialists live to a certain degree in symbiosis with capitalism. The workers' movement was conceived as a response to capitalism. . . . But in certain respects we have wanted the same things as capitalism. . . . The current crisis of capitalism is at the same time a crisis of industrial society. It is our task to rescue this society.

Bruno Kreisky:

> This is what was being said already in the 1930s. . . . Capitalism was incapable of resolving the problems of industrial society; Social Democracy was then to undertake their resolution. (Brandt, Kreisky, and Palme 1975)

The Social Democrats lost the elections in 1976 in Sweden and retained power in West Germany only by applying policies accompanying or favoring the restructuring of German capitalism then required by the crisis: the acceptance of a large increase in unemployment, the departure of immigrant workers, and pressure upon the buying power of the working world.

Social democracy—and more generally, the Western workers' movement as a whole—has staked nearly all its hopes on the strategy of the "national compromise," within the framework of an economy dominated by capitalist logic. Such a strategy has meant being caught in a trap: social democracy itself has been forced to seek means for reestablishing the "smooth functioning" of capitalism itself. Though this could possibly be done through negotiating a "new compromise," there are considerable obstacles to such a development. Two of them have to do with the international dimension of the problem.

• On the one hand, the national employers, at least their most concentrated and modern sections, have surpassed the national framework. These employers are in a position to act on a global scale and within a wide range of national situations.

• On the other hand, the countries of the Third World have demanded a new international order, while the ruling classes hope for a quite different division of wealth. Policies for industrialization are being instituted that involve changes in the international division of labor.

From now on, the "national compromises" are for the most part outmoded:

a "new compromise" must be elaborated on an international scale. In the world-wide discussion that, as best it can, struggles to take place, three categories of speakers are in a position to make themselves heard:

- the ruling classes of the developed capitalist countries;
- the ruling classes of the Third World;
- the organizations of the workers' movements in the developed countries.

Within this framework, the workers' movements in the developed countries face the following choice.

1. They can ally themselves with the regrouping set up—around powerful U.S. interests—by those segments of the employers in the principal capitalist countries who have chosen internationalization, and by the most authoritarian regimes of the Third World. Through such an alliance they may obtain a few crumbs, but only at the price of accepting the super-exploitation of workers in certain zones of the Third World. This would mean breaking the solidarity so often proclaimed between workers in the developed world and the peoples of the Third World.

2. Or else they can accept the perspective of a "compromise on a world level," a compromise that would take into consideration the interests of the ruling classes and the interests of the working world, not only in the industrialized capitalist countries, but also in a certain number of Third-World countries: newly industrialized countries, countries producing raw materials, less-advanced countries. Such a compromise has no chance to be carried out except within an expanding economy: lacking a "socialist road" for development and taking into account the limits that state collectivism encounters, it is capitalism's development on a world scale that appears most able to provide this expansion.

It is largely within this perspective that the Independent Commission on Problems of International Development, the Brandt Commission, elaborated its findings:

> It would be dishonest to cover up the differences of opinion and the conflicts of interest. But . . . in the middle as well as in the long term, North and South have more interests in common than is generally supposed. And experience shows that often lasting solutions are found once confrontation has ceased. . . . *Material* interests increasingly exist, interests that require a change in the character of cooperation. We now know that a stepped-up development of the South serves the populations of the North as well. (Brandt 1980)

Arguing in the same direction, for a planetary New Deal, Keynesianism on a world scale, Claude Cheysson, a member of the European Commission, elaborated the economic argument:

New investment of one hundred billion francs in the Third World would bring about nearly a one-percentage-point increase in growth in the industrialized countries—and we know the economic, social, and political importance of a percentage-point increase in growth. (Cheysson 1981a)

As minister of foreign relations he affirmed before the Commission of Ministers of the OCDE (Organisation de Coopération et de Développement Économique) that

the institution of a voluntarist policy, inspired by Keynesianism on a world scale, would greatly help our economies to emerge from the current troubling crisis. . . . The economies of the Third World contain tremendous potential for growth which should be developed, just as in the nineteenth century the potential was developed of the poorest strata of the populations in the industrialized countries. (Cheysson 1981b)

This movement is taking place within the current situation, and whether it is under the capitalist form or the state-collectivist form, the economies of many countries in the Third World are beginning to experience and will continue to experience significant growth in coming decades.

The paradox however is not insignificant.

Out of the spiritual nobility contained within the great variety of nineteenth-century socialist thinking, out of the impassioned battles against capitalist oppression and exploitation, social democracy arose in some places and state collectivism in others.

State collectivism has become the economic base for a new class society. Where capitalism has not yet attempted or succeeded in carrying out such steps, state collectivism has permitted the establishment of the foundations for industry, the creation of a working class, and the emplacement of mechanisms for accumulation relying upon state initiative. But at a certain point state collectivism comes up against inextricable economic difficulties, and beyond this point it encounters the aspirations of those in the working world and among intellectuals and young people: those who remain sensitive to the ideals of democracy and socialism.

Social democracy, thanks to the balance of forces that it established in relation to the ruling classes, incontestably permitted the working classes and the working world at the end of the nineteenth century to win substantial benefits and significant gains. By persisting along this road, social democracy contributed to the workers' obtaining new benefits during the 1930s and in the postwar period of prosperity. But at the same time social democracy helped create the conditions for a smoother functioning of capitalism and for a strengthening of the solidarity linking employers to the working world within capitalism itself. And while the working world has placed its confidence in the European social democracies, these social democracies, in order to safeguard the fundamental gains of the working world, are today forced to seek conditions that will provide smoother functioning for European capitalisms, and this involves the growth—either capitalist or state collectivist—of economies in the Third World.

The "national compromises" depended on capitalism's smooth functioning. A possible "world compromise" involves the development of capitalism on a world scale. Could such a compromise in fact take into consideration the interests of those who are least able to make themselves heard: the peoples and the producing classes of the Third World?

COMMENTS ON CHAPTER 9

The period following World War II has been unusual.

Never have references to socialism been so widespread: socialist revolutions in China, in Vietnam, in Cuba; references to socialism in Asia and in Africa when new nations gained independence and in Latin America when dictatorships were overthrown; the creation of popular democracies, and then the establishment of "socialist" regimes following the Soviet model in Eastern Europe; participation by socialists and by Social Democrats in governments of West European capitalist countries.

But at the same time, the socialist idea appears to have been diluted, to have been shattered, and sometimes to have been falsified.

Now on one side, of course, there is the Marxist-Leninist-Stalinist dogma.

1. The working class is the main force capable of overthrowing capitalism; the working class may accomplish this in alliance with the indigent peasantry, an alliance that the working class should lead.

2. At the forefront of combat there should be an organized and disciplined vanguard: the Communist party, the party of the working class, leader of struggle and revolution.

3. Since socialism is, in its main points, being constructed in the USSR, the USSR is simultaneously the leader of the world socialist revolution and the principal ally of Communist parties, and thus of working classes and revolutionary forces in each country.

This has been—and remains still— a sufficiently powerful and coherent dogma to be accepted by millions of militants throughout the world. Yet, in the eyes of many people, this dogma is cracking apart.

1. In most wars of liberation and anti-imperialist revolution, most

visibly the Chinese Revolution, it has been the peasant masses who have played a determining role.

2. In the revolutionary struggles carried out in Latin America and in the African independence movements, the Communist parties have not always been at the forefront of combat. This was demonstrated in Algeria and Cuba, among other places.

3. Tito's Yugoslavia early on rejected the leading role of the USSR. Later, China criticized the new orientation chosen by the USSR and accused the USSR of taking a road that would restore capitalism. And the USSR, in the name of socialism, dispatched its tanks against the workers of East Germany and then against popular movements in Hungary and Czechoslovakia, all the while keeping a watchful eye over the progress of the workers' and popular movement in Poland.

During this same period came the revelations about the gulag, about the purges, the rigged trials, mass repression, and oppression against opposition intellectuals, workers, and students. Is socialism, then, the gulag? Is it oppression?

In Cambodia the leaders extolled and then instituted, in the name of socialism, mass liquidations. In Afghanistan a similar process has begun. Is the decimation of a people by its own leaders, then, socialist?

Discord between the USSR and China rose to the point of threatening war. War actually broke out between China and Vietnam, ally of the USSR. Vietnamese troops invaded Cambodia . . . in order to avoid something worse. The same pretext was used for the occupation of Afghanistan by Soviet troops. Is war, then, socialist? Is the oppression of one people by another socialist?

Intellectuals and students criticized—some in the name of socialism and democracy—the entrenched system. Workers rose up, went out on strike occasionally, and in some cases rediscovered the great tradition of the Western workers' movement. When the yoke becomes intolerable, people move in the depths and rise up. Is there, then, socialist domination? Socialist exploitation?

Throughout the Third World, the flowering of socialisms in the period centered around the 1960s quickly sank back into military or authoritarian regimes, chaos, a capitalism dominated by the world market, or state collectivism. Is socialism, then, inefficient, illusory?

Finally, in the capitalist countries, the workers' movements, the socialist and Social Democratic forces, worked to broaden the gains won through the "national compromises." They largely succeeded in accomplishing this during the period of exceptional growth following the war. Governments with Communist and Socialist ministers in the immediate postwar period and with Socialist ministers in the next period forcibly put down liberation movements in colonized countries. And now, during the current crisis, the "national compromises" in the dominant capitalist countries can be maintained only on the basis of strong growth—whether capitalist or state collectivist—throughout the Third World. Is socialism, then, corrupt, compromised by capitalism?

Never has socialism been so powerful, so proclaimed throughout the world. But never has it been so controversial, so contested, criticized, and doubted, even by those who might expect socialism to provide their liberation, even by those who might have wanted to place their hopes in socialism. Never have the upholders of one form of socialism, the inheritors of one socialist tradition, been so hostile, so opposed to those in another tradition, who nonetheless also define themselves as socialists.

Sad, terrible winter of socialism.

10

SOCIALISM AS PROJECT

At the conclusion of works similar to this one, the convention is to pull from the hat of the analyst-magician *the* socialist truth, *the* road toward socialism, *the* model. This process involves, of course, condemnation of all other points of view and excommunication of those who hold them. Sometimes extenuating circumstances are mentioned, hypotheses are tested, and there may be, as an added bonus, the feeling of having helped rekindle enthusiasm.

During the recent "winter of socialism," some authors have broken with this "convention": socialism was a great and beautiful illusion of the nineteenth century; it had some grand moments and led to some lamentable errors. The proletariat, if it ever existed, did not expand as predicted; the working class has lost cohesion while increasing in numbers; capitalism itself has been surpassed: thus, socialism, too, belongs to the past.[60]

Our purpose is both more modest and more nuanced, and so is more contradictory and more complex.

On the basis of a balance sheet of accomplishments, advances, impasses, and diversions, our purpose is to *discover what resources and what forces might help—throughout the world in the closing years of the twentieth century—the conscious and collective reconstruction of the socialist project.*

1. THE HOPE AND THE ILLUSIONS

There has been utopianism, hope, enthusiasm, devotion, and an immeasurable commitment to socialism. There has been courage at the barricades, during strikes, and throughout everyday action. There have also been martyrs, shattered futures, and the individuals who have been sacrificed, mutilated, and crushed. These alone prevent one from speaking of the death of socialism, for does not this enumeration demonstrate

191

that socialism is still present and living in the collective memory, in the social consciousness, in the victories whose fruits we still enjoy, in our way of conceiving the future?

For this is *the heart of the socialist movement*: the fact that men and women, at first a few dozen, then thousands and finally millions, came to conceive of a future society that would be *other* than the society in which they had been formed and lived. In a world characterized by oppression and exploitation and in which the weakest members were crushed, intellectuals, producers, and common people *conceived the possibility of another world—free, interdependent, and equitable—and began to fight for this new world*.

This is the fundamental and vital point. Socialism has been the flag brandished during this fight, a fight that will continue on for a long time to come. Admittedly, this society of freedom and happiness has nowhere yet been achieved; still, in many places and in many different forms, steps have been made toward such a society. Certainly there have been defeats, errors, and false paths, but should these force us to drop the socialist flag? Suddenly to pick up a new flag—be it that of self-management or political ecology or liberation—will eliminate neither the obstacles nor the causes of errors and false paths. It is better to try to focus on these obstacles and causes.

We note that it is pointless to dwell on utopia and the utopians. Outside of a few individual misadventures and episodes of bitter disillusionment, they have caused barely any harm.

Much more serious has been Marx's "historical messianism"; the belief—which for a long time many people took as having been proved—that

- a "historical messiah" has arrived: the proletariat, which will free human societies from all oppressions;
- capitalism, in developing, will also develop its own negation: the proletariat, which, by overthrowing the regime of the bourgeoisie, will put an end to the last class society; and
- thus the era of socialism will ineluctably open, to be followed by communism.

And beliefs are terrible when they are reduced to certitudes of catechism and when this becomes, as it did with Stalin, state catechism.

Let us say it again, since it is still necessary: the analysis of capitalism that Marx produced was powerful, and it allowed him to understand the major lines of capitalism's evolution. By proclaiming how socialism would be born out of the ruins of capitalism, no doubt Marx was trying to infuse greater life into the workers' and socialist movement. But he also prepared the way for some awful developments, because

• capitalism in developing, in fact, first developed a working class and then developed low- and middle-level "techno-bureoisies," without at all destroying all the petty and middle bourgeoisies;

• it has, thus, been complex societies that have developed with capitalism, in the midst of which the dominant bourgeoisie has retained power for a very long time by manipulating alliances and by accepting "national compromises" with the working classes and then, more generally, with the working world;

• beyond this, the overthrow of capitalism—embryonic capitalism in Russia in 1917 as much as present-day developed capitalism—far from giving rise to a classless society, has led, rather, to a new class society, "state-collectivist society" dominated by what we call a "state techno-bureoisie."

Thus, in the name of socialism, another, new, class society has appeared and developed.

Important consequences have flowed from the fact of accepting that there exists a lasting break between objective and means, between the goal of a liberated society and the minority-led and authoritarian approach: Saint-Simon's leadership by technicians, Blanqui's insurrection, and ultimately Lenin's domination by a conscious vanguard.

Within such a framework the opposition reform/revolution has caused false splits and a squandering of strength and energy. On the one hand, who can deny that insurrection, the uprising of an oppressed people, revolution, may be necessary to overthrow tyrannical power, a dictatorship detested and rejected by an entire people? But on the other hand, who can deny that a long series of reforms, gains, and advances is necessary—whether or not a revolution has taken place—in order to transform a society to its core? In this regard, the conviction that the collective appropriation of the means of production will satisfy all needs has caused immense damage.

For if the private appropriation of the means of production and of the surplus value resulting from this production is a central characteristic of capitalism, what is at capitalism's heart is the relation of domination existing between a dominant class, the bourgeoisie, and an exploited class, the working class; it is the compulsion to produce *more*, to clear a surplus, the compulsion to surplus labor imposed by the bourgeoisie upon the working class. But the socialist movement has not thought out the question of production once capitalism is overthrown, or else it has thought it out only in terms that are vague and in many respects utopian, such as "freely associated producers." Were not the rich to make "restitution" for their ill-gotten gains? Wasn't abundance to reign? Well, no, reality has revealed itself to be not that simple; the minority that swept to power found it necessary to impose upon the peasants and workers norms, constraints, incitements, and sanctions. The minority in power has had to refind or reinvent means to force increased production, to clear a surplus. In other words, this minority has had to re-form itself into a dominating class that compels the producing classes to surplus labor. This was the chain of forces leading to state collectivism, a new class society, developing alongside capitalism and likely to outlast it.

Beliefs, illusions, errors. . . . Let us now take up the positive side of these negative reflections.

1. If capitalism is not the last class society and if the coming of socialism is not inevitable, then we must *take up socialism as a project*. Against certain possible futures—shattered societies, powerful and inegalitarian domination, modern tyrannies—the socialist movement proposes the consciously developed project of a democratic, equitable, and closely knit society.

2. If the proletariat is not the force whose development will ineluctably overthrow capitalism, then it is necessary to examine each situation in order to identify the forces capable—taking into account the condition of the society—of undertaking a step toward socialism: peasants and exploited workers, intellectuals, young people, women, elements of the middle classes, etc.

3. If it was wrong to believe that domination by a vanguard could lead to the liberation of the masses, and if in addition it was wrong to let the notion of the "(democratic) dictatorship of the proletariat" increasingly cover up dictatorship over the producing classes and the people as a whole, then it becomes necessary to accept, broaden, and deepen the democratic approach to socialism. In all organizations claiming to be socialist, in the countries choosing the socialist road, free debate, information, rights, and liberties should permanently prevail, along with a real possibility for the majority of the people to choose their destiny and to control and sanction those who carry out these choices. Only a democratic approach will allow progress toward a democratic society, and thus toward socialism.

4. If the problem of production has been neglected and if this neglect has indeed formed the basis of two disappointing avatars of socialism—in the West, accepting capitalism's efficiency while negotiating at the same time the most favorable compromise possible for the working world; elsewhere, the invention of an ersatz capitalism on a statist base, which imitates many of capitalism's methods, though with less capacity for initiative and adaptation—then we must no longer seek an easy way out of this impasse, for progress toward socialism here runs into a sizeable problem.

For a long time into the future, there will be jobs that are dangerous, unhealthy, nerve-wracking: in a word, jobs that are neither pleasant nor fulfilling to carry out. And for a long time yet, a minority—under forms that are more or less democratic, more or less dictatorial, centralized, or decentralized—will exercise the tasks of leadership, decision, coordination, and repression. This is a fundamental problem whose solution will be the key element of a new step toward socialism.

After a century, a century-and-a-half of historical experience to look back on, we are able to sort out the illusions from the hopes: *the illusion of the proletariat-messiah; the illusion of "capitalism as the last class society"; the illusion of "work carried out in joy" once the means of production are collectivized.*

We must reject the illusions, but maintain and strengthen the hope.

2. THE GAINS AND THE IMPASSE

Socialism—a free, just, and happy society—has nowhere been realized; no society, if we take into account all the richness and ramifications of the word, may be described as socialist. Does this mean that the struggle for socialism has in the end been crowned only by a grand constellation of defeats? Once again, this would be to see only one aspect.

For the successes, the gains, the accomplishments have also been considerable.

First of all, the *gains by the workers' movement* and more generally by the working world have been significant in the developed capitalist countries as a whole and in the state-collectivist countries. And certain developing countries have progressed in this area, though such gains have been nonexistent in some Third-World countries where a savage and especially cruel capitalism has developed, as well as in some other countries where pitiless statist systems have taken hold.

Making a list no doubt seems tedious to those interested only in what is "new," but the progress that has been made should be remembered—and a socialist from the end of the nineteenth century returning now would be surprised by the extent and depth of positive change: a reduction in the number of hours worked each day and each week; paid vacations; compensation in case of accidents, sickness, birth of a child, unemployment, or retirement; an increase in buying power; social services; committees within businesses; delegates and committees for health and safety; the regulation of labor; rights for unions; the right to strike; the right to self-expression within businesses, cooperatives, and mutual-aid associations; public and nationalized enterprises.

Certainly, much remains to be done, but we must neither minimize what has been accomplished nor consider these accomplishments as nothing more than paltry material advantages . . . which in any case reinforce the system. It is true that there exists a linked process "gains–concessions–recovery": paid vacations and the increase in buying power, for example, lead to the development of mass leisure and, thus, to new sources of profits and activities. Fundamentally, however, the gains that have been made correspond in fact to the essential demands of the workers' movement:

- more free time;
- more security;
- the possibility of influencing labor and production organization.

These gains have been more or less significant within the developed capitalisms (in the framework of the "national compromise," which we have analyzed) as well as within the state-collectivist regimes. Occasionally what has been won may be cast fundamentally into doubt by the ruling classes during times of crisis. But the advances may also be strengthened and broadened, as an integral part of the effort by the working world to transform society in the direction of socialism.

Then there are the *democratic gains*: universal suffrage, allowing the election of representatives on local, regional, and national levels; the fundamental rights and freedoms of thought and expression, of assembly, press, and association, of forming coalitions and of protesting; the right to formulate disagreements and critiques, to express claims, and to defend interests.

These gains, as well as the advances of the workers' movement, appear to us to be a constituent part of the process transforming societies toward socialism. For, as has been often repeated: there is no socialism that is not democratic, and democracy will be deepened, will blossom with socialism.

That the advances in this direction seem to us to be more significant in the developed capitalist countries is both clear and explicable: these countries, especially Great Britain and France, very early experienced an initial revolution in which the bourgeoisie, carrying the flag of democracy, freedom, and the rights of man, obtained the support of the popular classes in order to wrest power from the older oligarchies. The bourgeoisie, with the arrangement of property tax requirements for the right to vote, as well as the system of "respectable men," tried hard to keep for itself the advantages of this new system: a democracy limited to owners, to "men having goods." But with the development of the workers' movement, and within the compromise that the bourgeoisie was forced to make with the working world, the bourgeoisie conceded universal suffrage first for men and then for both sexes, first for one chamber and then for all representative positions. The ruling class next sought to control the system through trickery, restrictions, and alliances, or by using means open to it because of its wealth. Nonetheless, a system was in place that allowed a majority to elect the ruling group.

The state-collectivist countries and the developing countries have followed another route: a minority has taken power in the name of socialism. In the name of socialism, in the name of the working class—and no matter what the intentions may have been—this minority has formed itself into a ruling class, compelling peasants and workers to produce. The intellectuals, the workers, and the peasants have begun to win or regain rights and freedoms and to reconstitute democracy. Such a process involves pluralism at a fundamental level: the right to establish unions and associations, a plurality of electoral candidates, a plurality of parties, and the possibility of expressing divergent positions, disagreements, and critiques. Such a movement has begun in the state-collectivist countries as a whole: if it is stifled, this will mean the maintenance of a statist totalitarianism, which—we should clearly and tirelessly repeat—is quite opposed to socialism; if this movement develops, it will contribute, perhaps in innovative ways, to progress toward socialism.

Finally there is *the collective effort to control the direction of society's development*. From a voluntary decision by a woman or a couple to have a child, to the collective control of demographic growth; from educational efforts at a basic level, to a policy of technical and scientific research; from choices carried out within the framework of a village, a commune, or a city district, to the main lines of economic, industrial, or regional development: in all these domains there exist the elements of an effort to determine collectively (and in our view this process would best be accomplished through democratic procedures) what a society desires to be, what it desires to become. Planning is an essential tool, as are policies favoring active government intervention in income distribution. And in the context of an internationalizing capitalism that puts each social whole rooted in a given territory at the mercy of a "redeployment" of activities on a world scale, nationalized industries and agreements for cooperation and exchange between countries may help protect against capitalism's incursions.

In this matter, the central problem is one of balance: balance between the national interest and the interest of other nations (we are thinking especially of the weakest countries), between the collective interest and the individual interest, between choices carried out through planning and state and public projects, and those carried out through the market. Doubtless the state-collectivist countries are overly subject to central planning and to the state, while the capitalist countries—except for brief periods—are not subject enough to planning and the state. However, beyond economic planning, there is a whole process that needs to be invented so that a society may democratically control the main lines, the axes that determine its future, a future assuring mastery of modern technologies and the solution of major world problems.

Taken as a whole, though socialism—in the sense of a society without exploitation or class domination, a society that is equitable, interdependent, democratic, and able to control its future democratically—has nowhere been realized, nonetheless the partial and localized advances toward socialism have been many and significant.

A wider and more general step toward socialism—we must repeat this, for here lies the stumbling block where all previous efforts have faltered—must overcome the twin problems of production and political power. Whether for assuring the functioning of the great modern cities, for maintaining living standards in places where they have already risen, or for increasing production levels and productivity in underdeveloped regions, unpleasant, toilsome, and dangerous work remains necessary. Until socialists invent and institute a "socialist method" of resolving this problem, they must confide either to capitalism or to state-collectivism the burden of compelling people to work, of forcing people who would rather be doing something else to do these jobs.

In our view, this is the origin of the impasse in which the socialist movement currently seems to be caught.

For socialism proclaims that it is liberating, most of all for the working class and the working world. Yet the necessity to produce, to clear a surplus, to accumulate, remains very powerful; until the tedious, fatiguing, or dangerous jobs have been eliminated, compulsion—in one form or another—is still necessary. Within the leading capitalist countries, the workers' movement as a whole has come to accept the capitalist logic of production as the driving force, so long as it is more or less contained, so long as its most brutal effects are reduced and wealth is divided less unequally.

In the state-collectivist countries, certain capitalist methods of organization, compulsion, and incitement have been adopted, but without the logic of the capitalist whole, and with less efficiency, despite the politico-ideological campaigns.

Producing remains a burden. There is still a break between, on the one hand, those who rule, and on the other, those who produce, along with those who carry out labor that is not directly productive. The socialist hope was, and remains, that this break might become blurred and eventually disappear: this has in fact occurred nowhere.

Yet—and in our view this is the most serious aspect—this problem has not really been taken up by those calling themselves socialists.

In the state-collectivist countries with Marxist-Leninist ideology, the subterfuge has been in perfect readiness since Stalin's day: since collectivization has been carried out, the working class is the master of the means of production; since the party is the party of the working class and the state the state of the working class, the problem does not exist, cannot exist. Once that is established, worker discontent can only be due to either action by antisocialist elements, or else errors and abuse of power by cadres or leaders. All that is needed is to eliminate one or the other of these sources of discontent.

In some left circles in the capitalist countries, the problem has been complicated, if not denied outright, by a new myth of salvation: self-management. Certainly self-management takes place as part of the general movement of emancipation for the working world, if only by widening the field within which workers are able to exercise their control, influence, and power. But can it be claimed that self-management in the workplace or the commercial enterprise will bring about the withering away of the central power? Such a claim acts as if a certain form of "self-management" were not perfectly compatible with a capitalist or state-collectivist logic of production and accumulation.

To ignore this problem can only lead to what is occurring today in the state-collectivist countries: rumblings, and then one day the mass uprising of the working class against "its state," "its party," "its leaders."

In our view, we must at least take up the problem consciously, as a whole, and in some way, politically. This must be done first of all with those most directly concerned: the workers.

Since productive labor remains a burden, one may seek

1. to limit it, in a way that guarantees the satisfaction of basic needs and that avoids an excessive expansion of needs;
2. to divide it up more fairly; one may also, more pragmatically, make an inventory of the unhealthy, dangerous, unpleasant jobs, and then, on this basis, (i) seek technical means for reducing the number and severity of these sorts of jobs, and (ii) make sure that the same people do not, their whole lives, remain bound to perform such jobs.

3. CLASS STRUGGLES AND COMPROMISES

The vision was straightforward: a proletariat more and more powerful confronting a diminishing and isolated bourgeoisie. By overthrowing the bourgeoisie, the proletariat was to destroy the last class society and create a world without exploitation or domination.

Revolutionary romanticism made the picture beautiful and luminous:

the proletariat became a modern messiah, the class struggle an aposto-
late, and the revolution a purification and a deliverance. Starting at
the political and social level there arose a movement that traveled to
the domain of myth, the mystical, and the sacred.

On such bases, all excesses, all illusions, all false paths, became
possible.

Returning to reality, we note:

1. With capitalism, the bourgeoisie on the one side and the working
class on the other have certainly been strengthened; the confrontations
and struggles between these two classes have been violent and brutal,
involving fierce repressions. Still,

- the double polarization foreseen by Marx has not occurred: the
categories of employees, technicians, cadres, and "techno-bureoisies"
in particular have developed, while the petty and middle bourgeoisies, far from being eliminated, have undergone a certain degree
of renewal;
- the development, the organization, and the advance of the workers'
movement and more generally the struggles of the working world
have led to the establishment of a balance of forces that has permitted
the development, through successive gains and negotiations, of
"national compromises."

Socialism has thus not been achieved, but in its name, through a
linked chain of struggles, negotiations, conquests, and compromises, *a
process of transforming societies in the direction of socialism has begun* (gains
by the working world, the protection of those least well-off, democracy,
a partial effort to control the direction of social evolution).

What has been accomplished is both disappointing—in relation to the
dream of a fraternal and liberated society—and significant, in relation to
the cruel logic of capitalism. On this basis, new progress is possible:
through the democratic path, in pluralism, and thus with the conscious
support and participation of very wide strata of the population: the
working world and young people, of course, but also management and
businesspeople.

2. Where capitalisms or precapitalist regimes have been overthrown
by forces laying claim to socialism, a new ruling class has developed
and, insofar as this class has succeeded in pushing through the effort of
statist industrialization, a working class has developed, the peasantry
has been maintained at more or less significant levels, and the categories of cadres, technicians, employees, and "techno-bureoisies" have
developed. Thus,

- a new class society is possible, parallel to and beyond capitalism, a society in which from the very start a certain compromise as well as powerful forms of statist domination—simultaneously political, ideological, and police—are set into place, and in which new discontent, even short-lived uprisings, demonstrate that the class struggle has not been extinguished;

• the reference to socialism, the affirmation of the workers' character of the state and the party may contribute for some time to obscuring and blocking—repression and control helping here—the struggles of workers; but they may also, in other circumstances, become sources of ferment and even detonators of social explosions.

Thus, *the idea of a classless society*, even in its toned-down version of a society without conflict or antagonism, *should be reexamined*. On the one hand, in modern societies this idea lacks the first shred of reality, and on the other hand, it has served above all as an ideological weapon for covering up contradictions and silencing opposition. It has become, in the name of liberation, a tool of oppression.

And finally, to the extent that the objective of *reducing inequality and of strengthening solidarity* is circumscribed within the perspective of socialist struggle, to this same extent it will be useful to acknowledge the reality of classes in society as it is, and to allow each class, each strata, to express its dissatisfactions, complaints, and hopes. *We need to admit that class struggle and class compromise interact together, and will continue to do so for a long time into the future.*

3. Most fundamentally, one may ask whether socialism has not been, and whether it does not still continue to be, the ideology of a class alliance joining together significant sections of the working class and the working world, the intelligentsia, and various strata of the techno-bureoisie.

More exactly, and despite the reactions this may provoke, one must ask the following question: in the same way that democracy was the principle that allowed the bourgeoisie to win over to its side significant numbers of the common people against the old ruling classes, *is not socialism the principle that allows the middle and the upper techno-bureoisie to rally to its side broad sections of the working world and the producing classes against the bourgeoisie?* Carrying the flag of democracy, the rising bourgeoisie succeeded in taking power in England, in France, in the United States. Carrying the flag of socialism, sections of the intelligentsia have succeeded in taking power in Russia and in China; out of these initial core groups the state techno-bureoisies have developed into new ruling classes. Carrying the flag of socialism, techno-bureoisies in various parts of the world attempt either to widen their influence, to consolidate what power they already hold, or to win power outright.

If this hypothesis is correct, we see in it an additional reason for a suspicious attitude toward any absolute myths—self-management or control by workers, rupture or revolution—new or refashioned, which would lead to new illusions, new and enormous disappointment. And we see in this hypothesis yet another reason for reflecting on *the content of the compromise, on the progress and advances rendered possible by this alliance*. In what ways do workers, the peoples of the Third World, women, young people, and the various categories of oppressed and exploited people stand to gain from the alliance?

4. For more is involved here than classes alone.

Because twentieth-century socialism has centered analysis too much on class domination, exploitation between classes, and class struggle, it has neglected other forms of domination, exploitation, and struggle: colonization, national and racial domination, discrimination and domination between men and women.

However, once there no longer exists a supreme savior—neither the Proletariat, nor the Third World, nor Woman—*it is these dominations as a whole that, within a socialist vision, we must fight*. And insofar as these forms of domination are not parallel and compartmentalized, they combine with one another and in some cases multiply their effects. An example: a woman or girl from a repressive country where sexual mutilation is practiced emigrates with the head of the family to a capitalist country, or to a capitalist island in the Third World, where the man finds work as a laborer.

Once again, it is a question of not reducing everything to a single domination: either imperialist domination over the Third World (as some Third-World partisans have attempted to do in recent years), or domination by men over women (as some militant feminists attempt to do). It is rather a question of understanding the diversity and combinations of domination, and of fighting against them everywhere possible.

4. DIRECTIONS OF STRUGGLE AND GUIDING PRINCIPLES

If the arrival of socialism is not an ineluctable historical necessity; if socialist ideology has been the principle underlying an alliance through which the middle and upper techno-bureoisie has found support from the common people, and especially the working class, for establishing, broadening, or strengthening its power; if the necessity to produce and the compulsion to labor remain such that nowhere in the world today has the overthrow of a ruling class given rise to a society without classes, domination, or state—then for those who have kept and keep the socialist hope alive within themselves, three attitudes are possible:

1. disappointment and resignation: our youth fostered the socialist illusion, but now let us accept the world as it is, possibly attempting, should the occasion arise, to correct this or that situation;

2. blind flight and the invention of a new myth or a new mystique, whether Self-Management, Ecology, Convivial Society, or any other absolute in which to invest one's capacity for faith and hope, even at the risk of falling into new and cruel disillusionment;

3. on the basis of a balance sheet such as we have outlined, unburdening socialism of its utopian, mythic, or mystical elements, yet at the same time taking up socialism once again as a collective, conscious project, democratically elaborated and carried out, aimed at controlling the direction of evolution of our societies.

Within this third perspective there is neither inevitability nor historical necessity, though there are dangers and constraints; above all we accept the fact that *we are at a stage in the evolution of human societies where these societies can and should be aware of their own realities, as well as the possibilities and choices open to them.* Within this framework the socialist project proposes one possible option: progress toward an equitable, interdependent society that has eliminated exploitation and oppression of its weakest members; a society that has control over the collective direction of social evolution. Such direction includes a balance between the freedom for an individual to influence fundamental, collective, and long-term choices and the freedom for an individual to choose his own path, to conceive and fulfill his own destiny.

Since so many errors, abuses, and even aberrations have been committed in the name of these ideals, we believe it wise to foresee and to accept a few guiding principles, in particular democracy, pluralism, and decentralization.

Within this vision, *socialism* is no longer an ideal society toward which history leads; rather, it is *one of the main evolutionary directions possible for modern societies*, or more exactly it is *a project for society, elaborated on the basis of moral values built up through tradition and precedent dating back thousands of years*—fairness, freedom, solidarity, democracy, individual and collective responsibility—*and taken up collectively*, at first through tentative ideological and political efforts, and now *more and more consciously and democratically.*

Within this perspective, certain *directions for struggle* appear clearly out of the various battles carried out in the name of socialism over the last century-and-a-half.

• Struggle against suffering and the causes of suffering; struggle against exploitation of man by man, of one group by another group, of one class by another class; struggle against the crushing of society's weakest and poorest members; thus, in positive terms, social justice, fairness and equality, solidarity, an ever-widening possibility for the full development of abilities, and access to responsibilities.

• Struggle to reduce the number of unsatisfied needs, and thus to assure the satisfaction of basic needs; struggle to reduce the amount of necessary labor, of forced labor. This requires developing and mastering new technologies, yet without becoming a slave to these technologies. This also requires controlling the development of new needs, for recent decades have shown that society's increasing complexity generates new needs, or else makes social labor necessary where "the goodness of nature" had for a long time been sufficient.

• Struggle to expand the terrain open to conscious choice. For example, the new technologies will offer new ways of living, working, and producing; rather than letting ourselves be led along by the implantation of these technologies into various aspects of social life, wouldn't it be better first to define social goals, and then seek the technological and organizational means allowing these goals to be achieved?

These directions for struggle appear clear enough. In one way they appear so simple, so obvious, that they threaten to deceive us through their banality. In fact, *progress in any of these directions is extremely difficult*.

Consider for example the problem of poverty. Along with their ways of living, the richest, most developed societies also produce their norms, their networks for access to education, to health, to knowledge, to technical responsibilities, to leisure and rest, and most basically to the means for assuring food, life, and safety; in relation to these norms, these societies produce their own poor people as well.

Are some of these societies, for example the Scandinavian countries and, in another way, some of the state-collectivist countries, tending toward a certain equalization of income and ways of living?[61] Such a development risks being to the detriment of collective efficiency.

Finally it is certainly not sufficient to pose the problem of poverty and suffering on the level of a single country. It is, rather, on a world level that the problem must be taken up, since the wealth of the developed countries is drawn in part from labor carried out in the dominated countries. And here, the gap between the desirable and the real is shocking. Consider a single quantified indicator: the developed countries as a whole have not attained the objective of devoting 1 percent of their national product to helping the Third World, while armament expenditures account for 6 percent of spending worldwide.

Another case involves the problem of needs: tens or hundreds of millions of human beings in the world lack potable water; tens of millions of people will die from starvation or diseases that could have been prevented or treated. At the same time the production of gadgets and goods possessing secondary importance expands, superproductions swell, and unemployment grows.

Ultimately, *the socialist project* cannot be thought out on a single level; it *must be taken up and achieved on all levels*:

- at the *local* level of the commune or the district, the business enterprise or the school, for it is here in everyday life that people meet, work, and live together, and are able to decide most easily about their most direct concerns and about issues that depend primarily on their own initiative;
- at the *national* level, for here history has established links, networks of power and social life, bonds founded on compromises, and procedures for collective decision making; it is in this framework that steps forward—unequal and diverse—toward democracy and socialism have been accomplished;
- at the *global* level, for capitalism has been developing on a global level. Our survival as well as the quality of social life in coming decades will depend on the solution of problems on a planetary scale: the use and destruction of resources, maintaining essential balances, peace and war.

The task is immense. Advances can only be partial and progressive: let us hope they will be sufficient to avoid the worst, which is the condition for leaving open the path to something better.

These steps forward will be made starting from the world as it is: from the three continents of the Third World where new requirements and new approaches will develop; from the state-collectivist countries where working classes, intellectuals, and successive waves of young people desire new steps toward freedom and democracy; and from the developed capitalist countries where crisis necessitates the mastery of new technologies and the establishment of interdependent relations with the rest of the world.

No central power is able to conceive of or globally execute these advances. They *will be carried out*—if enough forces act together in this direction—*through vast numbers of actions by men and women where they live and work, through new "national compromises" to be negotiated and established, and through the "world compromise" whose features are in the process of clarifying.*

And, in our view, in each case as far as possible, advances forward have the greatest chances of succeeding through *a pluralist and democratic approach*. Put another way: no matter how strongly we believe we are acting for the common good, we need to remind ourselves of the ravages that have been caused by the leadership of active minorities and vanguards holding power. We must force ourselves to accept the mechanism of counterbalance, including an efficient system of critique and the possibility of alternatives. The population must be able to express its hopes, choices, and preferences through all the forms of democracy, and through the market as well.

• Thus, planning is an indispensable tool for carrying out collective social and economic choices (on regional, national, and multinational bases in both the short and the long term), but once it has been determined what shall be the priority of investments, the sort of social needs to be directly assumed by the public sector, as well as the degree of inequality of wealth and income, then everything else should be decided by consumers (private or public) acting through the market.

• And also, in the face of the worldwide logic of the huge capitalist companies, and in the face of the suffering and errors produced by the logic of profit on a short-term basis, protective barriers in the form of public (at present, mainly national) enterprises are solid points of support for controlling a collective destiny; space should remain, however, for non-state, private, cooperative, or mutualist initiatives.

• In the same way, the parties devoted to the socialist cause should accept not only the plurality of parties and alternation of power, but also pluralism in the very approach toward transforming society. Such transformation takes place also through unions, cooperatives, mutual associations, local and municipal action, and other movements of various types: out of these grow the fundamental importance of freedom of expression (and thus of critique), freedom to carry out union and strike activity, and freedom of association and assembly.

Tensions, propositions, critiques, disputes, opposition, compromise, consensus: *it is through a contradictory and conflictive process that steps along the road toward an equitable and interdependent society will be made.*

The same is true on a world scale. The United States is closed within its logic of domination and control, by means of the violence of authoritarian and dictatorial regimes, of zones that threaten to slip away from its grasp: the United States thus continues to be the principal adversary of the forces of liberation, independence, and social progress throughout the Third World. The USSR benefits from the fact that it is the main power able to oppose the United States. The USSR uses its ideology of "achieved socialism" or of socialism-being-achieved and its state-collectivist political and economic know-how, but it becomes increasingly apparent that the aid that it can give is connected with a will to power and to domination on a world scale.

From now on, *between these two colossal powers, these two superpowers, all people in the world who have chosen the road of democracy and of socialism in freedom should work to create a space*: through the development of exchanges, through strengthening aid and solidarity, through the development of joint projects and cooperative operations, through alliances and accords in all domains (art, health, techniques, science, information), *we need, throughout the world, to keep open and to widen a space where countless projects, approaches, and paths in the direction of democracy, socialism, and freedom may begin, develop, and deepen.*

At its heart, the socialist project cannot be reduced to a simple questioning of the logic of capitalist profit. While the battle against capitalist exploitation remains fundamental, the struggle has widened to include resistance to all kinds of exploitation—in particular statist, bureaucratic, and technocratic exploitation. Certainly the direction of society should not depend on the search after profit by the employing classes who are confined within their own selfishness or by worldwide companies often more powerful than many states, but neither should it depend on the will or interests of this group or that minority or class that has managed to take over state power.

The socialist project requires that the direction of our societies' evolution be taken up collectively and democratically, through many different paths and means. Fundamental social choices—justice, solidarity, dignity, full development, and achievement for each person—should thus take precedence over the particular interests of each stratum or class; these values should take precedence as well over the logic of profit, should this latter continue to exist.

The socialist project cannot be reduced to the development of transformations on a national scale alone, though democratic political life, union activity, planning, social and fiscal policies, and action for regional and local development are essential components of this project.

For the socialist project is also carried out in everyday life: in how problems are posed, taken up, and resolved within the neighborhood, the commune, the school, within business enterprises and offices, health services, and leisure activities. It is through an in-depth transformation of the social fabric, through the modification of mentalities, attitudes, and individual behaviors that new social relations are formed.

And the socialist project also involves the mastery of the major world problems: ending over-armament and creating the conditions for peace; preventing the excesses of nationalisms, both old and new; halting the population explosion; stopping the depletion of resources, the thoughtless waste of nonrenewable raw materials, the destruction of basic planetary balances; pushing back and overcoming hunger, suffering, poverty, and insecurity throughout the world; controlling and mobilizing new technologies in order to deal with the most urgent needs.

The ambition is immense: the future to be invented and realized together, working together in solidarity. And recent decades teach us that in order to advance in this task, prudence, modesty, and realism are needed.

A future to be reinvented, in Jean Ferrat's words, without idols, models, or sacred truths:

> A future born out of a little less suffering,
> With our eyes open wide to the real,
> A future led by our vigilance
> Toward all powers of earth and sky.

11

BETWEEN THE HAMMER AND THE ANVIL

Eight years already . . .[62]

Eight years ago I was completing the preceding text. During these eight years, my analyses have become more definite, more refined; the question of socialism appears to me to a certain extent to be extremely straightforward. Yet at the same time I am able to appreciate better how fragile, vulnerable, and in some ways, inconsequential, an analysis carried out by a few isolated intellectuals may appear when such analysis confronts the power of official truths and the inertia of received ideas.

1. A CLOUDED VISION

From the grand socialist hope of the nineteenth century to the current socialist project, which was to have given direction through all the present commotion, the continuity can be seen. *A "common ground" of socialism exists*: indignation toward all attacks against human dignity (suffering, disrespect, oppression); an aspiration toward solidarity, toward a certain amount of brotherhood, toward equity and social justice; a gut-level attachment to democracy and to freedom, at individual as well as collective levels; and finally, a certain feeling of responsibility: responsibility toward the world as it is; responsibility as well toward the future of the world and of humanity.[63]

Out of this grows a multiple refusal: a refusal to turn selfishly back upon oneself, a refusal of "laissez-faire," a refusal of fatalism and resignation.

Excited by these hopes, many people in the nineteenth century believed, and many still believe today in the twentieth century, that humanity faces a simple choice: capitalism or socialism; that in places

209

where capitalism crumbled, socialism would necessarily bloom. A similar belief arose that in circumstances where a revolution overthrew a bourgeois state, a brief phase of dictatorship by the proletariat would lead to the construction of socialism: a society without exploitation or oppression, without state or even political power, a society in which class differences would progressively diminish.

And finally, confronting capitalist industrialization in the nineteenth century, a dichotomized capitalism/socialism interpretive scheme was formed, which continues to function in our minds to this day.

IN REALITY	REPRESENTATION THROUGH IDEAS (IN THE MIND)	
Capitalist industrialization or capitalist development on an industrial base	Analysis of capitalist reality, especially the Marxist theory of the capitalist mode of production	Opposition capitalism/ socialism; idea that the collapse or end of capitalism would lead necessarily to the establishment of socialism
Destruction of previous social forms; extremely difficult living and working conditions	Hope for socialism, for a society without classes, exploitation, or domination	

However, since the end of the nineteenth century, new and important changes have taken place, either progressively or through separate movements.

1. *In the developed capitalist countries*, significant social progress has been made, due to the workers' movement and trade-union action, and it has been expressed in social compromise and legislation. The role of the state has widened, as much through the extension of the productive public sector as through the development of the welfare state.

2. *In the countries that have chosen "socialism" (for example, USSR, China)*, the collectivization of the means of production marks a major rupture with capitalism. The state has become the keystone in the organization of society and the economy, especially for the accumulation effort; statist domination expresses itself through severe attacks on democracy and basic freedoms, while at the same time social progress is achieved on a very unequal basis throughout society.

3. *In the dominated countries of the Third World*, the development of capitalism on a world scale and the effort of development on a national level (whether capitalist or statist), as well as on a local level, have led to the destruction of previously existing social formations. Concretely, this

has meant extremely difficult, often unacceptable, living and working conditions. In these countries the state—as necessary stage or as bastion—has become decisively important, within a process that leaves very little space for democratic or social progress.

When facing this complex reality—here extremely simplified—*the representational scheme inherited from the nineteenth century* hinders understanding more than it helps.

1. One cannot analyze *the developed capitalist countries* as other than capitalist. But, at the same time, they have often been considered, especially during the 1950s and 1960s, as "socialist," particularly in reference to their social achievements: French, British, Swedish "socialisms," with their achievements and limits. We then pass from one illumination to another . . . with the state being considered sometimes as a simple instrument serving capitalism, sometimes as the Trojan horse of socialism.

2. In *the countries that have broken with capitalism*, state truth, official ideology consecrated by constitutional texts, academic works, and the ideological apparatus as a whole leave no doubt: once the means of production have been collectivized, "socialism has been achieved";[64] and if the role of the state is decisive, no more is required than rebaptism as a "socialist state." But for the critical intellectuals who, since the 1930s, have refused to describe these societies as having achieved socialism, their one alternative is to describe them as capitalist. In addition, since the state plays a central role, the phrase "state capitalism" is employed, though the new reality these societies represent no longer has much to do with capitalism.

3. Among *the dominated countries of the Third World*, those linked to the USSR (which have—more or less—collectivized the means of production) call themselves socialist or on the path to socialism. Other countries in the Third World have also managed to call themselves socialist, though such a description has more to do with the intentions of their leaders and the needs of ideology than with actual social reality. Yet in all these countries, to varying degrees, it is the state, the statist reality, that prevails in the confrontation with the pressures of the world market and with the repeated disturbances endemic to societies undergoing rapid change.

It can be seen then that the vision of the world provided by the dichotomized interpretive scheme of the nineteenth century, in terms of capitalism and socialism, leads to profound incoherence: the collective appropriation of the means of production is the foundation of societies considered by some people to be socialist, and considered by others to be "state capitalist." Similarly, the social progress achieved on the basis of Western capitalism is considered by some to be a form of socialism, and by others to be only simple adaptations on the part of capitalism. The same reality is represented by some as capitalist, and by others as socialist, and the use of these words takes on an increasingly ideological dimension (usually apologetic or polemic). At one extreme, capitalism is viewed as an absolute evil, the exploiter and destroyer of man and society, while socialism is seen as luminous reality and ultimate hope. At the other extreme, socialism, symbolized by the gulag, is viewed as oppressive, dominating, and alienating, while capitalism is seen as bringing progress and support for democracy and freedom.

At this degree of confusion, it is no longer possible to speak, to make oneself understood. Are we forced to say "socialism" as soon as the means of production are collectivized? Or as soon as any social progress is made? Must we say "capitalism" as soon as a ruling class dominates the producing classes? Is it possible to reduce the appearance of new realities, especially the strengthening of the statist reality, everywhere evident, either to (state) capitalism or to (statist) socialism? Because we reply "no" to each of these questions, we find it impossible to retain the interpretive scheme "capitalism versus socialism." And because it is the state, the statist reality, that predominates in contemporary societies, we have attempted an analysis of the statist system.

2. A STATIST SYSTEM

A new social reality has appeared, extended, and strengthened itself. The state is its framework and it aims at the extension and centralization of power. It is a new class society existing today alongside capitalism, and which could, in the future, spread further, taking the place now occupied by capitalism.

In the preceding chapters (written eight years ago) and particularly in chapter 7, we referred to this new system as "state collectivism." Following many discussions and further reflection on this point, our initial view has become more definite: the object we are considering is a logic of power, which simultaneously develops and structures itself through organizations concentrating power, principally the state. And through the statist logic, a statist system is formed.

At issue is neither capitalism nor socialism, but another social reality, statism. This is a fundamental intuition, one of the essential interpretive hypotheses of this book.

For this new social reality cannot be reduced to capitalism, a system based on commodity relations (commodity production, labor power bought and sold as a commodity, commodity consumption), on money relations, and on the logic of profit (production of surplus value for accumulation, enlarged reproduction, ceaseless widening of the sphere of commodity exchange), accompanied by the two inseparable processes of growth and crisis.

The statist logic, the logic of power for the sake of power, of ever more concentrated and ever more centralized power, goes beyond money relations and far beyond commodity relations: it covers all aspects of individual and social life. Statist logic has assumed its harshest form, at the end of the twentieth century, in the national state within which it had already taken form and strengthened itself over several centuries. The two dimensions of statist logic are evident in the current period: domination (ideological, political, police) over civil society, and assertiveness (diplomatic, political, military) toward "the rest of the world," and especially toward other states. Each state exists simultaneously against, and yet by means of, the others.

All those who have tried to interpret this new reality in terms of capitalism (especially by using the concept of "state capitalism") have failed: where is the imperious mechanism of accumulation, the irresistible extension of the sphere of commodity exchange, or the wage-laborer free to sell his labor power? What the two systems in fact have in common is principally the ruling class's oppression and domination of the other classes. . . .

Similarly, if one remains committed to the essential aspects of the nineteenth-century socialist vision, one cannot describe this new statist reality as socialist. It is impossible to mix fire and water: socialism was to have been the end of exploitation, and the end of domination by man over man, with the beginning of the withering away of the state and even of all political power. By contrast, what we observe in the countries of "actually existing socialism" is the establishment of a new ruling class, the strengthening and generalization of state power, the extension and concentration of power. Whoever remains committed to the original content of the socialist project and the socialist hope must refuse the joining of these two words: "socialism" and "statism." This is true even though these words are too often put together in formulae such as "state socialism" or "statist socialism."

In fact, what has developed is indeed a new reality, irreducible to preceding systems: a global organization of the economy, society, and social relations, to which the state is both the backbone and the nervous system. It is a new class society, in which the ruling class establishes and reproduces itself through control of the state apparatus—and in some cases, through control of the single party that is the state's brain. In addition, the statist system represents a new economic logic, oriented less toward the production of commodities bearing surplus value than toward the accomplishment of objectives defined through the national collectivity. Underneath the appearance of wage-labor, the statist system is a new social reality that takes responsibility for each individual, from birth to death, in all areas of daily life, from education to health, leisure, culture, information, safety and security, from childhood to old age. And finally, in order to clarify our hypothesis, we propose the descriptive term of *statariat*: the social body as a whole is reduced to being a "statariat" under the power, but also the responsibility, of a new state ruling class, the "statocracy."

The statariat is, on the one hand, the working people, all assimilated into the bureaucracy: everyone becomes a "civil servant"; that is to say, everyone is guaranteed stable employment until retirement age, so long as each worker continues to provide the (state) apparatus with the certain minimum amount of labor that the state requires to function. On the other hand, for the statariat responsibility for collective needs is assumed by the state: protection (social or police), safety and security (individual, highway, social, national), and assistance (at home or while traveling, personal or social).

This statariat is assimilated by some analysts to the concept of wage-labor. Certainly they share certain characteristics: the insertion into a hierarchic structure and the regular collection of monetary income. However, if one examines the apparent similarity more closely, it becomes necessary to distinguish the two concepts: the main characteristics of wage-labor are the sale of labor power, the labor market, and the risk of unemployment. None of these is found (or in any case, not essentially) within the statariat, which is characterized by a relation of owing allegiance to, depending on, and being cared for by, the state and the statocracy. And, excepting the hopes for an increase in living standards, shared by different social strata, the logics and expectations of the statariat are not the same as those prevailing in a system of wage-labor: this is as true in the statist countries (with a predominant statariat) as in the capitalist countries (in which more or less significant strata of statariat have developed).

Once again, if we attempt to describe with a single word two categories that are fundamentally different, we will prevent ourselves from understanding reality. Positively, however, the distinction of these two categories, "statariat" and "wage-labor," allows us to understand one of the major issues at stake in the current reforms in the USSR, Eastern Europe, and China: to reduce the present predominance of the statariat in order to re-create or strengthen the position of wage-labor. Further, this distinction between the two categories allows us to un-

derstand the hesitation and resistance of many ensconced function-
aries [*statariés*] who fear the harshness of wage-labor, the labor market,
and unemployment.

The statocracy is the class that has succeeded in mastering the state
apparatus and that on this basis forms and perpetuates itself as a
dominating class. It is neither a bureaucracy (in the sense that this word
evokes images of the abuses and paper shuffling of clerks tangled up in
pointless administration) nor is it a technocracy (for this word brings to
mind the reign of technicians, specialists, and experts). Rather, the
statocracy may be seen as a descendant of the Old Regime aristocracy
and the conquering bourgeoisies of expanding capitalism. It is greedy
for power, recognition, and gratitude from all those it employs, helps, or
protects, or who profit from it. Statocracy inextricably links together the
accomplishment of social projects along with the accomplishment of its
own ambitions, even its own delusions. And, always, there is the issue
of power—not only its exercise, but its strengthening and concentration
as well.

Here again, too many authors, through inertia, facility, or polemic
intentions, describe the ruling classes of the statist countries as
"bourgeoisies." Of course, the statocracies—statist ruling classes—like
all ruling classes, benefit from wealth, privilege, and power. But the
bourgeoisie, in all its diversity, is linked to capital, which is itself not
uniform; the bourgeoisie's prosperity and influence depend on the
dynamic linking of its various enterprises (commercial, industrial, financial). The statocracies, for their part, form around power institutions,
primarily, during the last two or three centuries, the national states (and
secondarily, during recent decades, around inter- or multinational organizations). The statocracies draw their wealth, privileges, and power
from these power institutions; it is through such institutions that the
statocracies develop their strategies for strengthening and concentrating
power, and which lead them to seek power for the sake of power.

Power for the sake of power: absurd, some will say. But it is no more
absurd than wealth for the sake of wealth, profit for the sake of profit,
accumulation for the sake of accumulation. The logic of power for the
sake of power can be seen in associations, municipal councils, trade
unions, and the institutional structures of cooperatives and mutual
associations. Such a logic unfolds vigorously within political parties and
administrations; it becomes ever more concentrated, dense, and inflexible the closer one approaches the heights of state power. This is the logic
that joins the president to his most trusted friends as well as to his rivals,
the first secretary to his allies as well as to his adversaries, the dictator
to his acolytes. This is the logic underlying clan battles and factional

infighting; finally, this logic explains the irreducible, ultimate commitment to power by those who hold, or who have held, power.

Thus, alongside capitalism, with its complex and tenacious dynamics, instead of the socialism that had been hoped for or dreamed of, it is statism that has taken hold and strengthened itself everywhere.

Taking this analysis of statism as a supplementary tool, we believe we are able to give a more adequate account of contemporary reality.

1. The two dominant economic and social logics in the present period are capitalism and statism.

2. Capitalism is predominant in the dominant capitalist countries (the United States, Japan, West Germany, and so on), and by means of these, throughout the world.[65] However, statist logic is not absent from these dominant capitalist countries; it is merely secondary.

3. Statism is predominant in the countries that have rejected capitalism: the basis common to the rejection of capitalism and the development of statism has been the collective appropriation of the means of production, which has in fact led to the concentration of all powers within the hands of those who control the state apparatus (statocracy). But other logics (capitalist, commodity) are not absent from these countries.

4. Statism is also a means for national resistance on the part of weak capitalist countries (France, Italy, and so on), and, a fortiori, for the dominated countries within the hierarchical system of world capitalism. This implies that many national economies are mixed economies: capitalist *and* statist.

5. On the basis of these national economic foundations—capitalist, statist, and mixed—unequal social progress has been realized: advances by the workers' movement in the capitalist countries, achievements or concessions on the part of statocracies in power. Much of this progress can be considered as advances in the direction of "hoped for socialism."

6. But nowhere has a global logic of production/distribution/consumption/accumulation that could be considered socialist been established on the scale of an entire social formation (this is simply the other side of proposition 1).

7. The ideas, the discourse of socialism, the themes of socialism being built (or to be built) or existing (and to be defended) often constitute the ideology of statism; they are one of the means that statocracies, either in formation or already established, utilize to take hold of or keep power: this is "official-truth socialism."

8. This ideology is not without foundation: it is based, on the one hand, on the collective appropriation of the means of production (one of the elements of "socialism as seen from the nineteenth century") and on the other hand, on the reality of social progress accomplished within the

framework of the statist system. But in order to "stick," this ideology is forced to cloud over the other dimension of "socialism as seen from the nineteenth century": the movement toward a classless society, without domination or exploitation, without state or political power, or, at the very least, toward a society more deeply and widely democratic.

9. At the same time that socialism has become the official ideology of the statist regimes, in many countries of the world, and especially in the Third World, the suffering, poverty, oppression, and domination of the most downtrodden members of these societies call for, and perhaps prepare, a new rise in socialist hopes. "Hoped for socialism" has, then, been strengthened by new social and political dynamics, whose forms and effects are varied. Nonetheless it is difficult, given a historical perspective, to believe that these dynamics will very quickly lead to the construction of "socialist societies"; rather, they tend to prepare the ground for "official-truth socialism."

3. NEW DIRECTIONS

In order to get beyond the confusion of ideas, we propose, on the one hand, to analyze contemporary economic and social realities as capitalist and/or statist, and on the other hand, to use the word "socialism" in a precise, specific way. We distinguish, in particular:

- "hoped for socialism";
- "official-truth socialism";
- where appropriate, "scapegoat socialism" (bandied about by partisans of liberalism);
- "social and/or democratic progress in the direction of socialism" (achieved on the basis of capitalist, statist, or mixed economies).

The difficulty, of which we are well aware, is that such clarifications will not easily be accepted, partly because of the inertia of received ideas and the "habits of expression and language," but most of all because these clarifications conflict with powerful vested interests.

The ideologues and supporters of liberal capitalism clearly have no reason to demonstrate intellectual rigor: the easiest way out for them remains the tried-and-true method of amalgamating disparate elements: since the USSR and China call themselves socialist, socialism is, then, the oppression and institutional repression symbolized by the gulag; it is economic failure, unresponsiveness, and backwardness.

On the other hand, the leaders and the ideologues of the statist systems obviously have no interest in renouncing their official truth, for it is on their affirmation that "socialism has been achieved" (or "is to be achieved") that their legitimacy is based. In such circumstances, for these leaders to proclaim "We are the new ruling class of a statist society and we can guarantee only limited social and democratic progress" would be clearly suicidal. Moreover, faced with the discontent and demands of the population, especially young people, the denunciation of "counterrevolutionaries" and the call for a "defense of socialism" retain a certain utility.

Similarly, the leaders of revolutionary movements in the Third World—where the great socialist hope has recovered strength and inspiration—are unable to go beyond the well-worn vision of a dichotomized world; they promise socialism and a rosy future to the "popular masses." For how could the people be mobilized—and how could the verbal escalation of competing movements be resisted—if the leaders were to say only, "Socialism, you know, will not arrive tomorrow, or even the day after tomorrow; it is going to require a long detour by way of statism or by a mix of statism and capitalism for socialism to be achieved. . . ." Additionally, how on such a basis could the support of the statocracies calling themselves socialist—Soviet or others—be assured?

Finally, the leaders of socialist and Social Democratic movements hardly have the desire—and one can understand their situation—to take up an in-depth reflection on the difficulties, limits, and ambiguities of their position. And yet we believe such reflection is not simply the luxury of an intellectual observing the world as it goes by. It is an illuminating analytic path for all those who wish to act, and a fortiori for those who assume, or hope to assume, social responsibilities.

Illuminating path? Here we can only suggest a few directions and examples.

Consider France, governed by the left for the five years between 1981 and 1986, before experiencing two years of "cohabitation" between a Socialist president and a conservative parliamentary majority (1986–1988), and then, following the reelection of President Mitterrand in May 1988, a government supported by a relative Socialist majority. The common program of the left, signed in 1972 by the Communist and Socialist parties, promised new policies based mainly on nationalizations, democratic planning, and new rights for workers. The French Communist party hoped to reduce the grip and power of business monopolies; the Socialist party, seized in 1979–80 by the escalating rhetoric of the moment, spoke of "breaking with capitalism": planning, instead of the market, was supposed to assure "the global regulation of the economy."

And then, very quickly after 1981, France's presence and participation within the world market imposed their logic and constraints; the

attempt at economic reactivation through Keynesian and social measures was abandoned; the plan ended up defining mainly budgetary
priorities, many of which were not respected; nationalizations served to
strengthen the national industry and banking "units" within an increasingly harsh international economic war; the new rights for workers
gave opportunities to the most alert businesses for adapting their social
relations to the attitudes of the new generation of wage-laborers.

*The government was caught between the two major logics of capitalism
and statism*: it strengthened the statist pole in order to stand up better
to the international melee, but at the same time it refused a total slide
toward statism, which was perceived to contain the dangers of unresponsiveness and unacceptable inertia. Within the same movement, the
government accepted opening the economy to the world market and to
intercapitalist competition. Very quickly, the profitability of businesses
was restored, and the stock exchange was revived, though both these
were accomplished without falling into an absolute laissez-faire economy. Between capitalism and statism there remained no room for the
fine socialist dreams, and only very limited possibilities for advancing in
the direction of social justice or toward developing a tertiary sector.[66]

Since spring 1986 the Rocard government has tried to create for the
"new poor" a certain "minimum income for social reinsertion," as well as
to take into consideration the most unwavering social demands, though
without calling into question the system of wage limits as a whole. The
Rocard government has tried to leave businesses as free as possible, yet
without falling backwards toward extreme liberalism and deregulation.

Consider the USSR, China, and the countries allied to the Soviet
regime: countries having collective appropriation of the means of production along with centralized planning. It is evident to all observers
that these are class societies in which the state plays a determining role,
and that the ruling class has formed itself, since the Revolution, from
and on the basis of state control. Most often such control has occurred
by means of a single party. Beyond these evident statements, however,
one must ask: is the formation of these statist systems not rooted in
societies already possessing a long tradition of strong, centralized, and/
or authoritarian states?[67]

Generalized throughout a country, the statist system allows continuing adherence to a war economy, a successful phase of heavy industrialization, and the accomplishment of long-term programs (military
production, nuclear, and space exploration programs).[68] But the statist
system leads, at all levels, to inefficiency, bureaucratic inflexibility,
waste, and, too often, to corruption and misappropriation of resources.
Ultimately, statism reveals itself as unable to respond to diversified

demands and unable to accommodate the permanent adaptation required by changes in technology, products, and tastes. Out of such unresponsiveness grows the inefficiencies regularly denounced for decades in the USSR and its sister states; this unresponsiveness is also the source of the ever reborn debate on economic reform.

Out of this situation comes, too, the effort to find a better-adapted balance between the statist sector, basically predominant, and the market, including trade relations. For example, the market's influence may be increased in its final form as a market for consumption goods and as free choice for consumers—though in a situation of relative scarcity or excess buying power compared to available goods, the usefulness of this tactic remains limited—or in the form of reestablishing barter relations and the pitting of business enterprises one against the other in direct competition.[69]

Another indication of the process aimed at increasing market influence is the taking into account of the world market, especially the relative prices existing on this market, through a "controlled opening" to the Western market.

A third indication is the acceptance, sometimes explicit, of the various levels of the nonofficial economy, which, in our view, allows at least partial compensation for the blockages, dysfunction, and deficiencies of the statist economy.[70]

Especially interesting in this regard are the revisionist policies put into effect in China since the end of the 1970s. We cite a brief extract from a statement made by a group of Chinese economists:

> We were unable to properly regulate the relations between the state and business enterprises. The state has assumed too much power, while businesses have been too restricted. Planning has imposed overly rigid unification and has neglected the regulating role of the market. (Guangyuan 1983, 97)

One result of such changed thinking has been the restored importance of peasants in the countryside. Another result has been the emphasis on decentralization designed to restore commercial relationships between businesses; a third has been the "free zones" and the opening toward foreign investment.[71]

With its characteristic mixture of daring and carefulness, inertia and dynamism, China has moved down the road of economic reform. During the first years of reform, spectacular results were obtained in the agricultural sector, but afterwards, advances slowed. Similarly, the great increase in small-business activity, favorable to the proliferation of individual initiatives and ingenuity, has struck many observers. Yet here, too, the reforms have not been without consequences: there has been an increase in both unemployment and in tangible inequalities; these have been experienced directly by many strata of the population. In addition, price stability has in some areas been strained, leading to weaker buying power for persons living on fixed incomes. Reform of the price system has been a continuing difficulty, which threatens to upset many gains already established and which threatens as well to open the gates of inflation.

Moreover, economic liberalization, in a regime whose ideology is avowedly socialist, has contributed to the rekindling of fundamental hopes for freedom (freedom of opinion, expression, association . . .), and for democracy. Additionally, as in most countries of the Third World (among which group China represents a major share), Chinese demographic growth means that young people, having many deep-rooted hopes, come of age in a society whose jobs and positions of responsibility are already occupied by adults. These two factors undoubtedly contributed to the widescale movement by Chinese students and young people in May–June 1989. They called for freedom, more democracy, and more equality—especially in their denunciation of privileges and corruption. Their movement can be viewed within the perspective of "hoped for socialism." But the leaders of the country, relying on "official-truth socialism," justified intervention by the armed forces and police repression.

While China emphasized economic reform, Mikhail Gorbachev made a different choice for the USSR. Of course, many discussions have taken place regarding the USSR's economic reform: its various forms and pathways. But Gorbachev's reforms have above all emphasized political democratization and the electoral process (with a plurality of candidates). The field of debate opened up by the reformers has widened in scope to include new critical points of view (anti-bureaucratic, ecologist); questions that remained for a long time in the shadows have again come to the forefront (national claims and nationalist tensions). In a country that has been accustomed for so long to what might be called "concern to conform to the official line," it is difficult to differentiate, among the proliferation of texts and initiatives, those that are simply conforming to the reformist line from those that are in fact genuine attempts at reform.

In any case, whether one considers the USSR, China, or the countries of Eastern Europe, there will be a long road from generalized (or predominant) statism to a more efficient and flexible system. This is first of all because the interests of many different strata and classes will be affected, and in certain cases, threatened, by such changes. And in the second place, the road will be long because the dominant ideology easily incorporates socialism into statism: conservative forces will thus be able to make use of "defending socialism" in order to slow down or block the reforming process. The third reason reform will be difficult is that young people in the USSR and Eastern Europe confront a very contradictory field of action, where ideological reference points lack social confirmation, and where the middle and ruling strata are firmly committed to defending their advantages and privileges.

At a deeper level, beyond the reference to socialism, in the USSR, Eastern Europe, China, and many countries of the Third World, the great dream of a protecting state—simultaneously unifying society, modernizing the economy, guaranteeing development and progress, and leading the way toward socialism—has been broken. This is a dream that was indeed powerful during the period of independence movements in the Third World; think of the version expressed by Algerian president H. Boumediene in 1977

> of a coherent system that will cover all national activities, and that will extend its ramifications into even the furthest recesses of our country, which will reverberate with the presence and solicitude of state authority, like the human body whose vascular system carries life even to the body's furthest extremities. (Cited in Dahmani 1985, 510)

Instead of this vision, what has developed is a state in which citizens do not see their interests reflected in the state, which appears to them as a reality separate from their own, like a foreign body: "Trickery in order to steal from the state seems to have become the rule, as though the state were a foreign state" (cited in Dahmani 1985, 666).

This is of course not all: the foreignness of the state is accompanied by oppression, repression, and political, police, and ideological control over society;[72] but at the same time a social compromise is established between the statocracy and the population as a whole. The compromise is based on the fact that "the Communist mode of life also has its merits: a guaranteed minimum of material goods and protection for the citizen, the advantages of collective life, etc." (Zinoviev 1983, 116). The compromise may be summarized—or caricatured—in the following terms:

> The citizens give their freedom to the state, in exchange for which the state gives them the right (which it controls) to take advantage of their position and go around the law. At the same time the state guarantees minimal conditions of existence. (Heller and Nekrich 1982, 581)

Thus, the collective appropriation of the means of production—which had appeared as *the* condition for socialism in the nineteenth century—has led to societies quite opposed to what socialism was supposed to have been: free association of workers, disappearance of classes, wither-ing away of the state and of political power. Instead, a new ruling class has taken hold of the state apparatus in order to impose its domination over the other classes. This class uses the ideology of official truth about socialism (to be built, to be defended, and so on) to solidify its system of domination. Though each country must be studied individually, in general there exists a split of varying proportions between the stated intentions and the reality: the more or less significant achievements in the areas of housing, health, education, culture, nutrition, etc.

This process has functioned, and continues to function, today on a world scale: in the oppressed, dominated, or crisis-ridden countries the hope for a socialist solution is continually reborn; an active minority, often with noble intentions and not acting out of self-interest, becomes the vanguard of the socialist movement. If such a group manages to take power they very often require support from the USSR or from a nation allied to the Soviet bloc; Soviet methods of economic organization are instituted, and very quickly the new leaders come to adopt the official truth of actually existing socialism. This official truth, along with the magic, by now well understood and mastered, that "the socialist hope" exercises over the poor and dispossessed, favors the rise to power of new elites who form the core elements of new statocracies.

In conclusion, if one attempts, at the close of the 1980s, to take stock of the historical trajectory of socialism, the following elements stand out.

1. Nowhere has socialism, in the sense of an entire social alternative, been achieved, such as it was dreamed of or hoped for in the nineteenth century.

2. The socialist ideal and the battles for this ideal have, however, led to much progress and many advances in the areas of freedom, democ-racy, social justice, and solidarity; the socialist ideal can then only be judged country by country, for each different historical period.

3. The struggles carried out in the name of socialism have had effects in all countries of the world; but the changes have occurred at a deeper level in certain countries, which may be grouped into two different categories: (i) countries whose economic foundation has remained pri-marily capitalist, but in which significant transformations have been accomplished, either through action by Social Democratic parties and organizations (in northern Europe), or through the multiple and inter-connected actions of various left forces (France and southern Europe); (ii) countries whose modern economic development has taken place on a primarily statist base; countries that for many years have retained the construction of socialism as a project, and as an ideological reference

point. Within this perspective these countries have achieved results that the current fashion for the market and for liberalism will no doubt undermine.

The fact that these countries have been (and are) described as "socialist" or call themselves (and continue to call themselves) "socialist" is not without ambiguity.

4. This ambiguity explains a great deal of the deep ambivalence with which the reference to socialism is greeted in the world today.

• In certain countries, for certain social classes and generations, there exists disappointment over a hope that was too vast; disappointment and disillusion caused by the gap between the official discourses and the reigning reality.

• On the other hand, in countries characterized by destitution, poverty, suffering, great inequalities, and a lack of democracy, the socialist hope retains, again, for certain social classes and generations, all of its vigor and power.

Viewed globally, it is clear that the socialist project remains to be completed. The last few decades contain lessons that should be helpful to all those who are committed to the socialist project and who hope to inject it with a greater sense of realism, wisdom, and modesty.

As the world economy becomes ever more interconnected and interdependent,[73] new tasks will need to be taken up by those who are committed to the cause of socialism and democracy: to fight inequalities that are forming on a worldwide level, to invent concrete and useful bonds between human beings, to impose conditions that will guarantee a lasting balance between the forms of modern development and the earth's environment as a whole, and, at the deepest level, to learn to assume our new responsibilities toward present and future generations.[74]

For from now on we will have to act, not only at local and national levels, but also at a world level. We will need to create a "humanism of the twenty-first century."

NOTES

1. The very Catholic Thomas More, chancellor of England, and his *Utopia* (1516); the Dominican monk Tommaso Campanella, imprisoned insurrectionist, and his *The City of the Sun* (1602); the atheist priest Jean Meslier, who died in 1729, and his *Memory [of his] Thoughts and Feelings*; and among many others, Morelly, and his *The Basiliade* (1753) and *The Code of Nature* (1755).
2. See Beaud [1981] 1983a, chap. 2.
3. This law declared the voluntary destruction of machines or the buildings containing them to be a felony and provided the death penalty for such offenses. See Mantoux 1959.
4. Industry in the widest sense, understood as productive activity—M. B.
5. Industry understood, again, in the widest sense—M. B.
6. The word *socialism* is found in the journal *The Sower* in November 1831, in *The Globe* (Saint-Simonian) in February 1832, and in *The Phalanstery* (Fourierist) in 1833. Pierre Leroux claimed to have invented the word, in opposition to *individualism*; see Droz 1972–78.
7. The parentheses are in the manuscript; see the edition established by Abensour and Pelosse (1972).
8. A single illustration: from 1880 to 1910 steel production in Great Britain doubled, but in this same period it increased nine-fold in Germany and fifteen-fold in the United States; in 1880 British steel production was greater than German and U.S. production put together, but by 1910 it represented about half of German production and one-fourth of U.S. production. See Beaud [1981] 1983a, 117–44.
9. Books that characterize this period include H. M. Hyndman, *England for All* (1881) and *The Historical Basis of Socialism* (1883); W. Morris, *News from Nowhere* (1890); S. and B. Webb, *Industrial Democracy* (1897); and R. Blatchford, *Merry England* (1894).
10. Some of the fundamental questions debated within German social democracy at this time will be examined in the following section of this chapter.
11. On these points see Beaud [1981] 1983a, 117–44.
12. See Carr 1950–53, Ferro 1967–76, Bettelheim 1974–77, and Carrère d'Encausse [1972] 1979.
13. Once the decision to call for a Constitutional Assembly was made, Lenin had this to say: "It is an error, it is obviously an error which could cost us dearly! May it not cost the Revolution its head!"
14. Lenin, who had carefully prepared this dispersal of the Constitutional Assembly, said, "The dispersal of the Constitutional Assembly by soviet power is a complete and open liquidation of the democratic form in the name of the revolutionary dictatorship. May the lesson remain."
15. On this question, see Linhart 1976, 84–85.
16. Capitalism is here conceived of as a step on the way to socialism.

17. This second sentence was disavowed by the party; see Carrère d'Encausse [1972] 1979, 195.
18. Not counting members of the Communist party in the USSR, there were nearly 900,000 members of Communist parties throughout the world in 1921, around 300,000 in 1931, and over a million in 1939 (Kriegel 1964).
19. Despite its setbacks, the trade union movement, which counted eight million members in 1919, still had six million in 1926, nearly five million in 1930 and 1934, and again nearly six million just before the war. The increase in Labour votes continued throughout the 1920s: 31 percent in 1923, 33.3 percent in 1924, 37.5 percent in 1929 (Marx, R. 1973).
20. The net revenues from foreign investments were on the order of 200 million pounds per year between the wars: considerably more between 1925 and 1929, but less between 1930 and 1934 (Beaud [1981] 1983a, 117–44).
21. The number of members of the LO (Lutte Ouvrière [Workers' Struggle]) union rose from 280,000 in 1920 to 553,000 in 1930, 622,000 in 1937, and 1,150,000 in 1946 (Dolléans 1979).
22. The term *bureoisie* designates "the strata of civil servants, clerks, and wage earners in offices and various administrations" (Beaud [1981] 1983a, 245).
23. There were 900,000 unionized workers directly after the war, but more than 4 million at the end of 1936.
24. Thus, the CGT alone saw its membership increase from 375,000 in 1922 to 500,000 in 1925, 900,000 in 1932, and 1,000,000 in 1936, before reunification.
25. Danos and Gibelin 1972, vol. 2.
26. Remarkable, this economic base characterized as in "conformity with the Constitution"!
27. Remarkable, this state, an instrument that creates relations of production!
28. One might also cite here Munis 1946, Bordiga 1953, and Gluckstein 1955; regarding their positions, see Naville 1970.
29. We describe as the "bureoisie" the wage-earning office and business workers, as well as workers in the service sector. "Techno-bureoisie" designates the strata among the bureoisie who possess learning or techniques (industrial or social) that allow them to carry out management and leadership functions.
30. Regarding these questions, the straightforward reasoning of David Rousset is very sensible: "When they [the members of the International Commission against the concentration camps] declare that 'concentration camps of a considerable size exist in the Soviet Union and in the People's Republic of China,' this necessarily implies that these two states are not at all socialist, at least if one gives to this word the meaning that socialists in general and Marxists in particular have always given to it" (preface to Barton 1959).
    Reasonable also is this thought from P. Ivanov: "Means are not neutral: there is no socialist Taylorism; there is no socialist authoritarianism; there is no socialist parliamentary cretinism" (Ivanov 1974).
31. Cereal production, which had grown by 4.4 percent per year from 1890 to 1900 and by 2 percent per year from 1899 to 1913, rose by 7 percent per year from 1921 to 1927–28; during this latter period agricultural production as a whole increased, according to various estimates, from 8 percent to 12 percent per year (Zaleski 1962, 1:260).
32. One may observe in Preobrazhensky a significant step toward the assimilation of a "socialist economy" within the idea of a "state economy." The

expression "primitive socialist accumulation" had already been used by Smirnov at the time of the Gosplan, and by Trotsky in 1923 in his report to the Twelfth Congress; see Trotsky [1923b] 1975, 76.

33. During the five years between 1923–24 and 1927–28, the value of Soviet accumulation has been estimated at 26.5 billion rubles, of which 15.6 billion came from agriculture (Chambre 1967).

34. See especially Zaleski 1962, 1:148; see also Bettelheim 1939.

35. *On Right Deviationism in the Communist (Bolshevik) Party*, a speech in April 1929 to the Central Committee at the end of which Stalin condemned "Bukharin's group" (Stalin [1929b] 1974).

36. See pp. 71–73 of this volume.

37. See Linhart 1976; Schwarz 1952; and Chambre 1965.

38. We are thinking of the story by Slawomir Mrozek, "The Giraffe," which appeared in the collection *The Elephant* ([1958] 1964). A small boy asks his uncle, chief editor of a review, what a giraffe is:
    "Go look in the *Manual of the Perfect Propagandist*."
    "It's not there."
    "Well then, in Ludwig Feuerbach."
    "We've already looked, it's not there either."
    "Then in *Anti-Dühring*."
    "Nor there."
    "It should be there."
    "But it isn't . . ."
    "[Then] . . . it doesn't exist. Neither Marx nor Engels, nor any of their followers, have written anything about the giraffe. This means that the giraffe does not exist" (Mrozek [1958] 1964, 15–18).

39. The "state techno-bureoisie" is that fraction of the "techno-bureoisie" belonging to the state apparatus and exercising its functions within the state and in its name (see note 29).

40. Statistics from a study carried out by intellectuals within the French Communist party in 1978, *The USSR and Us*, published by Editions Sociales.
    One may compare these statistics with those given by K. Pomian (1978) for POUP in Poland in 1973:

10.2%	were peasants
39.4%	were workers
11.0%	were engineers, technicians, managers
6.2%	were retirees, pensioners
6.2%	were primary- and secondary-school teachers
5.0%	were economists, planners, accountants
2.8%	were agronomists, agricultural or forest specialists, university professors and researchers, doctors
20.2%	were others

41. Once again it is interesting to compare the situation of Poland in 1973. The following percentages of the indicated groups were members of POUP (Pomian 1978):

10.0%	of the population
5.3%	of the peasants
13.3%	of the workers
20.0%	of the doctors

24.7%   of the economists
28.4%   of the engineers and technicians
31.4%   of university professors and researchers
38.5%   of primary- and secondary-school teachers
60.0%   of the members of the state and judicial administration
100.0% of the members of the Party apparatus

42. Here again, one could draw a parallel with the "books" of ruling classes in other countries: genealogies of the nobility under the ancien régime; the "books" (not for sale) of the great bourgeois families; employers' guides published yearly and distributed sparingly; and books such as *Who's Who?*

43. Five years after Stalin's death, Mao, not without humor, told this story: "If [in 1937] we had followed the method of Wang Ming, that is, Stalin, the Chinese Revolution would not have succeeded. Even when it did succeed, Stalin declared that it was false" (Mao Tse-tung [1958a] 1975a, 485).

44. I thank Serge Vincent Vidal, a teacher in the Department of Political Economy at the University of Paris VIII, who made the texts of these two documents available to me.

45. One may read on this subject the very solid thesis in economics by Bruno Hébert, *State Enterprise in China*, University of Paris VIII, 1981.

46. In a book on *Socialism and Africa* (1966), L. V. Thomas remarked that some countries have openly chosen socialist development, often without being able to bring it wholly into being *politically* (power belonging to the workers) or *economically* (collective appropriation of the means of production for the benefit of the workers alone), and sometimes without defining "socialist development" rigorously enough (Tunisia, UAR, Mali, Senegal, Guinea, Ghana, Tanganyika). In addition, he considered other "states that are aware of the urgency of socialist policies (Kenya, Zanzibar, Uganda, Chad, Dahomey, Gambia) without yet having established such policies." Still others are opening only very slowly to the collectivist ideal (Somalia, Sudan, Libya, Morocco, Niger, Nigeria, Sierra Leone, Congo, Rhodesia) (Thomas 1966).

47. The USSR awards the label "socialist" only sparingly; it acknowledges cautiously that some countries have begun "the noncapitalist road toward development," either with a working class already formed (Syria, Algeria, Burma), or else with a working class in the process of being formed (Guinea, Congo, Tanzania, Yemen) (Oulianovski 1975).

48. For Cuba the course of events may be summarized as follows: in February 1960 a commercial agreement was made with the USSR, and in May 1960 diplomatic relations with the USSR were established. Then, American-owned refineries refused to process Soviet crude oil provided as payment for Cuban sugar. Castro took control of these refineries. The United States then stopped buying Cuban sugar. The USSR bought the entire sugar harvest, and Castro nationalized the thirty-six sugar refineries as well as the American telephone company. The United States then succeeded in having Cuba condemned by the Organization of American States. In October 1960 Castro nationalized thirty-two of the largest businesses, after which the United States decided on a trade embargo; Cuba then sought to develop trade relations with the USSR and other collectivist countries. "Less than ten years were required to form a system for which the USSR had been the prototype" (Martinet 1971).

49. "The experience of class struggle in the era of imperialism demonstrates that the only way the working class and the laboring masses can defeat the landowners and the armed bourgeoisie is through the use of guns" (Mao Tse-tung 1938).

"In countries where the state administration, the armed forces, and the police of the bourgeois class are still powerful, the proletarian class must continue to prepare itself for armed struggle" (Ho Chi Minh [1956] 1968, 156).

"Under the leadership of our party, with President Ho Chi Minh at its head, we have established the following great historical truth: a colonized people, who are weak but united in their common struggle, and who rise up to defend resolutely their independence and peace, are quite able to defeat the aggressive forces of an imperialist power" (Vo Nguyen Giap 1961).

"Let us create two, three, many Vietnams" (Che Guevara, to the Executive Secretary of the Tricontinental Congress, 1966).

50. "We believe that the Cuban revolution has brought three fundamental changes to revolutionary movements in the Americas by demonstrating that (1) popular forces can win a war against a regular army; (2) one should not always wait for all objective conditions to be present in order to create a revolution, for the central insurrectional source may itself provoke these conditions into appearing; (3) in underdeveloped America, the principal terrain for armed struggle should be the countryside" (Guevara [1962] 1971, 148).

"The guerilla will become the fundamental tactic of the revolutionary movement" (Castro [1967] 1968, 171).

51. A comment by Mao on Stalin's *Economic Problems of Socialism in the USSR*: "Stalin's basic error lay in his lack of confidence in the peasantry" (Mao Tse-tung [1958b] 1975b, 40).

"Revolution, in the colonial and semi-colonial countries, is first of all and above all a peasant revolution. It is inseparable from the antifeudal revolution. Alliance between the great peasant masses and the working class is the fundamental base upon which a wide and strong national front may be formed" (Ho Chi Minh [1957] 1968, 164).

"While it is true that in the underdeveloped countries of America the working class is generally small in numbers, there exists a social class which, given the inhuman conditions under which it lives, constitutes a great potential force in the struggle for national liberation. This is the class of peasants, who, led by the workers and the revolutionary intellectuals, will play a decisive role in our struggle" (Castro [1962] 1968, 42).

For his part, Senghor emphasized the importance of "Peasants, Fishermen, and Shepherds."

52. "Under the glorious banner of Marxism-Leninism, and following the path marked by the October Revolution, with total faith in the masses and absolute confidence in victory, we continue forward with courage and resolution toward the shining future of happiness, friendship, and lasting peace, toward a socialist society" (Ho Chi Minh [1957] 1968, 168–69).

"It was necessary to carry out an anti-imperialist revolution, a socialist revolution. . . . And the result is that socialism triumphs . . . that the era of socialism is established and is then followed by the era of communism" (Castro [1961] 1968, 95).

Other impressions from African countries shortly after independence: "I believe that only socialism can solve our problems of development. . . . Our socialism cannot be exactly that of Marx and Engels, which was thought out more than a hundred years ago in Western Europe" (Senghor, cited in Thomas 1966). "We believe that the political organization of the people as a whole may lead a country to socialism" (Kouyaté, cited in Thomas 1966). "Algerian socialism is a socialism that will have something in common with all socialisms: the elimination of privileges. But there will be no Marxist socialism in Algeria, because of certain principles deeply rooted in the Algerian people, such as their culture and religion" (Ben Bella, cited in Thomas 1966).

53. "Now we are going to begin the *zafra*, the sugar-cane harvest. How auspiciously it is starting! This cane belongs to our peasants; it will produce the hard currency with which we will buy equipment and factories" (Castro [1959] 1968, 106).

   "Push forward the movement of emulation: May each person work for two. Be determined to overcome all difficulties, to put forth all your strength" (Ho Chi Minh [1965] 1968, 176).

   "It is not justice that creates wealth; it is labor. All that justice can do is to distribute this wealth humanely, in a just manner. Justice may distribute what labor creates, but it cannot replace labor in the process of creating wealth" (Castro [1968] 1968, 105). And even more bluntly: "In Vietnam, people often emphasize that 'economic efficiency must be one of our primary goals'" (Brocheux and Hemery 1980).

   In the same vein is this statement by Carlos Rafael Rodriguez, vice-president of the Cuban Council of State: "Under capitalism there exists an automatic exploitative mechanism: he who does not work is fired. The foremen are there with their demands, which they make in the name of the company president or the boss. Socialism should replace them with comrades who direct the work in the name of the society and who cannot allow themselves to be indifferent about poorly done work. I will mention a difficulty that we have not yet completely overcome: the lack of an industrial tradition. Industrialization presupposes a certain discipline, which the developed countries acquired over decades of time" (Rodriguez 1980).

54. It is impossible not to mention here the thoughts that a Nicaraguan official expressed at a meeting of the Department of Political Economy at the University of Paris VIII in the spring of 1981. Essentially his point was this: "It is said that the working class forms the vanguard, that it is at the front line of combat. But in our country, it is above all the peasants, the young people, and the women who have led the struggle and brought victory. Then must we not question the old dogmas?

   "And now that we have won, we have been thrust into positions of responsibility: in government ministries and administrations, in the police. What can we do to prevent ourselves from becoming a new ruling strata, cut off from the people?" Even if no one has quick answers to these questions, it is nonetheless important that they continue to be asked once power has been won.

55. "The National Assembly of the people of Cuba condemns the exploitation of man by man, as well as the exploitation of the underdeveloped world by imperialist finance capital.

   "Consequently, the Cuban National Assembly proclaims to America:

• the right of the peasant to the earth, and the right of the worker to the fruit of his labor;
  • the right of children to education, and the right of young people to work;
  • the right of students to free, experimental, and scientific education;
  • the right of blacks and Indians to full human dignity;
  • the right of women to civil, social, and political equality;
  • the right of the elderly to protection in their old age;
  • the right of intellectuals, artists, and scholars to struggle through their work for a better world;
  • the right of states to nationalize imperialist monopolies in order to retrieve national wealth and resources;
  • the right of countries to free trade with all peoples on earth;
  • the right of nations to full sovereignty;
  • the right of people to transform barracks into schools, and to arm the workers, peasants, intellectuals, students, blacks, Indians, women, young people, and old people: in a word, to arm all of the oppressed and exploited so that they will be able themselves to defend their rights and their future" (cited in Castro 1968, 133–34).

"For Africa, communism is not the way; there can be no class struggle here, for there are no classes, only social strata. The basis of our society is the family and the village community" (Sékou Touré, cited in Thomas 1966).

"By using the word *Ujamaa*, we affirm that for us, socialism means building on the foundations of our past and building as we think best. There can be no question of importing into Tanzania a foreign ideology that will stifle and smother our own social models. . . . We want to try to create, through methods suited to Tanzania, something that belongs specially to us here" (Nyerere [1969] 1972).

"We have thus resolved to keep Marx's method, by which I mean the spirit and not the letter of Marx. We further resolve to create for our people, by beginning from the reality of their lives, and from the values of negritude and blackness, a new socialist model" (Senghor [1973] 1976).

Mao Tse-tung often emphasized that communism should accomplish the objective of the "well-being of the people," this world of *Datong* that Confucius strove for. . . .

56. A first outline of these reflections was published in *Le Monde Diplomatique* in May 1979 under this title, chosen following discussion with Claude Julien.
57. See Gallissot in Droz 1972–78; Fejtö [1952] 1971; and *Samizdat 1* 1969.
58. In the same speech Gomulka stated: "The working class has given a sobering lesson to party leaders and the government. By striking and by protesting in the streets . . . the workers of Poznan have shouted 'Enough! This cannot continue! We must abandon this false path!'
   "The working class has never taken the act of striking as a weapon to be used lightly. This is even more true at this time in Poland, with the government acting in the name of, and for, the workers. The working class has not taken such a step without considering the consequences. Certainly, their actions went too far. Yet, actions of such seriousness are always accompanied by certain risks.
   "The path of democratization is, given our conditions, the only path that will lead to a better model of socialism. We will not stray from this path and we will work with all our strength not to be led astray."

59. Gallisot in Droz 1972–78; see also Heller and Fehér 1981.
60. The death of socialism has been announced quite regularly by intellectuals on the right since the middle of the nineteenth century: the third issue of the *Information Letter* of the Horloge Club announces once again "the end of socialism" (see the article by A. Fontaine in *Le Monde*, 24 March 1981). Nowadays, however, the death of socialism is being announced by intellectuals on the left, such as Alain Touraine in *After Socialism* (Touraine 1980), and André Gorz in *Goodbye to the Working Class: Beyond Socialism* (Gorz 1980).
61. In both cases, an immense gap continues to exist between "the working world" (including middle-level management) and the upper-level leaders: the leading capitalist families in Scandinavia and the principal rulers within the state apparatus in the collectivist regimes.
62. This chapter was rewritten in July 1989, based on chapter 11 of the second French edition (1985).
63. Socialists have no monopoly on these ideas and ideals: many others— humanists, Christians, democrats, republicans—who do not call themselves socialists may also advance such ideals. On the other hand, members of socialist organizations or parties who fought for these ideals at an age or in a period when they still believed in the ideals may very well remain in these parties and organizations—through inertia or interest (electoral, power, or career)—though their actual beliefs have faded or have even been reversed.
64. "The socialist regime is the basic system of the People's Republic of China, and it is forbidden to all organizations and all individuals to attack it" (Article 1 of the Constitution of the People's Republic of China in 1982, cited in Tsien Tche-hao 1983, 109). "The USSR is a socialist state of the entire people, which expresses the will and interest of the workers, the peasants, and the intelligentsia" (Article 1 of the Constitution of the USSR of 1977, cited in Radvany 1982, 11).
65. See Michel Beaud, *L'économie mondiale dans les années 80* (Beaud 1989).
66. We have further developed these analyses in Beaud 1983b and Beaud 1985.
67. See, for example, Skopol 1985.
68. This point is developed particularly in Castoriadis 1981. Beyond what we describe as the statocracy, Castoriadis uses this same word to indicate leadership of the society by military power (Castoriadis 1981, 22). This hypothesis is also discussed by Morin 1983, 211–12.
69. See Drach 1984, and Lavigne and Andreff 1985.
70. See Archambault and Greffe 1984.
71. See Dumont 1984.
72. See, among many others, Morin 1983.
73. See Beaud 1989.
74. See Vézelay 1988.

REFERENCES

Alexandrian. 1979. *Le socialisme romantique*. Paris: Editions du Seuil.
Archambault, E., and X. Greffe. 1984. *Les économies non officielles*. Paris: La Découverte.
Attlee, C. 1937. *The Labour Party in perspective*. London.
Bahro, R. [1977] 1978. *The alternative in eastern Europe*. London: New Left Books.
Barbeyer, D. 1980. DEA thesis, Université de Paris VIII.
Barbusse, H. 1936. *Staline, un monde nouveau vu à travers un homme*. Paris: Flammarion.
Barton, P. 1959. *L'institution concentrationnaire en Russie, 1950–1957*. Paris: Plon.
Bauer, O. [1921] 1968. "Le 'cours nouveau' en Russie soviétique." In *Otto Bauer et la révolution*. Paris: EDI.
Beaud, M. [1981] 1983a. *A history of capitalism, 1500–1980*. New York: Monthly Review Press.
———. 1983b. *Le mirage de la croissance*. Paris: Syros.
———. 1985. *Le grand écart*. Paris: Syros.
———. 1989. *L'économie mondiale dans les années 80*. Paris: La Découverte.
Bernstein, E. 1899. *Socialisme théorique et social-démocratie pratique*.
———. [1920] 1974. *Présupposés du socialisme*. Paris: Editions du Seuil.
Bettelheim, C. 1939. *La planification soviétique*. Paris: M. Rivière.
———. 1974–77. *La lutte des classes en URSS*. 2 vols. Paris: Seuil-Maspero.
Blanqui, A. [1868] 1972. *Instructions pour une prise d'armes*. Edited by M. Abensour and V. Pelosse. Paris: Editions de la Tête de Feuilles.
Bobowicz, R. 1973. *Crises, les socialismes*. Paris: SEF.
Bordiga, A. 1953. *Dialogues avec Staline*. Milan.
Borissov, V. 1980. Interview in *Le Monde*. 26 June.
Bouloiseau, M. 1972. *La république jacobine*. Paris: Editions du Seuil.
Brandt, W. 1980. *Nord-Sud, un programme de survie*. Paris: Gallimard.
Brandt, W., B. Kreisky, and O. Palme. 1975. *La social-démocratie et l'avenir*. Paris: Gallimard.
Bravo, G.-M. 1970. *Les socialistes avant Marx*. Vol. 1. Paris: Maspero.
Brocheux, P., and D. Hemery. 1980. Article in *Le Monde Diplomatique*. March.
Buci-Glucksmann, C., and G. Therborn. 1981. *Le défi social-démocrate*. Paris: Maspero.
Bukharin, N. [1925–27] 1974. *Le chemin du socialisme et le bloc ouvrier-paysan*. Paris: UGE.
Bukharin, N., and E. Preobrazhensky. [1919] 1968. *ABC du communisme*. Vol. 1. Paris: Maspero.
Carr, E. [1950–53] 1969. *La revolution bolchevique*. Paris: Editions de Minuit. *The Bolshevik revolution*.
Carrère d'Encausse, H. [1972] 1979. *Lénine et Staline*. Paris: Flammarion.
Castoriadis, C. [1949] 1973. *La société bureaucratique*. Paris: UGE.

———. 1981. *Devant la guerre*. Vol. 1, *Les réalités*. Paris: Fayard.

Castro, F. [1959] 1968. Discours. 15 December 1959. In Castro 1968.

———. [1961] 1968. *Sur la formation du PURS*. In Castro 1968.

———. [1962] 1968. Second Declaration of Havana. In Castro 1968.

———. [1967] 1968. Speech at the close of the first OLAS conference. In Castro 1968.

———. [1968] 1968. Discours. 9 April 1968. In Castro 1968.

———. 1968. *Citations de Fidel Castro*. Paris: Editions du Seuil.

Chambre, H. 1965. *Le marxisme en Union Soviétique*. Paris: Editions du Seuil.

———. 1967. *Union Soviétique et développement économique*. Paris: Aubier-Montaigne.

Chavance, B. 1980. *Le capital socialiste*. Paris: Le Sycomore.

Cheysson, C. 1981a. Article in *Le Monde*. 30 April.

———. 1981b. Cited in *Le Monde*. 18 June.

Coriat, B. 1978. *L'atelier et le chronomètre*. Paris: Bourgeois.

Crosland, C. A. R. [1952] 1954. *L'avenir du travaillisme*. Paris: Editions Ouvrières.

Dahmani, A., 1985. "Contribution à l'étude d'un nouveau type d'état dans le Tiers Monde: le cas algérien." Ph.D. thesis, Université de Paris VIII.

Danos, J., and M. Gibelin. 1972. *Juin 1936*. Vol. 2. Paris: Maspero.

de Man, H. [1926] 1929. *Au-delà du marxisme*. Paris: Editions du Seuil.

Denis, H. 1966. *Histoire de la pensée économique*. Paris: Presses Universitaires de France.

Desobre, G. 1977. *Les quatre constitutions soviétiques, 1917–1977*. Paris: Savelli.

Dolléans, E. 1936–56. *Histoire du mouvement ouvrier*. 3 vols. Paris: A. Colin.

———. 1979. *Qu'est-ce que la social-démocratie?* Paris: Editions du Seuil.

Dommanget [1922] 1970. *Sur Babeuf et la conjuration des égaux*. Paris: Maspero.

Drach, M. 1984. *La crise dans les pays de l'est*. Paris: La Découverte.

Droz, J., ed. 1972–78. *Histoire générale du socialisme*. 4 vols. Paris: Presses Universitaires de France.

Dumont, R. 1984. *Finis les lendemains qui chantent . . .* Vol. 2, *La Chine décollectivise*. Paris: Editions du Seuil.

Feinberg, V. 1978. Interview in *L'Unité*. 28 April.

Fejtö, F. [1952] 1971. *Histoire des démocraties populaires*. Paris: Editions du Seuil.

Ferro, M. 1967–76. *La révolution de 1917*. 2 vols. Paris: Aubier-Montaigne.

———. 1980. *Des soviets au communisme bureaucratique*. Paris: Gallimard.

Ford, H. 1922. *My life and work*. New York: Doubleday, Page, and Company.

Gide, A. [1936] 1937. *Retour de l'URSS*. Paris: Gallimard.

Gierek, E. 1970. Radio speech, cited in *L'Humanité*. 21 December.

Gluckstein, T. 1955. *Stalinist Russia: A Marxist analysis*.

Gorz, A. 1980. *Adieux au prolétariat, au-delà du socialisme*. Paris: Galilée.

Guangyuan, Y. 1983. *La modernisation socialiste de la Chine*. Vol. 1. Peking: Editions en Langues Étrangères.

Guérin, D. 1970. *Ni Dieu, ni maître*. 4 vols. Paris: Maspero.

———. 1973. *Bourgeois et bras nus—1793–1795*. Paris: Gallimard.

Guevara, E. [1962] 1971. "La guerre de guérrilla, une méthode." In *Oeuvres I: Textes militaires*. Paris: Maspero.

Gurvitch, G. 1965. *Proudhon*. Paris: Presses Universitaires de France.

Handbook of Political Economy. (No author). [1954] 1956. Paris: Editions Sociales.

Heller, A., and F. Fehér. 1981. *Marxisme et démocratie*. Paris: Maspero.

Heller, M. 1974. *Le monde concentrationnaire et la littérature soviétique*. Paris: L'Age d'Homme.

Heller, M., and A. Nekrich. 1982. *L'utopie au pouvoir*. Paris: Calmann-Lévy.

Ho Chi Minh. [1956] 1968. "Allocution à la 9ᵉ session du comité central du Parti des travailleurs du Viêt-nam." In Ho Chi Minh 1968.

———. [1957] 1968. *La Révolution d'octobre et la libération des peuples de l'Asie*. In Ho Chi Minh 1968.

———. [1965] 1968. Discours. 15 April 1965. In Ho Chi Minh 1968.

———. 1968. *Action et révolution*. Paris: UGE.

Ivanov, P. 1974. Article in *Politique-Hebdo*. 14 February.

Jaurès, J. 1900. *Bernstein et l'évolution de la méthode socialiste*. Paris: Bibliothèque du mouvement socialiste.

———. 1969. *Histoire socialiste de la révolution française*. Paris: Editions Sociales.

Kania, S. 1980. Cited in *Le Monde*. 17 October.

Kautsky, K. 1899. *Le marxisme et son critique Bernstein*.

———. 1919. *Terrorism and communism*.

Kollontaï, A. [1921] 1974. *L'opposition ouvrière*. Paris: Editions du Seuil.

Korsch, K., P. Mattick, and A. Pannekoek [1934] 1973. *Thèses sur le bolchevisme*. In *La contre-révolution bureaucratique*. Paris: UGE.

———. [1935] 1973. "Les conseils ouvriers et l'organisation de l'économie." In *La contre-révolution bureaucratique*. Paris: UGE.

Kriegel, A. 1964. *Les Internationales ouvrières*. Paris: Presses Universitaires de France.

Kupferman, F. 1979. *Au pays des soviets: Le voyage français en Union Soviétique, 1917–1939*. Paris: Gallimard.

Lavigne, M. 1970. *Les Économies socialistes soviétique et européennes*. Paris: A. Colin, 1970.

Lavigne, M., and W. Andreff, eds. 1985. *La réalité socialiste—crise, adaptation, progrès*. Paris: Economica.

Lazitch, B. 1956. *Les partis communistes d'Europe*. Paris: Les Iles d'Or.

Lenin, V. I. [1895] 1943. "Draft and explanation of the programme of the Social-Democratic party." In *Selected works*, vol. 1. New York: International Publishers.

———. [1902] 1943. "What is to be done?" In *Selected works*, vol. 2. New York: International Publishers.

———. [1905] 1943. "New tasks and new forces." In *Selected works*, vol. 3. New York: International Publishers.

———. [1913] n.d. Article from "Pravda." In *Oeuvres complètes*, vol. 18. Paris.

———. [1914] n.d. Article in *Oeuvres compèletes*, vol. 20. Paris.

———. 1915. *The failure of the Second International*.

———. [1917a] n.d. *April theses*. In *Oeuvres complètes*, vol. 24. Paris.

———. [1917b] 1932. *The state and revolution*. In *Collected works*, vol. 21, part 2. New York: International Publishers.

———. [1917c] n.d. "To the population." In *Oeuvres complètes*, vol. 26. Paris.

———. [1918a] n.d. *Seventh Party Congress*. In *Oeuvres complètes*, vol. 27. Paris.

———. [1918b] n.d. *Immediate tasks of Soviet power*, in *Oeuvres complètes*, vol. 27. Paris.

———. [1918c] n.d. First draft of *Immediate tasks of Soviet power*. In *Oeuvres complètes*, vol. 42. Paris.

————. [1921a] n.d. "L'impôt en nature." In *Oeuvres complètes*, vol. 32. Paris.

Leroy, M. 1950. *Histoire des idées sociales en France*. Vol. 2, *De Babeuf à Tocqueville*. Paris: NRF.

Levesque, J. 1980. *L'URSS et sa politique internationale de 1917 à nos jours*. Paris: A. Colin.

Ligou, D. 1962. *Histoire du socialisme en France (1871–1961)*. Paris: Presses Universitaires de France.

Linhart, R. 1976. *Lénine, les paysans, Taylor*. Paris: Editions du Seuil.

Löwy, M. 1980. *Dialectique et révolution: Essai de sociologie et d'histoire du marxisme*. Paris: Anthropos.

Luxemburg, R. [1918] 1961. *The Russian revolution*. Ann Arbor: The University of Michigan Press.

Mantoux, P. 1959. *La révolution industrielle au 18e siècle*. Paris: Génin.

Mao Tse-tung. 1938. *De la guerre prolongée*.

————. [1956] 1975a. "On the ten important relationships." In Mao Tse-tung 1975a.

————. [1958a] 1975a. "Comments at the Cheng conference of 10 March 1958." In Mao Tse-tung 1975a.

————. [1958b] 1975b. "Regarding Stalin's *Economic problems of socialism in the USSR*." In Mao Tse-tung 1975b.

————. [1960] 1975b. "Notes on reading the Soviet Union's *Manual of political economy*." In Mao Tse-tung 1975b.

————. 1975a. *Textes 1949–1958*. Paris: Editions du Cerf.

————. 1975b. *Mao Tse-toung et la construction du socialisme*. Paris: Editions du Seuil.

Martinet, G. 1971. *Les cinq communismes*. Paris: Editions du Seuil.

Marx, K. [1844] 1970. *Critique of Hegel's philosophy of right*. Cambridge: Cambridge University Press.

————. [1847] n.d. *The poverty of philosophy*. New York: International Publishers.

————. [1850] n.d. *The class struggles in France, 1848 to 1850*. Moscow: Foreign Languages Publishing House.

————. [1852] 1983. "Letter to Weydemeyer, 5 March 1852." In *Marx-Engels collected works*, vol. 39. New York: International Publishers.

————. [1871] 1940. *The civil war in France*. New York: International Publishers.

————. [1875] 1933. *Critique of the Gotha program*. New York: International Publishers.

Marx, K., and F. Engels. [1844] 1947. *The German ideology*. New York: International Publishers.

————. [1848] 1955. *The communist manifesto*. New York: Appleton-Century-Crofts.

Marx, R. 1973. *La Grande-Bretagne contemporaine*. Paris: A. Colin.

Morin, E. 1983. *De la nature de l'URSS, complexe totalitaire et nouvel empire*. Paris: Fayard.

Mrozek, S. [1958] 1964. *L'éléphant*. Paris: A. Michel.

Munis, G. 1946. *Les révolutionnaires devant la Russie et le stalinisme mondial*. Mexico City.

Naville, P. 1970. *Le nouveau Léviathan*. Vol. 3. Paris: Anthropos.

Nyerere, J. [1969] 1972. *Liberté et socialisme*. Yaounde: Editions de la Clé.

Oulianovski, R. 1975. *Le socialisme et les pays libérés*. Moscow: Editions de Moscou.

Picard, R. 1910. *Les cahiers de 1789 et les classes ouvrières*. Paris: M. Rivière.
Political Economy of Socialism. (No author). 1967. Moscow: Editions de Moscou.
Pomian, K. 1978. In Il Manifesto, ed., *Pouvoir et opposition dans les sociétés post-révolutionnaires*. Paris: Editions du Seuil.
Preobrazhensky, E. [1926] 1966. *La nouvelle économie*. Paris: EDI.
Radvany, J. 1982. *Le géant aux paradoxes: Fondements géographiques de la puissance soviétique*. Paris: Editions Sociales.
Rakowski, M. 1977. *Le marxisme face aux pays de l'est*. Paris: Savelli.
Rizzi, B. 1939. *La bureaucratisation du monde*. Paris: Hachette.
Rodriguez, R. 1980. Interview in *Le Monde*. 19 April.
Roumiantsev, A. 1969. *Economie politique du communisme*. Moscow: Editions de Moscou.
Rovan, J. 1978. *Histoire de la social-démocratie allemande*. Paris: Editions du Seuil.
Samizdat 1. 1969. Paris: Editions du Seuil.
Schwarz, S. 1952. *Workers in the soviet union*. New York.
Senghor, L. [1973] 1976. *Liberté 3*. Paris: Editions du Seuil.
Servier, J. 1967. *Histoire de l'utopie*. Paris: Gallimard.
Sinyavsky, A. 1979. Interview in *Le Monde*. 17 July.
Skopol, T. 1985. *Etats et révolutions sociales—La révolution en France, en Russie, et en Chine*. Paris: Fayard.
Stalin, J. [1906] 1952. *Anarchism or socialism*. In *Works*, vol. 1. Moscow: Foreign Languages Publishing House.
———. [1929a] 1977. *The year of the great turning-point*. In Stalin 1977.
———. [1929b] 1974. *On right deviationism in the Communist (Bolshevik) party of the USSR*. Paris: Editions du Centenaire.
———. [1933] 1977. *The balance-sheet of the first five-year plan*. In Stalin 1977.
———. [1936] 1977. *Regarding the project of the Constitution of the USSR*. In Stalin 1977.
———. [1938] 1968. *Le matérialisme dialectique et le matérialisme historique*. Tirana: Editions de Tirana.
———. [1939] 1977. "Report to the 18th Congress of the Communist Party of the USSR." In Stalin 1977.
———. 1952. *Les problèmes économiques du socialisme*. Paris: Editions Norman Béthune.
———. 1977. *Les questions du Léninisme*. Peking: Editions de Pékin.
Thomas, L. 1966. *Le socialisme et l'Afrique*. Le Livre Africain.
Thorez, M. 1937. *Fils du peuple*. Paris: Editions Sociales Internationales.
Tingsten, H. 1973. *The Swedish social-democrats: Their ideological development*. Bedminster Press.
Touraine, A. 1980. *L'après-socialisme*. Paris: Grasset.
Trotsky, L. [1923a] 1972. *Cours nouveau*. Paris: UGE.
———. [1923b] 1975. *La lutte antibureaucratique en URSS*. Paris: UGE.
———. [1936] 1963. *The revolution betrayed*. In *De la révolution*. Paris: Editions de Minuit.
Tsien Tche-hao. 1979. *L'empire du milieu retrouvé: La Chine populaire a trente ans*. Paris: Flammarion.
———. 1983. *La Chine: Constitution de 1982 et institutions*.
Vandervelde, É. 1933. *L'alternative: Capitalisme d'état ou socialisme démocratique*. Brussels: L'Eglantine.

Varga, E. [1920] 1922. *La dictature du prolétariat (problèmes économiques)*. Paris: Librarie de l'Humanité.

———. 1970. *Le testament de Varga*. Paris: Grasset.

Vézelay. 1988. *La Déclaration* and *L'appel*. Unpublished documents issued by the Groupe de Vézelay, rue Bonnette, 89450 Vézelay, France.

Voline. [1947] 1972. *La révolution inconnue*. Paris: P. Belfond.

Vo Nguyen Giap. 1961. *Guerre du peuple, armée du peuple*.

Wilson, H. 1961. *Que veulent les travaillistes?*

Zaleski, E. 1962. *Planification de la croissance et fluctuations économiques en URSS*. Paris: Sedes.

Zinoviev, A. 1978. Interview in *Le Monde*. 2 September.

———. 1983. *Ni liberté, ni égalité, ni fraternité*. Lausanne: L'Age d'Homme.

INDEX

ABC of Communism, The, 70
Africa: communism in, 146, 147;
  socialism in, 144, 228n.46
Agrarian law, the, 8–9
Agriculture: in China, 152–53;
  growth figures for, 226n.32,
  227n.33; in Russia, 125–26, 128–29
America, working class in, 107–8
l'Ange, François, 6–7, 18
Apology for the French Revolution, 9–10
April Theses, 65
Arago, François, 34–35
Attlee, Clement, 101

Babeuf, François-Nöel, 7–9, 18
Bahro, Rudolph, 134
Bakunin, Mikhail, 34, 36
Barbusse, Henri, 97
Bauer, Otto, 79, 80
Beaud, Michel, ix, x–xii
Bella, Ben, 230n.52
Benbow, William, 30
Béranger, Charles, 21, 22–23
Bernstein, Eduard, 48–49, 79–80
Blanc, Louis, 22, 25
Blanqui, Louis-Auguste, 21, 26,
  28–29
Blum, Léon, 89, 90, 105–6
Bolshevism: and the Communist
  International, 92; and the Russian
  Revolution, 65, 67–69, 70, 77–81,
  130–31
Borissov, Vladimir, 178
Boumediene, H., 222
Brandt Commission, the, 186
Bukharin, Nikolay, 68, 70, 75, 81,
  111, 112–13, 125
Buonarotti, Philippe, 7, 8
Bureaucratic Revolution, The, 120
Bureaucratization of the World, The,
  119–20

Burke, Edmund, 9

Cabet, Étienne, 27–28
Capital, 33–34
Capitalism: Lenin's views on, 74–75;
  100–11; overviews of, 192–93;
  comparison to socialism, 209–12;
  Stalin's views on, 113–15;
  comparison to state collectivism,
  131–33, 140–41
Capitalist countries: and the national
  compromises, 179–88; socialism in,
  x
Castoriadis, C., 120–21
Castro, Fidel, 157, 158, 228n.48,
  229nn.50, 51, 52, 230nn.53, 54
Catechism of the Industrialists, 13
Celebration of Sunday, The, 24–25
Cheysson, Claude, 186–87
China: agriculture in, 152–53;
  communism in, 146–48, 149–57;
  economic reforms in, 220–21;
  industrialization of, 152–54;
  influence of Russia on, 150–51;
  statism in, 220; working class in,
  153
Civil War in France, The, 38
Class Struggles in France, The, 47–48
Closed Commercial State, The, 11
Communism: development of in
  Europe, 86–91; membership in
  Communist parties, 226; attacks
  against social democracy, 91–99.
  See also Socialism
Communism, examples of: in Africa,
  146, 147; in China, 146–48, 149–57;
  in Czechoslovakia, 174–76; in
  Germany, 170–71; in Hungary,
  172–73; in India, 146; in Latin
  America, 146; in Poland, 171–72,
  176–77

Communist International: and
  Bolshevism, 92; establishment of,
  87–89; influence of outside
  Europe, 145–47, 148–49
Communist Manifesto, The, 33
*Complaints and Remonstrances of a
  Citizen Decreed to Be Passive to
  Citizens Decreed to Be Active,* 6
Considérant, Victor, 21–22, 26–27
Conspiracy of Equals, 7, 9
Cooperative movement, development
  of, 24, 36
Critique of the Gotha Program, 38
Crosland, C. A. R., 183
Cuba, revolution in, 228n.48,
  230nn.53, 54
Czechoslovakia, communism in,
  174–76

Dallin, 79
De Man, Henri, 109
Doctrine of Science, 10–11
"Document of Twenty Points,"
  155–56
Doherty, John, 30
Dubcek, Alexander, 174–75

Eastern Europe, influence of Russia
  on, 167–73
Economy, and socialism, 110–16,
  124–28
Eden, William, 2–3
Enfantin, Barthélemy, 21
Engels, Friedrich, 31, 33, 38,
  47–48, 53
England: and the Industrial
  Revolution, 29; socialism in, 29–31,
  43–44; unionism in, 29–31, 35,
  43–44; working class in, 29–31,
  35, 57, 99–101, 180–81, 183

Feinberg, Victor, 138
Ferrat, Jean, xiii–xiv, 208
Ferri, Enrico, 144
Fichte, Johann, 10–11, 18
Fielden, John, 30
"Five-Dollar Day," the, 107–8
Five-Year Plan (First), in Russia,
  126–27
Ford, Henry, 107–8

Fordism, x–xi
Fourier, Charles, 14–18
France: socialism in, 20–29, 45–46;
  statism in, 218–19; unionism in,
  23–24, 45–46; working class in,
  20–29, 34–35, 104–5, 180–81, 184
French Revolution: l'Ange's views
  on, 6–7; Babeuf's views on, 7–9;
  Fichte's views on, 10–11;
  Mackintosh's views on, 9–10;
  Paine's views on, 10; working class
  during, 4–6
Friedmann, Georges, 117
Frossard, 90

Germany: communism in, 170–71;
  socialism in, 32–34, 44; unionism
  in, 44; working class in, 32–34,
  103–4, 170–71
Gide, André, 117
Gierek, Edward, 139, 176–77
"Giraffe, The," 227n.38
Godwin, William, 3–4, 18
Goelro Plan, 126
Gomulka, Wladyslaw, 231n.58
Gorbachev, Mikhail, 221
Gosplan, 126
Grenier, Fernand, 117–18
Grignon, 23
Guesde, Jules, 48, 53
Guevara, Ernesto "Che," 229nn.49,
  50

Handbook of Political Economy, 115
Hansson, Per Albin, 102
Hardie, Keir, 46
Henri Saint-Simon to the Workers, 14
*Hierarchical National/World System,
  The,* xi
"Historical messianism," 192
Ho Chi Minh, 147, 229nn.49, 51, 52,
  230n.53
"House of Tomorrow," 99–100
Hungary: communism in, 172–73;
  working class in, 172–73

Immediate Tasks of Soviet Power, 72
India, communism in, 146
Industrial Revolution: in China,
  152–54; destruction of machinery

during, 2, 225; rise of in England, 29; Godwin's views on, 3–4; in Russia, 124–30; steel production during, 225; working conditions during, 2–4

Instructions for a Taking Up of Arms, 28

Internationalism, 52–56

International Workingmen's Association (IWA), 35–38

Ivanov, P., 226n.30

Izvestia, 73–74

Jaurès, Jean, 46–47, 50–51, 52, 54, 59, 60

Jouhaux, Léon, 87

Julliard, Jacques, ix

Kania, Stanislaw, 177

Kautsky, Karl, xii, 49, 80, 81, 85–86

Keynes, John Maynard, 108

Kollontaï, Alexandra, 112

Kreisky, Bruno, 185

Kronstadt Commune, 73–74

Kropotkin, Pyotr, 63, 77

Labor unions. *See* Unionism

Labour Representation Committee, 43–44

Lamennais, Fr. Hughes de, 22

Latin America: communism in, 146; socialism in, 143–44

Lenin, V. I.: on capitalism, 74–75, 110–11; on reformism, 85; on the Russian Revolution, 61, 65–68, 70, 86, 225nn.13, 14; on Taylorism, 71–73, 127

Leroux, Pierre, 225n.6

Letters from an Inhabitant of Geneva to His Contemporaries, 12

Liber, 79

Lowett, William, 30

Luxemburg, Rosa, 69–70

Mackintosh, J., 9–10, 18

Manual of a Stock Exchange Speculator, 25

Mao Tse-tung, 149–53, 228n.42, 229nn.49, 51, 231n.55

Marx, Karl, 31–38, 53, 130, 168, 192–93

Merleau-Ponty, Maurice, xii

Mill, John Stuart, 46

"Mill fever," 2

Modern Slavery, 22

Mrozek, Slawomir, 227n.38

Myrdal, Gunnar, 102

Nabat Federation, 77–78

Nagy, Imre, 172–73

"National compromises," 179–88

New Christianity, The, 14

New Economic Program (NEP), in Russia, 74–75, 125

Nguyen Ai Quoc, 147

Noiret, Charles, 24, 26

Novotny, Antonín, 174–75

Nyerere, Julius, 231n.55

October Revolution. *See* Russian Revolution

Of the People, 27–28

On the Federative Principle, 25

On the Reorganization of European Society, 13

"On the Ten Chief Relationships," 151–52

Organization of Labor, The, 22, 25

Paine, Thomas, 3, 10, 19

Palestine, socialism in, 144–45

Palme, Olaf, 185

Parable, 12

Paris Commune, 37–38

Parvus, 79

People's Tribune, 8–9

Perpetual Cadastre, 7–8

Petition of a Proletarian to the Chamber of Deputies, 21, 22–23

"Plebian Manifesto," 8–9

Plekhanov, Georgy, 78–79

Poland: communism in, 171–72, 176–77; POUP membership figures, 227nn.40, 41; working class in, 171–72

Political Economy of Communism, 116

Political Economy of Socialism, 115–16

Politics, 13

Pomian, K., 227–28nn.40, 41

Preobrazhensky, E., 70, 75, 111, 113, 125–26

Problematic Notions on the General Estates, 6
Proletariat. *See* Working class
Proudhon, Pierre, 24–26, 34

Radiant Future, The, 138
Rafael Rodriguez, Carlos, 230n.53
Rakowski, M., 136
Rappoport, 89
Rectification of Public Judgment on the French Revolution, 10
Reflections on the French Revolution, 9
Reformism, Lenin's views on, 85
Reybaud, Louis, 35
Rizzi, Bruno, 119–20
Road to Socialism and the Worker-Peasant Alliance, The, 125
Roosevelt, Franklin D., 108
Rousset, David, 226n.30
Roy, Manabendra Nath, 146
Russia: agriculture in, 125–26, 128–29; critiques of Soviet regime, 117–23; industrialization of, 124–30; influence of on China, 150–51; influence of on Eastern Europe, 167–73; intellectuals' movement in, 173–74; political reforms in, 221; revolution in, 60, 64–84; ruling class in, 135–36; socialism in, ix–x, xi–xii, 60–84, 117–21, 133–40; state collectivism in, xi–xii, 130–33, 140; working class in, 72–76, 86–87, 127–30, 173
Russian Revolution: and Bolshevism, 65, 67–69, 70, 77–81, 130–31; critiques of, xi, 77–81; Lenin's views on, 61, 65–68, 70, 71–73, 74–75, 86, 225; overviews of, 60, 82–84; Stalin's views on, 62–64

Saint-Simon, Claude-Henri de, 11–14, 18
Scandinavia, working class in, 101–2, 183
Senghor, L., 229–30n.52, 231n.55
Shachtman, Max, 120
Shlyapnikov, 112
Simple and Easy Methods for Assuring the Permanent Abundance of Bread at a Fair Price, 6–7

Sinyavsky, Andre, 178
Soboul, Albert, 7
Social Democratic party, 44
Social Destiny, 21–22, 26–27
Socialism and Africa, 228n.46
Socialism: comparison to capitalism, 209–12; in capitalist countries, x; and the split with communism, 85–91, 106; decline of, x; and economy, 110–16, 124–28; future predictions about, 191, 193–95, 198–99, 202–8; originators of, 1, 225; overviews of, xiii–xiv, 18–19, 46–52, 81–82, 122–23, 162–64, 188–90, 191–92, 199–202, 223–24; problems in implementing, 166–70. *See also* Communism, Statism
Socialism, examples of: in Africa, 144, 228; in England, 29–31, 43–44; in France, 20–29, 45–46; in Germany, 32–34, 44; in Latin America, 143–44; in Palestine, 144–45; in Russia, ix–x, xi–xii, 60–84, 117–21, 133–40; development of in the Third World, 143–45, 157–62, 164–65
Spence, Thomas, 3
Stalin, Joseph, 71, 92, 169; on capitalism, 113–15; and China, 150; on the Five-Year Plan, 126–27; on the Russian Revolution, 62–64; on socialism, 133–34, 137–38, 148; on the working class, 129
Statariat, definition of, 214–15
State and Revolution, The, 66–67
State collectivism: comparison to capitalism, 131–33, 140–41; overviews of, 123, 156–57, 193–94, 197–99; in Russia, xi–xii, 130–33, 140
State of the Poor, The, 2–3
Statism: in China, 220; in France, 218–19; overviews of, 212–18, 219–20, 221–23
Statocracy, definition of, 215, 232n.68
Steel production, during the Industrial Revolution, 225n.8
Stephens, Reverend Mr., 30–31
Stinnes, Hugo, 103–4
Ströbel, Heinrich, 79

Studies and Critique, 155–56

Taylorism, 71–73, 127
Teng Hsiao-p'ing, 155–56
Testament of Varga, 138
Theoretical Socialism and Practical Social Democracy, 48–49
Theory of the Four Movements and of the General Destinies: Prospectus and Announcement of the Discovery, 15
Theses and Additions on the National and Colonial Questions, 146
Theses on Bolshevism, 119
Theses on the Struggle against the Imperialist War and the Tasks of Communists, 93–94
Third World, socialism in, 143–45, 157–62, 164–65
Thomas, L. V., 228n.46
Thorez, Maurice, 97
Tiger, Christophe, 5
Tolain, 35
"To the Population," 67
Touré, Sékou, 231n.55
Trade unions. *See* Unionism
Trotksy, Leon, 71, 73, 112, 118–19
Turati, Filippo, 86

Unionism: in England, 29–31, 35, 43–44; in France, 23–24, 45–46; in Germany, 44; establishment of the IWA, 35–38; membership figures, 226nn.21, 23, 24; overviews of, 25–26
USSR. *See* Russia
Utopianism: Cabet's views on, 27–28, Considérant's views on, 26–27; Fourier's views on, 14–18; Saint-Simon's views on, 11–14

Vabsenter, 26

Vandervelde, Emile, 118
Varga, Eugene, 111–12, 127–28, 138
Voline, 76–77, 120
Vo Nguyen Giap, 229n.49

Williams, Raymond, xii
Wilson, Harold, 183
Working class: in capitalist countries, 179–88; in communist countries, 177–79; in developed countries, x–xi; Fourier's views on, 16–17; gains made by, 195–96; and industrialization, 2–4, 43; and internationalism, 52–56; overview of nineteenth-century movement, 38–41, 56–59; Saint-Simon's views on, 12–14; and "social democratic compromise," 107–9; support of the Soviets by, 95–99, 106–7; and Taylorism, 71–73. *See also* Unionism
Working class, examples of: in postwar America, 107–8; in twentieth-century China, 153; in nineteenth-century England, 29–31, 35, 57; in postwar England, 99–101, 180–81, 183; in nineteenth-century France, 20–29, 34–35; in postwar France, 104–5, 180–81, 184; during the French Revolution, 4–6; in nineteenth-century Germany, 32–34; in postwar Germany, 103–4, 170–71; in Hungary, 172–73; in Poland, 171–72; in twentieth-century Russia, 72–76, 86–87, 127–30, 173; in postwar Scandinavia, 101–2, 183

Zetkin, Clara, 87, 89
Zinoviev, Alexander, 71, 138, 178